Very Special Episodes

Very Special Episodes

Televising Industrial and Social Change

EDITED BY JONATHAN COHN AND JENNIFER PORST

Rutgers University Press
New Brunswick, Camden, and Newark, New Jersey, and London

Library of Congress Cataloging-in-Publication Data

Names: Cohn, Jonathan, editor. | Porst, Jennifer, editor.
Title: Very special episodes: televising industrial and social change / edited by Jonathan Cohn and Jennifer Porst.
Description: New Brunswick: Rutgers University Press, [2021] | Includes bibliographical references and index.
Identifiers: LCCN 2020045039 | ISBN 9781978821156 (paperback) | ISBN 9781978821163 (cloth) | ISBN 9781978821170 (epub) | ISBN 9781978821187 (mobi) | ISBN 9781978821194 (pdf)
Subjects: LCSH: Social problems on television. | Television Programs—Social aspects—United States.
Classification: LCC PN1992.6 .V479 2021 | DDC 791.45/655—dc23
LC record available at https://lccn.loc.gov/2020045039

A British Cataloging-in-Publication record for this book is available from the British Library.

∞ The paper used in this publication meets the requirements of the American National Standard for Information Sciences—Permanence of Paper for Printed Library Materials, ANSI Z39.48-1992.

www.rutgersuniversitypress.org

Manufactured in the United States of America

In memory of Simon Cohn, who loved earnest television almost as much as Jackie Chan films

Contents

Preface and Acknowledgments

In 2016, I considered teaching a television studies senior seminar that gave something akin to a "People's History of TV." In the process of researching for the course, I was surprised to realize that many of the most interesting episodes to discuss in such a class were "very special." I hate-watch this earnest genre as much as anyone for the half-assed way it offers easy answers to some of the most complex questions in our world. Yet on reflection, these episodes are often the television industry's most meaningful attempts at addressing social ills and traumas. Without taking these shows into account in teaching a course on the history of television in American culture—and around the globe—would be a grave disservice to the topic.

My next surprise was that so little has been written not only on these shows but also on their series. Together, as a group of editors and authors, we felt that making it easier to teach these episodes could also make it easier for us to teach television history from a social justice angle that is sorely needed. Early on, Lisa Banning and Diane Negra expressed enough enthusiasm and encouragement to start us off. Phil Scepanski was also excited about this idea, and together we started cold-calling many of the most important scholars in television studies to ask them to contribute—not only because we wanted this to be the best collection possible, but also with the express understanding that the more people who signed on, the more graduate students, adjuncts, lecturers, postdocs, and other early-career academics we could also give space to. Many did sign on, and we thank them wholeheartedly for it. Those who couldn't often suggested or contacted other professors or departments on our behalf. Special thanks to John Caldwell and Mimi White for connecting us to a number of our writers. And extra special thanks to the UCLA Film and Television Archive and the fountain of knowledge that is Mark Quigley for helping us through our early research phase.

When Phil Scepanski had to step down as editor due to his ever-increasing workload, Jennifer Porst fortunately stepped in. The truly wonderful irony is that Porst knows way more about television history than I do. Together with Christine Becker (an endless source of positive vibes and fantastic encouragement), we put together a Society for Cinema and Media Studies (SCMS) panel on the topic, and at this crucial moment the audience really brought their a-game and gave us much thoughtful advice that went directly into our chapters. We also received a great deal of useful advice and encouragement from our anonymous readers, and even though one of them singled my chapter out as needing particular attention (no grudge—we're cool), their advice made every chapter better. This project would not have been possible without the collective energy and work of all of the contributors, and Jennifer and I thank everyone involved for going above and beyond to make this collection truly amazing. And, of course, thank you to Jaimie for everything.

Jonathan Cohn

Very Special Episodes

A Very Special Introduction

JONATHAN COHN AND
JENNIFER PORST

Ask anyone to identify a very special episode (VSE) of television, and there is a good chance that they will tell you about Jessie Spano's addiction to caffeine pills in the "Jessie's Song" episode of *Saved by the Bell* (NBC, 1989–1993). The second season of the series was mostly occupied with characters dealing with crushes, attending school dances, and learning to drive, but "Jessie's Song" (November 30, 1990) featured a story line in which Jessie (Elizabeth Berkeley) gets hooked on caffeine pills. When confronted by her friend Zach Morris (Mark-Paul Gosselaar), she reacts, as the episode's writer Peter Engel has described, "more like a heroin addict than someone on NoDoz." Engel continued, "It's sometimes laughed about now, as a lot of people look back and say, wait a minute, caffeine pills? Really?"[1]

A staple of television in the network era, VSEs have typically been thought of as a particularly corny brand of well-meaning television where family- and teen-oriented sitcoms like *Saved by the Bell* address topical and challenging social issues in overly simplistic ways. Arnold Drummond (Gary Coleman) gets molested. Alex P. Keaton (Michael J. Fox) mourns the death of a friend. The Fresh Prince (Will Smith) is shot, and Carleton (Alfonso Ribeiro) buys a gun. And numerous high schoolers like Jessie Spano have gotten hooked on over-the-counter drugs. Very few scholars or critics have taken these episodes seriously, and those scholars who have discussed VSEs often do so incidentally and without offering a clear definition of the form. Instead, their reference rests on a shared assumption of what is meant by a "very special episode," and more often than not, that shared assumption is dismissive and pejorative.[2] Although no one has yet offered a clear definition of the VSE, most discussion of such episodes characterizes the VSE as a form that represents deeply painful social issues as simplistic, gimmicky, and easily solved.

When academics have discussed VSEs in a positive light, they have not called them VSEs, perhaps in the belief that the term is so tarnished that it now applies only to garbage. For instance, Sasha Torres writes about how both *L.A. Law* (NBC, 1990–2010) and *Doogie Howser, M.D.* (ABC, 1989–1993) produced special episodes in response to the 1992 Los Angeles Uprising, and although those episodes can be viewed as VSEs, Torres did not use that frame in her analysis.[3] Likewise, other scholars have written about *Maude*'s "Tax Audit" episode (February 12, 1974), in which she confronts a man who sexually assaulted her years before, and "Maude's Dilemma: Part 1" (November 13, 1972), in which she considers having an abortion, without ever referring to them as VSEs.[4] Other historically important VSEs have simply not been studied, including such episodes as "Edith's 50th Birthday" (*All in the Family*, October 16, 1977), in which Edith is nearly sexually assaulted; "The Bicycle Man" a two-part episode in *Diff'rent Strokes* (NBC, February 5 and 12, 1983), which features a pedophilic bike shop employee; the *Sanford and Son* episode "My Brother-in-Law's Keeper" (NBC, February 14, 1975), in which Fred confronts his own racism; and *Fresh Prince of Bel-Air*'s "Bullets over Bel-Air" (NBC, February 6, 1995), in which Will is shot at an ATM and Carlton suffers from post-traumatic stress disorder. None of these episodes has been seriously discussed, researched, or critiqued by academics. Even "Jessie's Song" has been ignored by a whole generation of television scholars who grew up watching it over and over again in syndication.

But these fascinating episodes diverged from their series' typical formats and were produced in response to particular cultural traumas and concerns in ways that are similar to that of many of the episodes under investigation in this volume. As the work in this anthology demonstrates, focusing on the specialness of episodes like these brings into view both how varied the VSE is and how problematic it is to attempt to divide the special from the ordinary—especially when what often made these episodes special was their ability to consider racism, classism, sexism, and other social ills in ways that television ordinarily did not.

The lack of a serious interrogation of the VSE has led to labeling only the most saccharine, simplistic, misguided, and problematic episodes as VSEs. Glossing over the complexity and cultural specificity of VSEs has made those episodes a totemic bad object for television producers and scholars who have used them primarily to argue for the comparative value of their particular creations or objects of study. Take, for example, Joss Whedon's statement that "there will never be a 'Very Special Episode' of *Buffy*."[5] Whedon was arguing against a particular kind of VSE that Rhonda Wilcox identified as claiming "redeeming social value by focusing episodes on unmediated presentations of social topics such as AIDS and alcoholism."[6] The relevant shows (Whedon cited *Beverly Hills, 90210* [Fox, 1990–2000] as a major offender) tended to provide simplistic answers to morally and socially complex questions. Yet when viewed through the lens of our more rigorous definition of the VSE genre, several *Buffy the Vampire Slayer* (WB, 1997–2001 and CW, 2001–2003) episodes could be considered VSEs. For example, several holiday episodes broke with ongoing narrative concerns, and both "Hush" and "Once More with Feeling" broke with the formal/aesthetic qualities of the series. Other episodes addressed social issues of import to young people, including relationship violence, drug abuse, and school shootings. These *Buffy* episodes are primarily distinguishable from those in series like *Saved by the Bell* by the fact that *Buffy* was taken seriously as a "quality" program.

As Whedon's comments demonstrate, since the 1990s the television industry and much of television scholarship have ignored stereotypical VSEs in favor of middlebrow "quality" television along the lines of *The X-Files* (Fox, 1993–2002), *The Sopranos* (HBO, 1999–2007), and *Breaking Bad* (AMC, 2008–2013).[7] These discussions valorize the supposed cinematic artistry and narrative complexity of these series that make them worthy of formal analysis and critical acclaim. At the same time, another strain of television studies focuses instead on the daily normative flow of televisual content. Following Raymond Williams's discussion of television programming as a sequence or flow, these scholars are less interested in the artistic potential of television than they are in the ideologies it represents and the ways in which viewers use it for their own ends.[8] As a result, they avoid focusing on "special" events that disrupt this flow.[9] Neither approach has included the VSE, and indeed, all of them have overlooked VSEs for being neither artistic nor normative enough. By focusing on the VSE, this collection hopes to blur the lines between these two trends and question many of the assumptions on which they are based: What do we mean when we call an episode artistic or serious? What makes television quotidian? What makes a special episode special? How can VSEs deepen our understanding of the history of the television industry and its place in American culture?

These questions merit serious consideration because discourses about the VSE affect how we imagine the limits and potential of television more generally. First, we must recognize and move beyond the stereotypical assumptions about VSEs, which include but are not limited to the ideas that VSEs

- do not represent the typical stylistic or narrative elements of a series.
- are saccharine and excessively earnest.
- misstate or overly simplify complex, real-world problems.
- are thinly veiled public service announcements masquerading as narrative television.
- are merely marketing tools and ratings gimmicks.

- should not be taken seriously because they target younger, often female, audiences.
- are bougie middlebrow garbage for bougie middlebrow garbage people.

But these assumptions reveal conceptions of the VSE that are both too limiting and too derisive. They obscure the vast majority of VSEs in favor of focusing only on the worst examples of the genre—which, even if they exemplify the characteristics listed above, can still, as much as any other televisual text, contribute to our understanding of television history and the time periods in which specific television shows were produced. Intervening in these discourses and avoiding the various sexist, racist, and classist biases woven into the more pejorative definitions of the VSE will open up new ways of viewing these episodes and television more generally. It will also validate the experience of the many audience members who have found important meaning in these episodes.

Perhaps even more importantly, studying the VSE allows us to trace the history of television's engagement with many of the most important political, aesthetic, economic, and social movements that continue to challenge our society today. In doing so, the chapters in this collection demonstrate the fact that throughout its history, the VSE has helped television define itself and its relationship to the world around it.

Thus, this "specialness" has more broadly shaped the boundaries of normal, everyday television. Most recently, during the COVID-19 pandemic, this quality of the VSE became clear as the normal television production schedule shut down, and networks and streaming services rushed to create a wide variety of special episodes—including several new episodes of sitcoms like *30 Rock* (NBC, 2006–2013) and *Parks and Recreation* (NBC, 2009–2015), telethons, and (ironically, given its title) taped-from-home episodes of *Saturday Night Live*. This trend became so widespread that *South Park* (Comedy Central, 1997–) even created a meta-"Pandemic Special" (September 1, 2020) to critique the economic incentives of the format itself. And even more recently, the VSE structure of *WandaVision* (Disney+, 2021–) has been hailed for how it comments on the strange temporality and spatiality of pandemic living and our transforming relationship to televison.[10] Collectively, these VSEs recognized the uniqueness of this global moment and worked to return a sense of normality, audiences, and all-important ad buys that typically come with the television schedule and the shared communal experiences and catharsis that it can generate. During this time of social isolation and economic and industrial disruption, the VSE ironically became a symbol of normality. Yet much of the discourse around VSEs suggests that the VSE was born and died in the 1980s and 1990s era of television. While that certainly was a high point of the form, the VSE has been foundational to television programming since its earliest moments and continues to inform how the industry sees itself in this era of digital antennas, rampant cord cutting, and the proliferation of streaming services.

In this anthology, we attempt to catch up to the television industry's and popular critics' new, if unconscious, appreciation of VSEs by reappraising our own historical and scholarly accounts of how television has treated comparable subjects in the past. The chapters in this collection historicize and interrogate the role of VSEs in the television industry and its surrounding cultures. In particular, they examine these episodes as indicative of a broader impulse throughout television history to address significant social issues with event programming. In the process, the VSE has become an important way for the television industry to respond to and shape social change, cultural traumas, and industrial transformations.

Like many terms that arise from publicity departments and popular culture, the term "very special episode" is often used as an advertising buzzword to generate excitement and tends to evade clear distinctions between what is and what is not very special. The term "very special episode" is actually used far less often by the television industry, advertisers, or the general public than one might think. A survey of *TV Guide* from the period 1980–1993 revealed not one use of the term in the *Guide*'s content or advertisements for individual programs. A search of the Peabody Awards Collection Archives database similarly found no use of the term in the descriptions of the episodes submitted for consideration or in the materials produced by the Peabody Awards board. One of the instances that comes closest to the use of the term is MTV's entry for *The Tom Green Show*'s episode "The Tom Green Cancer Special" (MTV, May 23, 2000). In this case, MTV's Peabody entry form states, "MTV has prepared a very special edition of 'The Tom Green Show.'"[11]

Instead, it seems that the term "very special episode" developed over time from the use of the word "special" in network promos and the warnings that would appear at the top of certain episodes to prepare audiences for the mature themes and topics in store. For example, in a press release from September 1977, CBS announced "a special one-hour episode of 'All in the Family'" that would air in October and featured a story line in which "Edith is confronted by a rapist and a life-threatening trauma that neither she nor her family will ever forget."[12] Almost a decade later, in a promo aired by ABC for the episode of *Diff'rent Strokes* titled "Speak No Evil" (November 29, 1985), that featured Arnold and Drummond in conflict over, as the announcer explained, a "racist group that threatens to divide a family," the announcer described the episode as "a very special *Diff'rent Strokes*." For other VSEs, one of the stars of the show often provided the audience with a warning of challenging content ahead. As Jonathan Cohn discusses in his analysis of a *Bewitched* VSE that dealt with race and racism (chapter 2), Elizabeth Montgomery introduced the episode as a "Very Special Bewitched" and urged the audience to take its discussion of racism seriously and in a positive spirit. Other later examples, like *The West Wing*'s "Isaac and Ishmael" episode (NBC, October 3, 2001), began with a brief disclaimer to clarify that the episode was a rupture from the show's overarching narrative and dealt with a topic (in this case, 9/11) in ways some viewers might have found difficult. As these examples demonstrate, even though the historical usage of the term "very special episode" has been inconsistent, if we were to include just episodes that were named VSEs in the moment, this would be a very short collection.

Despite the fact that the use of the term has historically been uneven, we can identify certain elements common to VSEs. At their core, all VSEs are distinct from the rest of their series and often from the televisual landscape of their time. As the chapters in this collection demonstrate, these episodes also have certain formal qualities that unite them:

- In the VSE there is a noticeable rupture in the series' text (visually, thematically, narratively, socially, and so on). The VSE is a series' attempt to do something that stands out and rises above the flow of its "normal" diegetic world. As Barbara Selznick points out in her contribution to this volume, a topic "that is special for one show may not be for another simply because of what's expected of the programs, based on their places within the television industry." While comedic VSEs typically express their specialness through transformations in characters, stories, and locations, dramas and "quality" television shows are most often "special" in form and style. Christine Becker's chapter demonstrates this through her analysis of an *EastEnders* (BBC, 1985–present) VSE, which blends the fictional diegetic mode with documentary-style testimonials.
- VSEs are often educational and use a character or group of characters that the audience has laughed with and cared about over a series of normal episodes to convey an important lesson. At times, this lesson responds to major social traumas and provides a road map for how to think about and deal with a particular issue. The main characters manage to avoid serious harm, which typically happens offscreen and is instead endured by a supporting or guest character. Allowing the main characters, much like the home audience, to observe the dramatic situation and learn from it without actually experiencing it helps the episodes contain the traumas they present.
- VSEs raise questions and provoke discussion. In the process, they enable non-normative and more engaged modes of spectatorship, and encourage audiences to view the episodes with family, friends, and sometimes even in classroom settings. Although some VSEs raise questions seemingly only to provide definitive answers to them within the diegesis (for example, you should not use drugs under any circumstances), even in more simplistic cases they often end with a phone number for a hotline or a suggestion that viewers talk to their parents. Suggestions such as those make evident the producers' realization that the complex

issues dealt with in their VSE often require ongoing debate and discussion.

- The demands of the television industry—in particular, the content restrictions imposed by advertisers, network standards and practices departments, and federal regulators in the Federal Communications Commission (FCC) have often resulted in VSEs intertwining important social messages with entertainment in ways that provoke discussion without alienating or offending any segment of the audience. As demonstrated in the case of *Saved by the Bell*'s "Jessie's Song," this can make them purposefully bland.

Rather than restrictively defining the VSE, the analyses contained in this collection help illuminate many of the VSE's core characteristics and thereby the breadth of the genre. As Ron Becker argues in his chapter, rather than accurately defining "special" television, we should attempt to more clearly understand the discourse of the VSE and how it functions to produce the idea that certain episodes of television are "special" for different reasons at different times.

The fact that VSEs have evolved over time but still have many common characteristics illustrates how the VSE has become its own televisual genre. As Jane Feuer argued in her seminal work on television genres, "One of the goals of film and television genre criticism is to develop more theoretical models for these historical genres, not necessarily remaining satisfied with industrial or commonsense usage."[13] This collection moves beyond the uneven industrial and popular usage of the term "VSE" and seriously considers the ways that VSEs "regulate the production of difference by producing their own differences within very circumscribed structures of similarity."[14] As Feuer argued, "From the television industry's point of view, unlimited originality of programming would be a disaster because it could not assure the delivery of the weekly audience, as do the episodic series and continuing serial."[15] VSEs offer a series the opportunity—even if only for one episode—to escape the normal bounds of its narrative or aesthetic world. But the VSE contains those ruptures through its generic conventions that assure the audience that soon, often by the next episode, things will return to normal.

The controlled difference of the VSE disrupts the expected flow of television and allows television producers the ability to avoid monotony while maintaining familiarity. Examples of this kind of controlled difference in television are often most explicit in specials produced as stunt programming and for sweeps weeks. As John Caldwell outlined in *Televisuality: Style, Crisis, and Authority in American Television*, special programming allowed for specific episodes in a larger televisual text to rise above the rest of a series' episodes and attract larger audiences.[16] As Arthur Smith, an assistant curator at the Paley Center for Media, explained, "I think [they] might have had something to do with cynical marketing opportunities as much as a desire to serve the public. [Very special episodes] were always scheduled for sweeps weeks, and so clearly had ratings expectations."[17] Given the industrial roots of the VSE in the persistent drive for higher television ratings and the importance of episodes that draw viewers by standing out from the normal flow of television programming, the VSE deserves more attention as a way the television industry has also used its specialness to rise above ordinary television. That distinction then helps define what is not special: what is normal.

Indeed, from the very beginning of network television, the VSE helped standardize and clarify viewer expectations of what television should typically look like; what topics it should address; how its programs should be scheduled and promoted; and in the process, what its role should be in society more generally. During the early days, as television schedules were becoming normalized, presenting out-of-the-ordinary content during nonstandard times ironically became a way to highlight the value of the normal weekly programming schedule. For example, one of the earliest and most famous VSEs was the birth of Little Ricky on *I Love Lucy* (CBS, 1951–1955). This episode, "Lucy Goes to the Hospital" (January 19, 1953), was the culmination of months of advertising that linked Lucille Ball's real pregnancy with that of her character and largely focused on guessing the gender of the baby. Among other things, this episode gave rise to the first issue of *TV Guide*—the handbook for all aficionados of standardized television programming—which featured a photo of Desi Arnaz Jr. and the caption "Lucy's $50,000,000 baby."

While extraordinarily crass in many ways, this VSE set the stage for the next fifty years of television promotion and advertising. Over 70 percent of all American households watched this episode to see not just Little Ricky but the real Desi Jr. for the first time and celebrate with the characters on-screen and the American public as a whole. This destabilization of the relationship between actors and characters, or the real and the fictitious, is one type of rupture that the VSE especially affords.

As an early example of a VSE, "Lucy Goes to the Hospital" was something of a contradiction. On the one hand, by introducing Little Ricky, it helped introduce him as a regular, if minor, character in future episodes. On the other hand, this episode is significant in being anomalous. Lauren Berlant has pointed out that much of what makes this episode and narrative arc special is that it was the first time marital sexuality was discussed on national television—a topic that decades later would become central to many family sitcoms.[18] In its conflation of the real-life Lucille Ball's ten-year struggle to have a baby and the on-screen Lucy's tears, Berlant argues that this episode exemplified modern quotidian "struggles of intimate existence" in a world where the lines between public and private, as well as real and fiction, were rapidly dissolving. In synthesizing these ideas, the episode demonstrates how Little Ricky, the VSE, and the creation of nonstandard television programming helped reinforce what normal, everyday television was and, in many ways, continues to be. This clarification of

FIG. I.1 $50,000,000 is a bargain for those cute cheeks!

television's narrative and generic rules highlights how central the relationship between scheduling and content (and between normal and special television) has always been.

While many VSEs have focused on the birth of children, sexuality and reproduction have also been frequent topics. Those episodes often provide revealing looks into what was considered acceptable, or not, in each episode's time. For example, in the two-part "Maude's Dilemma," a critically important VSE of *Maude* (CBS, 1972–1978), Maude decided to get an abortion, bringing what had been a private issue into television's public forum. This episode aired in 1972, a year before the U.S. Supreme Court ruled in *Roe v. Wade* that the procedure was protected by a pregnant woman's fundamental right to privacy. According to an interview conducted in the 1990s with Norman Lear, the writer and executive producer of *Maude*, the two-part episode initially aired without controversy, but by the time it was rerun in August 1973, the religious right had mobilized against it.[19] However, newspaper coverage from 1972 reveals that Lear's memory may not have been entirely accurate. In fact, two CBS affiliates had refused to air the two-part episode, which was the first time that any CBS station had refused to run an episode of a continuing series. A New York station reportedly received 373 angry phone calls compared to only 10 favorable ones, and CBS had enough concerns that it originally refused to pay for the two-part episode.[20] For the repeats, not one corporate sponsor bought commercial time, and CBS received more than 17,000 letters of protest. Despite, or more likely because of, the protests and controversy, the double episode earned huge ratings and was number one in its time slot on both nights, which moved the series into the Nielsen top ten.[21]

The backlash against VSEs such as "Maude's Dilemma" reveals why many VSEs have suffered from networks and advertisers self-censorsing rather than confronting potentially controversial topics during family hours. Often the cringe-worthiness of a stereotypical VSE resulted from decisions made in response to the concerns of advertisers, network standards and practices departments, the FCC, and a general desire to avoid pushback—particularly from more conservative segments of the audience. As Peter Engel, the writer and executive producer of *Saved by the Bell*, recounted about the VSE "Jessie's Song," "When I originally wrote the episode with Tom Tenowich, Jessie was hooked on speed, not caffeine pills. But Standards and Practices, the censorial department of NBC, vetoed it, saying speed was too serious for Saturday mornings. I insisted that we needed to start dealing with more important issues than we had in the past, and that speed was a vehicle not only for exploring drug use but also the pressure that kids put on themselves to achieve. But Standards and Practices wasn't budging."[22]

Beyond the fear that explicit discussions about controversial subjects might make audiences uncomfortable, there is also concern that those depictions could cause more harm than good. Most recently, *13 Reasons Why* (Netflix, 2017–present), which Taylor Nygaard and Jorie Lagerway argue could be considered a very special series, was criticized for its explicit depiction of teenage suicide. During production, Netflix consulted with Dan Reidenberg, the executive director of Suicide Awareness Voices of Education, who advised it not to air the series at all, but Netflix ignored that warning and argued that it hoped the series would act as a "catalyst for conversation."[23] While it undoubtedly sparked conversation, a study suggested that it may have also led to an increase in teen suicides.[24] While other studies have since concluded that *13 Reasons Why* was not the culprit, Netflix decided to recut past episodes to excise the suicide from view. The virtually instantaneous and universal condemnation that Netflix received illustrates much of the complexity around the double bind faced by producers of VSEs: if they illustrate the problem in complex detail, they may be accused of glamorizing it; but if they choose instead to avoid the problem or treat it metaphorically, they may be accused of not taking the issue seriously enough.

This double bind in television's efforts to deal with difficult contemporaneous social issues is integrally related to the history of broadcasting's convoluted role as educator and creator of the public sphere. For example, VSEs have some characteristics in common with programming such as ABC's *Afterschool Specials* series that aired from 1972 until 1997 which was aimed at an audience of young teenagers who were underserved by the cartoons for children and the adult fare in soap operas, talk shows, and prime-time programming. As Amanda Renee Keeler documented, Squire D. Rushnell, vice president of children's programming at ABC during the late 1970s and early 1980s, described these after-school specials as "'realistic problem dramas' that featured 'relevant and entertaining' stories meant to help teenagers find resolutions to their troubles."[25] As Alisa Perren, Erin Copple Smith, and David Craig have detailed elsewhere, the rise of cable channels like Lifetime, Nickelodeon, Hallmark, and ABC Family in the 1990s provided a new space for what Craig called "television message movies."[26] Those made-for-TV movies shared many of the characteristics of stereotypical VSEs of the 1980s, and the movies' rise in the 1990s and a shift toward "quality" cable and network programming help explain the evolution of venues and the form of VSEs in that decade. As Stephanie Anne Brown has argued, "narrowcasting and niche programming allows for increasingly nuanced narratives that deal with complicated issues like sexuality, suicide, bullying, racism, misogyny, and sexual assault. While these narratives indeed represent opportunities for conversation and education, they also put a strain on television networks' ability to guide online conversations responsibly."[27] Series like *13 Reasons Why* clearly demonstrate this dynamic in the streaming era.

Even though the exact form, format, and venue of VSEs have evolved over time, one of the characteristics shared by all VSEs is the fact that they confront and often contain ruptures between the diegesis of a series, the production culture, and the larger world that surrounds it. This can occur for any of a number of extratextual reasons, from a production issue such as a strike to the arrival of a holiday or the Super Bowl. They may be produced in response to a traumatic event that affected the producers and viewers enough that the series creators felt that they must address it, as was the case with several VSEs about the Los Angeles Uprising or terrorist attacks—including *The West Wing*'s "Isaac and Ishmael" VSE, which took a very self-referential break to explain the complex U.S. role in the Middle East to a group of high schoolers. Just as often, VSEs are less a reaction to an acute trauma than an attempt to deal with a prolonged injustice and/or anxiety related to issues ranging from racism and sexism to global epidemics. There are also rare occasions when episodes of television manage to accomplish both. For example, *black-ish*'s (ABC, 2014–present) episodes "Hope" and "Juneteenth" were considered VSEs when they were originally broadcast in 2016 and 2017, respectively: "Hope" because it responded to the murder of unarmed Black teens like Tamir Rice and Michael Brown by the police by depicting the Johnson family's reactions to a court case involving a Black teenager who was the victim of police violence, and "Juneteenth" because it departed from the generic and stylistic norms of the sitcom by transforming it into a musical set in the past about the holiday that marks the end of slavery. Then, when ABC chose, in the aftermath of yet another police murder of an unarmed Black man, George Floyd, and the Black Lives Matter protests, to re-air the episodes in June 2020, Kenya Barris, the creator of *black-ish*, lamented in a tweet, "It's been 1,562 days since we first shared that episode ['Hope'] with the world and it breaks my heart on so many levels that this episode feels just as timely as it did then and eerily prescient to what's happening to black people in this country today. I'm grateful to ABC for choosing to re-air 'Hope' and 'Juneteenth' tonight, but this is more than one night of television. This is about coming together as a country and as humankind to say enough is enough."[28] Even while pointing out television's limitations, the rebroadcast of the episodes in 2020 once again responded to acute social and cultural traumas and, as demonstrated by their relevance years after their original airing, dealt with ongoing injustices.

At other times, VSEs take on joyous holidays, as with the yearly "Treehouse of Horrors" episodes of *The Simpsons* (Fox, 1989–present). They may also feature different or trendy formal or generic characteristics, such as a sudden switch to animation or a musical (as in the case of *Buffy*). Often these episodes are programmed for sweeps weeks, when ratings have historically held particular importance for networks, and are designed to make an otherwise staid series suddenly seem to be on the cutting edge, if only for a moment. And yes, the term "VSE" can also describe those cheesy examples from the 1980s that, despite some clumsiness in writing and performance, attempted to produce ethical television for young people in an era when deregulatory policies had largely excused broadcasters from creating children's programming that met any standard whatsoever. After all, who knows how many children learned from Punky Brewster's near-fatal error of playing hide-and-seek in a junkyard refrigerator.

This collection wrestles with different examples over the entire span of television history to identify a more coherent, useful, and expansive conception of the VSE. From a variety of perspectives, the chapters focus on episodes that rethink the complex and ever-changing relationship between television producers and viewers, as well as that between aesthetics and politics. Through studying the VSE, this anthology traces television's perennial engagement with many of the most important political, aesthetic, economic, and social movements that continue to challenge our society today. In doing so, the authors collectively argue that the VSE has always helped television and its audience conceive of themselves and their relationship to the world around them.

We considered various ways of organizing this collection but ultimately realized that simply placing the chapters in chronological order made the most sense, and that organizational logic had the added benefit of highlighting the historical transformations in the VSE as a televisual form. Reba Wissner begins by focusing on the VSE in 1950s and 1960s and demonstrates the fact that historically, the U.S. government played a role in sponsoring VSEs that were designed to make Americans aware of the dangers of the atomic bomb. She pays particular attention to how various episodes used music and sound to depart from their official message, while also intensifying the gravity of the nuclear age. Jonathan Cohn then analyzes how the VSE became a tool to fight racism in the 1970s. He considers a Christmas VSE of *Bewitched* from 1970 that was written by a class of Black high schoolers in which magical blackface is presented as a way to solve racism. His analysis demonstrates the complex and often misguided ways in which television tried to address the civil rights movement both on and off camera.

The heart of our anthology deals with the 1980s and 1990s, an important period of fruition for the VSE form. Philip Scepanski focuses on perhaps the most famous type of VSE—the 1980s antidrug special episode. He explains how these episodes became platforms not just for Nancy Reagan's "just say no" campaign, but also for Ronald Reagan's efforts at economic deregulation. Scepanski argues that the VSE was not simply a reaction to contemporaneous anxieties but was part of a concerted effort to amplify them for political and economic gain. Barbara Selznick then considers the role of the mother-child sex talk in 1980s sitcoms to explore the boundaries between what types of conversations become labeled as special while others remain normal. Her analysis of episodes from *Kate & Allie* (CBS, 1984–1989) and *Valerie* (NBC, 1986–1991) demonstrate the ways in which a program's sociocultural contexts, industrial goals, distribution platforms, and target audiences all contribute to the ways that they are understood as "special."

Another important aspect of the VSE is its role in representing and facilitating a conception of a national identity—resulting in the fact that holidays, which play an important ideological role, have also played an important role in many VSEs. Jennifer Porst traces the history of Thanksgiving holiday VSEs by focusing on *Cheers* (NBC, 1982–1993) and its famous episode, "Thanksgiving Orphans." She describes how Thanksgiving VSEs helped redefine the conception of the American family during periods of massive social transformation. These episodes also highlight the ways in which VSEs functioned as an industrial tool to earn ratings during the 1980s, when the television industry was undergoing significant shifts. Halloween has also been an occasion for a myriad of themed episodes, and David Scott Diffrient explores how they often provide an opportunity for series to follow their most subversive instincts. Diffrient focuses on how Halloween episodes from the original *Roseanne* (ABC, 1988–1997, 2018) voiced some of the more damaging unconscious and repressed impulses of mainstream American culture that would later come to haunt Roseanne Barr.

The 1990s featured many iconic VSEs that dealt with issues of race and racial conflict throughout the period. This is particularly evident in Lindsay Giggey's analysis of how *The Fresh Prince of Bel-Air* represented the complexity of the Los Angeles Uprising from a Black perspective. At the same time, VSEs during this period were also a chance for series to experiment with the formal and narrative limits of their genres. Erin Copple Smith considers NBC's 1994 experiment in offering an entire evening of "Must-See Thursday" programs, all set during a blackout in New York City. She foregrounds the deep relationship between VSEs and other forms of stunt television and argues that although most definitions of "specialness" focus on narrative, this case serves as an example of the ways that institutional structures and strategies mark an event as special.

The high point of the VSE during this period may well have been *Ellen*'s "The Puppy Episode," in which Ellen comes out. Ron Becker argues for the existence of what might be called the TV-milestone VSE and highlights the influence of television networks' promotional goals on the function of a VSE. In so doing, he makes the important distinction between television's actual social impact and the discourses about its impact. He considers the fact that during this moment when television audiences were fragmenting, the momentousness of this episode marked a transition in the television industry away from its status as the dominant mass medium.

Erin Giannini discusses how the U.S. government continued through the 1990s to use VSEs to weigh in on cultural debates and provide health information to citizens. During the late 1990s, the WB and other networks accepted money from the Office of National Drug Control Policy (ONDCP) in exchange for the networks' creation of several antidrug episodes on various teen-centric series. Giannini analyzes the ONDCP's program and the continuing role of government social policy and embedded messaging on television. She focuses on an episode of *Buffy* that was rejected for funding by this program for subverting messaging about government social policies.

From the 1990s to today, the VSE has also functioned to legitimize television by reflecting on its long history. Mimi White illustrates this tendency in her analysis of how *The Simpsons* and *Animaniacs* (Fox Kids, 1993–1995; Kids' WB, 1995–1998; Hulu, 2020–present) use the VSE format to comment on American media forms and histories. She argues that these VSEs transform the series' routine reflexivity and serve to amplify, rather than disrupt, routine television. At the same time, the VSE has also mined normative aspects of early television as a way to comment on contemporary television. Brett Mills analyzes episodes of comedy programs that were broadcast live to analyze how such broadcasting functions as "special" and to better understand television's relationships to liveness both as a medium and technology. He focuses on live episodes of the BBC program *Two Pints and a Packet of Crisps* (BBC Two, 2001; BBC Three, 2001–2011) and *30 Rock* (NBC, 2006–2013) to consider the formal elements of the VSE and especially how liveness has played a central role in marketing VSEs' specialness.

At the same time, the VSE has never been more controversial or central to television than it is right now. Aprryl Alexander and Jennifer Porst chronicle the controversies surrounding ABC's attempts to influence the content of several VSEs. Their comparison of an unaired episode of *black-ish* with the airing of other episodes from *black-ish* and *Scandal* (ABC, 2012–2018) highlights the limits of the modern VSE and the ways that the differences between the content regulation of broadcast television and that of streaming platforms play a role in the exodus of Black producers to over-the-top platforms, where they may have more creative control.

While this collection is primarily focused on the VSE in the American context, Christine Becker follows Brett Mills across the pond to the U.K. to explore an episode of another BBC series, East Enders, which focused on the problem of knife crimes in England. Becker considers how this format has functioned in a more transnational context as well as in the heavily serial soap opera narrative. In the process, Becker also considers how this episode, which includes the stories and relatives of real victims of knife crimes, uses the VSE format to challenge the limits of modern social realism. To conclude, Jorie Lagerwey and Taylor Nygaard look at series like *UnREAL* (Lifetime, 2015–2018; Hulu, 2018) to consider whether or not the VSE format in the era of streaming has been reimagined as a very special season that appeals to certain fragmented audiences and encourages binge watching. In the process, they argue, the streaming era is also stretching, breaking, and redefining the limits of the VSE.

Together, these chapters foreground the problems, potentials, and limits of television's mediation and representation of cultural traumas and anxieties. The chapters make it clear that television has never been simply the province of escapism. They show that the transformations in the television industry from the golden age to the network era, the postnetwork era, and the streaming era have paralleled the evolution of the form of the VSE. The chapters also highlight the relationship between industrial conditions and the ways in which television creates and mediates the special. And they demonstrate the fact that the discourses within and around VSEs have encouraged viewers to debate and critique representations of often challenging subjects and thus themselves. In the process, we offer in this volume a study of television that foregrounds its relationship and responsiveness to the world around it—one that allows us to explore television's very special history of industrial and social change.

Notes

1 Peter Engel, "Jessie Spano Originally Took Speed, Not Caffeine Pills, on *Saved by the Bell*," *Vulture*, November 15, 2016, https://www.vulture.com/2016/11/saved-by-the-bell-jessie-spano-caffeine-speed-excerpt.html.

2 Rhonda V. Wilcox, "There Will Never Be a 'Very Special' Buffy: Buffy and the Monsters of Teen Life," *Journal of Popular Film and Television* 27, no. 2 (January 1, 1999): 16–23; Kelly Kessler, "They Should Suffer Like the Rest of Us: Queer Equality in Narrative Mediocrity," *Cinema Journal* 50, no. 2 (Winter 2011): 139–144; Jack Holland, "'When You Think of the Taliban, Think of the Nazis': Teaching Americans '9/11' in NBC's *The West Wing*," *Millennium* 40, no. 1 (September 1, 2011): 85–106.

3 Sasha Torres, *Black, White, and in Color: Television and Black Civil Rights* (Princeton, NJ: Princeton University Press, 2003).

4 Kirsten Marthe Lentz, "Quality versus Relevance: Feminism, Race, and the Politics of the Sign in 1970s Television," *Camera Obscura* 15, no. 1 (2000): 45–93; Nicole S. Kypker, "Laughter and Ideology: A Critical Discourse Analysis of Changing Representations of Rape in Norman Lear's Sitcoms," *Comedy Studies* 8, no. 1 (January 2, 2017): 13–21.

5 Wilcox, "There Will Never Be a 'Very Special' Buffy," 16.

6 Ibid.

7 Robert J. Thompson, *Television's Second Golden Age: From* Hill Street Blues *to* ER (Syracuse, NY: Syracuse University Press, 1997); Michael Z. Newman and Elana Levine, *Legitimating Television: Media Convergence and Cultural Status* (New York: Routledge, 2011); Lynn Spigel and Jan Olsson, *Television after TV: Essays on a Medium in Transition* (Durham, NC: Duke University Press, 2004); Janet McCabe and Kim Akass, eds., *Quality TV: Contemporary American Television and Beyond* (repr., London: Tauris, 2010); Jason Mittell, *Complex TV: The Poetics of Contemporary Television Storytelling* (New York: New York University Press, 2015).

8 Raymond Williams, *Television: Technology and Cultural Form* (London: Routledge, 2003).

9 Maggie Andrews, *Domesticating the Airwaves: Broadcasting, Domesticity and Femininity* (London: Continuum, 2012); Frances Bonner, *Ordinary Television: Analyzing Popular TV* (London: Sage Publications, 2003); Amanda D. Lotz, ed., *Beyond Prime Time: Television Programming in the Post-Network Era* (New York: Routledge, 2009); Anna McCarthy, *Ambient Television: Visual Culture and Public Space* (Durham, NC: Duke University Press, 2001); Philip W. Sewell, *Television in the Age of Radio: Modernity, Imagination, and the Making of a Medium* (New Brunswick, NJ: Rutgers University Press, 2014).

10 James Poniewozik, "'WandaVision' Lives Inside TV, Just Like We Do," *New York Times*, February 23, 2021.

11 "Peabody Awards Collection Archives Record," *The Tom Green Show. [No. 309, 2000-05-23], Cancer Special.*, 2000, http://dbs.galib.uga.edu/cgi-bin/parc.cgi?userid=galileo&dbs=parc&ini=parc.ini&action=retrieve&recno=10&format=_citation.

12 CBS Television Network Press Information, "Edith's Fiftieth Birthday Is Anything but a Happy One, On 'All in the Family' One-Hour Episode, October 16," September 28, 1977.

13 Jane Feuer, "Genre Study and Television," in *Channels of Discourse, Reassembled: Television and Contemporary Criticism*, 2nd ed., ed. Robert C. Allen (Chapel Hill: University of North Carolina Press, 1992), 140.

14 Ibid., 142.
15 Ibid., 144.
16 John T. Caldwell, *Televisuality: Style, Crisis, and Authority in American Television* (New Brunswick, NJ: Rutgers University Press, 1995).
17 Quoted in Tyler Moss, "The Evolution of T.V.'s 'Very Special Episode,'" *Atlantic*, July 20, 2015, https://www.theatlantic.com/entertainment/archive/2015/07/very-special-episode/398432/.
18 Lauren Berlant, *The Queen of America Goes to Washington City: Essays on Sex and Citizenship* (Durham, NC: Duke University Press, 1997), [illegible].
19 "Norman Lear on the Controversial Abortion Episode of *Maude*," Television Academy Foundation, February 26, 1998, https://interviews.televisionacademy.com/interviews/norman-lear?clip=19187#show-clips.
20 Aljean Harmetz, "Maude Didn't Leave 'Em All Laughing," *New York Times*, December 10, 1972.
21 Lewis Beale, "Maude's Abortion Fades into History," *Chicago Tribune*, November 13, 1992.
22 Engel, "Jessie Spano Originally Took Speed."
23 Quoted in Stephen Marche, "Netflix and Suicide: The Disturbing Example of '13 Reasons Why,'" *New Yorker*, May 6, 2019, https://www.newyorker.com/culture/cultural-comment/netflix-and-suicide-the-disturbing-example-of-13-reasons-why.
24 Thomas Niederkrotenthaler, Steven Stack, Benedikt Till et al., "Association of Increased Youth Suicides in the United States with the Release of *13 Reasons Why*," *JAMA Psychiatry* 76, no. 9 (2019): 933–940.
25 Quoted in Amanda Renee Keeler, "Premature Adulthood: Alcoholic Moms and Teenage Adults in the ABC Afterschool Specials," *Quarterly Review of Film and Video* 33, no. 6 (2016): 483.
26 David Craig, "Calling Western Union: The Cultural Mission of Television Message Movies," *Journal of Popular Film and Television*, 2014, 60–70. See also Alisa Perren, "Whatever Happened to the Movie-of-the-Week?," in *Convergence Media History*, ed. Ellen Staiger and Susan Hake (New York: Routledge, 2009), 161–170; Erin Copple Smith, "A Form in Peril? The Evolution of the Made-For-Television Movie," in *Beyond Prime Time: Television Programming in the Post-Network Era*, ed. Amanda D. Lotz (New York: Routledge, 2009), 139–155.
27 Stephanie Anne Brown, "Millennial Fandom and the Failures of *Switched at Birth*'s Sexual Assault Education Campaign," in "Social T.V. Fandom and the Media Industries," ed. Myles McNutt, special issue, *Transformative Works and Cultures* 26 (2018), https://journal.transformativeworks.org/index.php/twc/article/view/1138.
28 Kenya Barris, @funnyblackdude, August 10, 2020. Twitter, https://twitter.com/funnyblackdude/status/1292910630600638434/photo/1.

1

Listen to Save Lives

Music and the Atomic Bomb in Cold War Very Special Episodes

REBA WISSNER

During the 1950s and 1960s, the U.S. government wanted to make Americans aware of the dangers of the atomic bomb. To do this, the Federal Civil Defense Administration (FCDA) worked in tandem with popular anthology series (series that aired weekly and had different characters, locales, and stories each week) and drama series to air very special episodes (VSEs) related to civil defense, often concluding with the delivery by civil defense officials of a message for the audience. Even more importantly, the music in these VSEs—if there was any—served to amplify the message: music that was distinctly Soviet in style illustrated who was responsible for the fictionalized attack, and American music implied that civil defense was the patriotic thing to do.

The music in VSEs was used to persuade the public to pay attention to the important message on the screen. It underscored the destructive power of the atomic bomb and relayed the significance of following civil defense protocols to save lives. For the episodes without music, its lack was abnormal for that series: some VSEs were the only episodes without music, which intensified the gravity of the message. Part of the specialness of a VSE includes its soundtrack, and such soundtracks need to be better understood in their contexts if we are to better understand how the VSE functions more generally.

This essay considers three civil defense VSEs—*Medic*'s "Flash of Darkness" (NBC, February 14, 1955), *Playhouse 90*'s "Alas Babylon" (CBS, April 3, 1960), and *Armstrong Circle Theatre*'s "Briefing from Room 103" (CBS, April 26, 1961)—and their role in disseminating important information to the public in the guise of a fictional television episode. I argue that not only was the message in each episode carefully crafted to increase the audience's awareness of the importance of civil defense, but so was the music. I will briefly discuss both VSEs during the 1950s and 1960s more generally and how these episodes fit into the long history of using music to signal specialness on TV. Ultimately, I consider the role of music in early television anthology and drama series to illustrate how these three episodes depart from this role, specifically highlighting the government's message to say what could not be said in words.

Early Cold War VSEs: A Short History

Depending on the show, fictional television is one of the most effective ways to spread information about a subject. As the tagline used in Noel Murray's *A.V. Club* website, "A Very Special Episode," states, "a single television episode can exemplify the spirit of its time," and that was especially the case during the early Cold War.[1] During the early Cold War, VSEs were indeed very special: they aired so infrequently that when there was an announcement of one, many people would tune in. VSEs tended to be part of anthology series. Some of these episodes were also docudramas or dramatized documentary episodes, as we will see below in the case of the *Armstrong Circle Theatre.*

Some of the episodes that we now consider to be VSEs were not marketed as such. Thus, there may be some disagreement about what qualifies as a VSE in the 1950s and 1960s. For example, the famous episode of *Lassie*, "Lassie's Pups" (November 14, 1954), in which Lassie gives birth to a litter of puppies, became known as a VSE given its content. Even before that episode, there was a VSE in *I Love Lucy*, "Lucy Goes to the Hospital" (January 19, 1953). Other episodes became known as VSEs only after their airing. One example is an episode of *Takedown*, "The End of the World" (May 9, 1958), which recently has been in the media. While it was not intended as a VSE, if we look at it retrospectively, we can see that it was one. Aside from childbirth, other sensitive topics found their way into VSEs. One example is an episode of *Leave It to Beaver*, "Beaver and Andy" (February 13, 1960), which discussed alcoholism. Other series used VSEs to touch on weighty topics such as terminal illness. One such episode is "Christmas Came a Little Early" (November 11, 1968), from *A Family Affair.*

Given that television was a relatively new medium in the 1950s and 1960s, composers were still developing techniques for using music on television. Some composers came from film and as a result had to learn to compose for a technology that had different sound capabilities, sometimes necessitating the use of certain instruments.[2] As Shawn VanCour has noted, "Music formed a prominent part of early television programming, defining the sounds of everything from dedicated musical programs to commercial advertisements and regular news and dramatic series."[3] This is true when it comes to the sound of specialness in VSEs. In general, however, music often signaled specialness in two ways. First, within the context of a specific episode, change of instrumentation and/or musical style might signify that a person, place, or event should be watched carefully. Second, within the context of an entire series, an episode's sonic specialness could be signified by a different musical style from that of the series overall or the lack of music in a series that used it in regular episodes.

Despite the unique sound of VSEs, it is also important to consider that in the 1950s and 1960s, television network music libraries were often used, meaning that once composers had their cues recorded for a certain episode, the network would have the right to reuse them whenever it saw fit, so not all television episodes had a unique score. But it should be noted that when an episode had a certain theme or character in which library music would not be appropriate, a composer was commissioned to write an original score for it. Indeed, this applied to most, if not all, early VSEs.[4] The exceptions to this rule are VSEs that do not feature any music at all, even when the rest of the series does.

In general, when music is used, it often serves to highlight emotional moments. Typically, upper strings such as violins play the melodies, which occur in minor keys with short musical phrases that are combined for a longer melody. For instance, in "Lassie's Pups," we get somber violin music as Jeff (Tommy Rettig) goes to the barn when Lassie is in labor and whimpering in pain. In later episodes, such as "Christmas Came a Little Early," there is a somber repeated musical motif that returns each time Buffy (Anissa Jones) and her Uncle Bill (Brian Keith) discuss Eve (Eve Plumb) or when Eve is present and we see how weak she is.

This type of music even occurs in comedy VSEs, mixed with music that is typical in serious VSEs. The music in these episodes can also represent emotional states and actions, consistent with the earliest television shows.[5] In "Beaver and Andy," the music that plays as Andy (Wendell Holmes) pours his alcohol in the bushes sounds slightly off-kilter (representing his drunkenness) and moves from a major to a minor key (illustrating the seriousness of his alcoholism). We later get a slow violin version of "My Darling Clementine," which Beaver (Jerry Mathers) was singing earlier, as Andy asks Beaver to give him some brandy that Ward (Hugh Beaumont) received as a gift. We hear the violin version again later, as Ward and June (Barbara Billingsley) try to explain to Andy that he had some "trouble." The music becomes sad, lyrical, and somber as Beaver admits to his parents that he gave Andy the alcohol that started his drinking habit again. In "Lucy Goes to the Hospital," the music uses jaunty, comical, and bouncy melodies played by woodwinds to highlight the anticipation of Ricky (Desi Arnaz) as he waits in his living room for Lucy (Lucille Ball) to go into labor. As we will see below, music—or the lack thereof—was just as integral to the civil defense VSEs as they were to those mentioned above.

Medic, "Flash of Darkness"

Many VSEs aired during the early Cold War used "what if" scenarios, but some were much darker than most audiences anticipated. One Valentine's Day episode was particularly grim: *Medic*'s "Flash of Darkness." This episode is atypical of the series: unlike the other episodes, there is no nondiegetic underscoring—or even diegetic music (that is, music that is part of the narrative and that both the characters and the audience can hear)—in the entire VSE. It does not even use Victor Young's theme for the series, which immediately sets it apart from the other episodes. The lack of music draws our attention to the matter at hand, as the episode focuses on the unforeseen detonation of an atomic bomb and its aftermath.

Typically, *Medic* focused on little-known medical conditions to educate the public about them, and this still applies in the VSE, which illustrates the effects of radiation on the human body after a nuclear attack. This episode's ultimate purpose, however, is to show both what could happen to Americans if they were unprepared and what could happen if civil defense tactics were used after an attack.

The episode opens with the protagonist, Dr. Konrad Styner (Richard Boone), getting a phone call about a state of yellow alert. Unsure whether it is another exercise or the real thing, he asks his nurse. Helen Mitchell (Nan Boardman), to send the patients in the waiting room home. Shortly after Styner, Mitchell, and the other volunteers arrive at their post, the warning siren sounds, and the volunteers gather in a shelter from which they see a bright light followed by a shock wave: this is no exercise, it is the detonation of a bomb. The volunteers begin to worry about their friends and family members who are downtown, where the bomb inevitably struck. The volunteers attempt to travel to the Morningside Armory, where they had been directed to set up a command center, but they cannot get there because everything is destroyed. Thus, they set up the center in a school across the street from the shelter that survived the blast and is clean of radioactive fallout. The volunteers begin to treat victims, some of whom have only minor injuries and who then help others. Later that evening, the volunteers begin to run out of supplies, including morphine, and have to choose who to give the remaining morphine to—deciding not to give it to people who are dying but to save it for those who will live.

The Control of Electromagnetic Radiation system (CONELRAD) then warns people that the warning siren indicated that the enemy had released biological contamination.[6] A person who delivers new supplies tells Styner that

FIG. 1.1 Setting up the civil defense command center in "Flash of Darkness."

people outside are panicking and that he has never seen anything like it. The CONELRAD announcer addresses this by telling people that the civil defense director has ordered that anyone caught looting will be shot on sight and that any illegal activity only aids the enemy. CONELRAD also indicates that the United States has retaliated and the enemy has suffered a crushing blow. Styner asks that he and the other volunteers be relieved, and his request is granted. They will rest and then be reassigned to another post to help further. The episode closes with Boone out-of-character giving a public service announcement about what would happen if a thermonuclear bomb was dropped on the United States and the importance of civil defense. He closes by stating that the nation's civil defense is sick and that the only ones that can cure it are government agencies and citizens.

Silence is often used on television as a marker of death.[7] The silence in this episode foreshadows the destruction once the bomb explodes. Many other television episodes that feature the detonation of an atomic bomb also lack music, whether or not they are VSEs. Many television episodes of the 1950s and 1960s that focus on the bomb, like "Flash of Darkness," do not show a mushroom cloud. When they do, it is usually accompanied by a single chord called a stinger chord, or accompanied by silence. This is often done to draw attention to the magnitude and power of the cloud rather than underscore it through music, which could draw attention instead to itself.

Playhouse 90, "Alas Babylon"

In 1960, *Playhouse 90* aired a television adaptation by David Shaw of Pat Frank's novel *Alas, Babylon*. The broadcast introduction noted that this was a special presentation and that for the evening, it would replace both the *Ed Sullivan Show* and *General Electric Theatre*. In fact, the script's title page calls it "*Playhouse 90* Special."[8] The episode centers on the protagonist, a nuclear war denier who comes to believe in the possibility of such a war only after hearing about an imminent attack over the radio. The production of the play was first scheduled by CBS in July 1959 as the series' season premiere, but three weeks later the network postponed the broadcast without explanation. It was eventually rescheduled for production and airing in April 1960 and announced in February 1960.[9] One explanation for this change was that Charlton Heston, the episode's star, had a prior commitment that conflicted with the first date.[10] However, we can speculate that the delay was also because CBS wanted to ensure the accuracy of the teleplay, as evidenced from the final line of one announcement: "CBS said the office of civil defense and mobilization would assist in insuring [*sic*] the authenticity of its play."[11] Another possibility is that the topic could have been too controversial just several months earlier.[12]

The episode was known for its special effects, which made it seem real, and this is likely also why the only music used came from the radio. According to one review, "the real stars of this TV adaptation . . . are the special effects achieved by the camera in providing the necessary jolt for the fictional atomic war."[13] The footage of the bomb detonation was provided by the Office of Civil and Defense Mobilization (OCDM) from the Bikini Atoll tests. This footage was superimposed over that of a town "to show what the 'Biggest War' might be like."[14] In fact, the OCDM was billed as having "provided experts in the field of civil defense for advice and technical consultation" and worked closely with the producer and story adapter both at OCDM headquarters in Washington, D.C., and its operations center in Battle Creek, Michigan.[15] The footage of the small town is representative of a suburb, used for the fictional town of Fort Repose in central Florida. In this period images of suburbia were often used as the location of atomic bomb television episodes—and Cold War television episodes in general—because life in suburbia represented a contrast to what existence under Soviet occupation would be like.[16] Typically, television episodes set in suburbia would have music typically associated with the locale at the opening. However, "Alas, Babylon" does not, which immediately makes it stand out.

"Alas, Babylon" takes place in Fort Repose, a fictitious town that becomes isolated from the rest of the nation due to an atomic bomb attack on various other parts of the country. However, Fort Repose is still contaminated by radioactive fallout, and the episode centers on how the community wills itself to survive. The title comes from a line in the Bible and was used as a code name among the main characters. At the outset, we find out that the episode's narrator is dead. In this story, the nuclear war between the United States and the Soviet Union is started accidentally. The climax of the episode comes when the city of Orlando is annihilated by the bomb.

The episode's conclusion also caused a lot of controversy among viewers, one of whom wrote: "My plea is that people will see the ridiculousness of the conclusion advocated by Playhouse '90' [*sic*] after the show—namely that everyone build an underground shelter and stock it well with supplies as a 'deterrent' to atomic war."[17] However, it was at this conclusion that the former director of the FCDA, Val Peterson, came on screen to urge everyone watching to take the proper precautions to prepare themselves for a potential atomic attack.

As mentioned above, the episode included only diegetic music. Nondiegetic music, or underscoring, was excluded to lend the film a sense of reality. Like other episodes that focus on the atomic bomb, silence accompanied the detonation, not only marking death but also the gravity of the situation. The use of diegetic music in the series was enough for one critic to remark on the absurdity of its use: Harriet Van Horne noted specifically the absurdity of using it in the scene in which the town's only doctor lies dying of radiation poisoning. She writes: "There was also a scene in which a small, radiation blinded child sat by the bandaged doctor's death-bed and asked, 'Shall I play the phonograph?' On came a crashing, grating jazz record, at which point the doctor breathed his last."[18]

Most of the episode's music was jazz, and some of it came from the CBS stock music library. Other music can be found in later episodes of *The Twilight Zone*, for example, such as the cue "Natural Rock," composed by Bruce Campbell. Jazz was often used in 1950s and 1960s television as a musical marker for the outside world, both for a world untouched by the bomb and for the representation of normalcy despite the bomb. Jazz becomes a trope on television in the period for the frenetic and hectic character of city life. However, the jazz used in "Alas, Babylon" is a deliberate signifier for the state of the faraway city that no longer exists due to the bomb blast. This conscious choice represents not only the loss of life but its now slower—even stopped—pace.

However, the style of the episode's music keeps going back in time, beginning with rock 'n' roll, turning to 1950s big band music, and ending with 1920s jazz. This is a musical representation of the reversion to an innocent age in which people might have to rebuild the world that people believed might exist after a nuclear attack.[19] Society's reversion to primitive days frequently appears in postapocalyptic bomb films, but while those people in this episode do not revert back as far as that, the use of early jazz does indicate the return to a simpler, more innocent time. Typically, in anthology television shows, any diegetic music is used to create an atmosphere. In this case, the music used represents a point in time and how the atomic bomb is forcing society to continually revert to an earlier time. This is unlike any other use of diegetic music in anthology series.

Armstrong Circle Theatre, "Briefing from Room 103"

Armstrong Circle Theatre aired a docudrama on April 26, 1961, called "Briefing from Room 103." The episode was originally titled "Civil Defense" and focused "on the important moral, ethical, and psychological problems that faced Americans concerning the building and use of fallout shelters."[20] The new title refers to the Washington headquarters of the OCDM.[21] This episode was publicized as "the first dramatization of fallout shelter behavior ever presented to the public and notably aired as part of that year's Operation Alert."[22] That evening, viewers were greeted by the announcement that the evening's episode of *Armstrong Circle Theatre* would be a VSE, produced in conjunction with the FCDA. One of the things that made this episode—especially within this docudrama series—so unusual for the typical anthology television show is that it was a dramatization of an experiment in which adults and children were locked in a nuclear bomb shelter to study the emotional effects such confinement would cause. Although *Armstrong Circle Theatre* was the first long-standing docudrama series, many of its episodes provided analyses of current events.[23]

The host, Douglas Edmunds, opens the episode by telling viewers that what they are about to see dramatizes a test that required placing thirty people in a room resembling a community fallout shelter to see how they would react, noting that "a few hours ago, these people were strangers." Interpolated into the dramatization are appearances by prominent officials from the OCDM such as Paul C. McGraff, the organization's Planning Board assistant; Charles K. Schaffer, plans officer; Lewis E. Berry, assistant director of the Plans Office for War and Peace; and Frank B. Ellis, director (and a member of the National Security Council). The messages that these men provided were sometimes instructional and sometimes opinion, and they often conflicted. For instance, McGraff remarked that "in my judgment, the general nuclear war cannot happen," while Schaffer implied that it could, stating that "it would not mean the end of everything." The episode closed with a simple message to viewers: "Survive, Recover, Win."

Unlike "Flash of Darkness" and "Alas, Babylon," "Briefing from Room 103" contains nondiegetic music (composed by Ethel Huber, who was also the series' music director). The music is strategically placed to heighten the impact of the events on screen and to create a sense of drama and urgency. As was typical for each episode of the series, "at the close of each act, a stab of music intensifies the dramatic impact, before the camera is faded out."[24] The placement of these so-called stingers is written in the script.[25] This is significant because it means that the music was considered an important enough part of the production that its placement and type should be precisely indicated.

But the music consists of more than just stingers. The episode's sonic style distinguishes between American civil defense and a potential Soviet attack. Having a musical reference to a specific country is not unusual in television or films of the period. However, specifically identifying the enemy could be dangerous, even if everyone knew that identity. But this film, like others of its type, used music to differentiate Americans from Soviets and outline how Americans could survive if they took proper precautions. In the process, this film musically represents the disasters that the Soviets could cause without actually naming them.

Whenever the episode refers to the Soviet civil defense instead of that of the United States, for example, we hear music that sounds like early twentieth-century Russian music, such as that by Dmitri Shostakovich or Sergei Prokofiev—implying the identity of the nation whose actions could necessitate the use of fallout shelters. The Soviet music often consists of brass and percussion, playing in minor keys. These melodies, which emphasize the interval of a minor third, was a recognizable trademark of Russian music. Both of these musical styles appear at their appropriate moments, implying either American know-how or Soviet sabotage.

Several types of music represent American civil defense protocols. March music played by low percussion and cellos is used to represent American operations such as those of the North American Aerospace Defense Command. A seven-note ostinato (or repeated bass pattern) played by the clarinet appears several times in the episode, functioning as a leitmotif (or a melody that is associated with a person, place, or event—in this case, in a film or television episode). The melody is associated with the OCDM, as we often hear it when the organization is mentioned. At moments that represent obedience—for example, when the participants enter the shelter—we hear triumphant, lyrical music played by high instruments such as the trumpet, violin, oboe, and French horn, all using their highest registers. This music borrows heavily from the musical language of Aaron Copland, with its wide-open intervals evoking the expansiveness of the American West. This use of music to represent America versus the Soviet Union began in the televised civil defense films of the 1950s, so the music's use here derives from a short history within the genre of the civil defense telefilm.[26] The American sound here also often borrows from the victory music of newsreels that depicted the American triumph in World War II.

The music in this episode presents thinly veiled messages about American power and Soviet danger. The contrast between American and non-American sound and between calmness and anxiety reflected the juxtaposition of emotions that were all too common in the United States during the Cold War. The messages were thinly veiled, but the music was not: it revealed a message that could not be verbally acknowledged on screen and therefore functioned as a tool of propaganda. The trope of Soviet versus American music, therefore, was common in civil defense films but not in fictional television episodes.

Conclusion

In early television, VSEs had a variety of topics. However, those that garnered the most attention from the media were those that served to provide the public with useful information regarding what to do in the event of a nuclear attack. The ways that music was used to signal specialness in these episodes varied from the use of no music at all to the use of only diegetic music or nondiegetic music. Thus, there is no consistency in the way that music was used in these VSEs, likely because at this point the genre of VSEs was relatively new. However, the music in these early VSEs also contrasts with that in other episodes in their series, marking their place in the overall oeuvre.

The use of music to convey both specialness and seriousness for these episodes is varied. For "Flash of Darkness," the episode's specialness is evoked through the lack of music. For "Alas, Babylon," the use of only diegetic radio music gives it a sense of realness that is important for the audience to understand what could happen. In the case of "Briefing in Room 103," the highly descriptive musical representations were used to persuade the public to pay attention to the important message on the screen, underscore the destructive power of the bomb, and relay the need to follow civil defense protocols to save as many lives as possible.

As this chapter has shown, these three VSEs are part of a continuum of such episodes that deal with topics including childbirth, terminal illness, and alcoholism. Those other episodes topically signaled their difference from not only the other episodes in their respective series but also from other television shows of the time, and their music also marked them as unique. With minor keys, specific instrumentation, and styles typically not used in television of the day, the sound of these VSEs is just as distinctive as the episodes themselves. Therefore, the music—or lack of it—of atomic bomb VSEs works in different ways to highlight the same message: civil defense can save lives.

Notes

1 Noel Murray, "A Very Special Episode," *A. V. Club*, accessed March 12, 2019, https://www.avclub.com/c/a-very-special-episode.

2 For more on the consideration of sound technologies for composing early television music, see Reba Wissner, "'I *Am* Big, It's the *Pictures* That Got Small': Sound Technologies and Franz Waxman's Scores for *Sunset Boulevard* (1950) and *The Twilight Zone*'s 'The Sixteen-Millimeter Shrine' (1959)," *Journal of Film Music* 7, no. 1 (2014): 79–95.

3 Shawn VanCour, "Television Music and the History of Television Sound," in *Music in Television: Channels of Listening*, ed. James Deaville (London: Routledge, 2011), 67.

4 For more on network library music, see Reba Wissner, *A Dimension of Sound: Music in The Twilight Zone* (Hillsdale, NY: Pendragon Press, 2014), chapter 1.

5 Shawn VanCour, "From Radio to Television: Sound Style and Audio Technique in Early TV Anthology Dramas," in *The Routledge Companion to Screen Music and Sound*, ed. Miguel Mera, Ronald Sadoff, and Ben Winters (Abingdon, UK: Routledge, 2017), 172–173.

6 The CONELRAD system was designed to take over radio and television stations in an emergency and ask people to tune their radios to the designated system stations,

640 or 1240 AM, for further instructions. CONELRAD stations worked in clusters in each city, meaning that they broadcast a single program in alternation to prevent bombers from homing in on a single location. Some radio broadcasts warned people to follow only the information given on CONELRAD stations. See Federal Civil Defense Administration, "Dial CONELRAD" (Washington: Federal Civil Defense Administration, 1956), 4.

7 Janet K. Halfyard, *Sounds of Fear and Wonder: Music in Cult TV* (London: I. B. Tauris, 2016), 70.

8 David Shaw, "Alas, Babylon," teleplay script as telecast, April 9, 1960, private collection.

9 "CBS to Do Alas, Babylon April 3," *Orlando Sentinel,* February 6, 1960.

10 "Playhouse 90 Postpones Alas Babylon," *Orlando Sentinel,* August 25, 1959.

11 "'Alas, Babylon' Scheduled Again," *Des Moines Register,* March 6, 1960.

12 TV Scout, "Atomic Disaster Novel Dramatized on Playhouse 90," *Pittsburgh Press,* April 3, 1960.

13 "Today's TV Key," *Battle Creek Enquirer,* April 3, 1960.

14 TV Scout, "Atomic Disaster Novel Dramatized on Playhouse 90."

15 "Nuclear Age on Stage," *Express and News* (San Antonio, TX), August 23, 1959.

16 Rupa Huq, *Making Sense of Suburbia through Popular Culture* (London: Bloomsbury, 2013), 85.

17 Barbara T. Snipes, "This Threat to Civilization," *Bristol Daily Courier* (Bristol, PA), April 8, 1960.

18 Harriet Van Horne, "'Alas Babylon' Loses Out to Good Fun on Showcase," *El Paso Herald-Post,* April 4, 1960.

19 In fact, the notion of reverting back even to the Stone Age may have come from a statement made by Albert Einstein: "I don't know what weapons will be used in World War III; I do know that World War IV will be fought with clubs" (WBNT interview, "H-Bomb and Atomic Energy," February 12, 1950, quoted in "Can We Live with the Atom? An Answer by Scientists and Physicians" [Hollywood: Southern California Chapter of the National Council of Arts, Sciences, and Professionals, n.d.), 6. The Left Literature Collection of Pamphlets and Periodicals, Identifier 0100, Box 6, University of Southern California Libraries Special Collections, Los Angeles, CA).

20 Memo from James T. Ramey, Joint Committee on Atomic Energy, to Wallace F. Bennett, "Comments on *Armstrong Circle Theater* Script Entitled 'Civil Defense,'" February 14, 1961, Chester Earl Holifield Papers, Identifier 0220, Box 42, Folder: Civil Defense 1961, University of Southern California Libraries Special Collections, Los Angeles, CA.

21 Arthur Cantor, "Three Government 'Experts' to Appear on Armstrong Circle Theatre 'Actual' 'Briefing from Room 103,'" 1, undated press release, Arthur Cantor Papers, 1951–1965, box 21, folder 12, Wisconsin Historical Society, Madison, WI.

22 "Civil Defense TV Program Set," *Wellington Daily News* (Wellington, KS), April 21, 1961.

23 Tom W. Hoffer and Richard Alan Nelson, "Docudrama on American Television," in *Why Docudrama? Fact-Fiction on Film and TV,* ed. Alan Rosenthal (Carbondale: Southern Illinois University Press, 1999), 68.

24 Myron Berkeley Shaw, "A Descriptive Analysis of the Documentary Drama Television Program, *The Armstrong Circle Theatre,* 1955–1961," PhD diss., University of Michigan, 1962, 96.

25 Harold Gast, *Armstrong Circle Theatre,* "Civil Defense," second revised script, February 27, 1961, Arthur Cantor Papers, 1951–1965, box 21, folder 12, Wisconsin Historical Society, Madison, WI.

26 For more on the music of early televised civil defense films, see Reba Wissner, "'Once You Hear This, Act Fast': Music in Civil Defense Television Advertisements of the Fifties," in *The Oxford Handbook of Music and Advertising,* ed. James Deaville, Ronald Rodman, and Siu Lan Tan (Oxford: Oxford University Press, 2021).

2

Blackface on a White Christmas

Bewitched's "Sneaky Racism"

JONATHAN COHN

During its run on ABC from 1964 to 1972, *Bewitched* was one of the most popular series on television, and it continues to be widely syndicated around the globe. Like other fantastical sitcoms of the period—such as *I Dream of Jeannie* (NBC, 1965–1970), *Lost in Space* (CBS, 1965–1968) and *My Favorite Martian* (CBS, 1963–1966)—*Bewitched* capitalized on the global interest in space travel and the promise that much of what was once considered science fiction, fantasy, or magic would soon become reality. Like these other series, *Bewitched* routinely used rapid technological and cultural transformations as a chance to question the sexism and racism explicit in the white flight and suburban lifestyle of the white American nuclear family.[1]

Bewitched traces the suburban malaise of Samantha Stephens, a somewhat rebellious witch played by Elizabeth Montgomery, who surreptitiously uses her powers to teach lessons to bigots and jerks and to counteract her meddling relatives, who disapprove of her "mixed" marriage to Darrin Stephens (played first by Dick York and later by Dick Sargent), a nonmagical Mad Man-esque advertising executive who does not approve of using magic in public. Clearly, this general setup (not to mention the specific plots of many episodes) suggests a strong desire to use magic as a way to tell stories about women's liberation and racial conflicts in the United States in the years immediately following passage of the Civil Rights Act of 1964. Yet during this period—defined by a ceaseless struggle for the most basic rights for people of color and the concomitant unrelenting assassinations, unrest, rebellions, marches, and strikes—*Bewitched* rarely dealt overtly with racism or even featured nonwhite characters. Instead, the series confronted racism almost entirely at the level of metaphor. This has led many scholars to argue that its liberal messages and feminist tone disguise a sneaky racism, an underlying ideology aligned with a white patriarchal perspective. For example, Phoebe Bronstein suggests that "entirely absent of bodies of color," the series ends up focusing only on the concerns of white bourgeois women.[2] As Lynn Spigel points out, there is some value in centering on this subject, especially as doing so critiques and pokes fun at the idealized image of the 1950s subservient housewife.[3] One could also argue that the series strategically focused on racism only at the level of metaphor to sneakily challenge the stereotypes of those viewers most reluctant to consider their own racism. Yet this strategy comes at the price of erasing people of color from the picture.

That said, here I focus on a rare occurrence in which *Bewitched* attempted to tackle racism head-on in the form of a very special Christmas episode. Montgomery introduces this episode, "Sisters at Heart" (December 24, 1970), as a "very special *Bewitched*, conceived in the image of innocence and truth." While very special episodes (VSEs) often present images of diversity, equity, and social justice in their content, their production methods rarely change and continue to rely on inequitable studios and largely white crews. In contrast, "Sisters at Heart" was written in large part by a class of Black students at Jefferson High School in South Los Angeles, California, making it very special not just in its content, but also in its attempt to imagine a more equitable mode of production. For its efforts and discussion of race, the episode won a prestigious Governor's Award Emmy. I am specifically interested in how its attempts to combat bigotry intersect with and are structured by the industrial goals and format of the VSE and its belief that making problems visible is a necessary step to solving them. In addition, I argue that *Bewitched*'s method of combating racism is also guided by the logic of the epiphany (which is only fitting, given its Christmas theme episodes)—that is, the idea that merely making a problem visible can lead to sudden, profound, and even miraculous transformations.[4]

At the beginning of "Sisters at Heart," Lisa (Venetta Rogers), the Black daughter of Darlene (Janee Michelle) and Keith Wilson (one of Darrin's colleagues played by Don Marshall), has a sleepover with Samantha and Darrin's daughter, Tabitha, who is excited to gain a temporary sister. At a park, Tabitha learns from another child that they cannot be sisters because they are different colors. As a solution, Tabitha first turns her friend white, then turns herself Black, and then turns them both polka-dotted.

The white and Black Lisas are portrayed by different actresses, while the Black Tabitha is portrayed by the actress who played the white Tabitha in blackface.

FIG. 2.1 Tabitha and Lisa claim their sisterhood through polka-dotted skin.

In the meantime, Brockway, a rich client of Darrin's, mistakenly assumes that Lisa (who at this point is Black) is Darrin's daughter and reacts by taking his business away from Darrin's company. Like Tabitha, Samantha decides that the solution to this racism is to make Brockway suddenly see everyone around him, including himself, as Black (spoiler alert: it works!). While this effect could have been accomplished in any number of ways, nearly every character is at least briefly done up in blackface or whiteface. Brockway comes back the next day to apologize, announcing that yesterday he discovered he was a racist—not the usual kind, but a "sneaky racist," one so sneaky that he did not realize his own prejudice. The episode makes this racism visible, and (as Darlene's father, Keith, suggests in the conclusion) it attempts to adequately define the problem to then solve it. But in its bizarre attempt to solve racism through the use of blackface in half an hour, *Bewitched* could be said to suffer from this same sneaky racism.

A great deal of attention has been paid to the television industry's efforts in the civil rights era to confront the explicit and intense racism with its segregation, violence, and assassinations through antiracist content, protests, and boycotts. For instance, Steven Classen has focused on how series like *Bonanza* (NBC, 1959–1973) at once attacked and profited from the blatant racism in the South in the early 1960s, and Aniko Bodroghkozy has discussed how series like *The Smothers Brothers* (CBS, 1967–1969) incorporated critical activist methods into their productions.[4] But much less attention has been paid to television's attempts to confront the often less visible and visual forms of everyday racism that many more white Americans have continually been guilty of, whether they realize it or not (that is, sneaky racism). Whether in the form of making assumptions about people and/or hiring them based on their race—or in Brockway's case, the race of their loved ones—this racism is often just as harmful as the more traumatic forms of racism that tend to garner far more headlines. In the early 1970s, this change in tactic from addressing racism as an extreme and purposeful evil to one based more on carelessness signals a sudden transformation in how television imagined and dealt with racism after many of the major fights of the civil rights era. Far more attention has been paid to television's antiracist achievements in the early to mid-1960s than to those in the early 1970s, which makes complete sense considering the many important transformations that took place during the earlier period. Yet this focus has elided the efforts to tackle racism by people who mean well but still manage to unthinkingly perpetuate racist attitudes and otherwise make a mess of things. It took a VSE to tackle this everyday racism, although the episode also unwittingly participates in it.

"Sisters at Heart" offers a chance to consider the sneaky ways in which television attempted to tackle sneaky racism. But *Bewitched*'s reasons for doing so are a bit confusing and its methods—especially its use of blackface—are hardly ideal. Why focus on sneaky racism at all, and why call it that? While there is a kinship between "sneakiness" and more recent terms like "dog-whistle politics" and "microaggressions," all of these terms imply a difference in who intends what and who is aware of the racism at hand. "Dog-whistle politics" describes situations in which someone intentionally employs racist, sexist, or otherwise harmful language and/or acts in a way that a particular audience will grasp but that other people may not even notice. In contrast, microaggressions are clearly seen as racist and/or sexist by their targets, but their perpetrators and other observers are often unaware of the prejudice inherent in their words or actions. Those words and actions may be framed as so minor that they do not rise to the level of needing to be called out or deserving of becoming upset over. While both of these forms of racism are "sneaky," the racism on *Bewitched* is different because while Brockway is unaware of his own racism, it is obvious to everyone around him. As this racism also effects Darrin's business, it has an immediate and demonstrable economic effect and should not be considered minor or micro in scale.

The racial politics of this episode are also deeply inflected and shaped by its unique production. Indeed, the way the episode was made may be more interesting than the episode itself. "Sisters at Heart" was written by a class of twenty-four Black students at Jefferson High School. Articles published at the time describe Jefferson as a "ghetto school" full of "filth, broken windows, pill pushers, pimps, students on drugs and students struggling to stay off drugs, students from broken homes and low-income families, students who know poverty and hunger."[5]

These same articles describe the students' novice white teacher, Marcella Saunders. According to one article, "faced with a despairing lack of motivation from her students, most of whom felt the system had 'shut them out,' Marcella began searching for a common ground, a bridge between her world and that of her pupils. She found it in television."[6] Saunders used television episodes to teach the short story and contacted producers from her students' favorite series, including *Room 222* (ABC, 1969–1974), *Julia* (NBC, 1968–1971), and *Bewitched*, to see if they could visit a set and watch the filming of an episode.

William Asher, a producer-director for *Bewitched* and Montgomery's husband, apparently liked the idea of using television to teach reading and analysis skills and paid to bus fifty students to the studio on three occasions. The producers gave each student a script so they could follow what was going on during filming and sent the school scripts for thirty other episodes to use in class.[7] Saunders's students had the idea of writing an episode themselves as a thank-you present, and they sent it to Asher and Montgomery. In their episode, the *Los Angeles Times* reported, these students wanted "to say that racism has to be taught. That children 4 or 5 years old do not see color in racist terms. You have to teach a child how to be a racist and hate. We'd like to say that it's not what you look like but what you are that counts."[8] In other words, they used their script to describe the structural inequities they experienced every day.

These students were already well versed in discussing and fighting against these inequities. Two years earlier, students at Jefferson, in solidarity with those at other schools across Los Angeles, staged a boycott to protest the treatment of Hispanic students and to ask for more Mexican American studies in their curriculum.[9] These efforts also challenged the impoverishing and maligning ways newspapers described these students and their community that were later reflected in coverage of the *Bewitched* episode. Whether or not these descriptions exaggerated the decrepitude of Jefferson—a school that is only a few blocks from the campus of the University of Southern California and that has produced many accomplished musicians, actors, politicians, and judges, as well as the Nobel Peace Prize recipient Ralph Bunche—these articles focus on the distance both between Saunders and her students and between these students and *Bewitched*'s assumed audience to make television's ability to bridge these divides and unify audiences all the more miraculous.

"Sisters at Heart" is staged as a series of discussions about different types of racism and how to best combat them (which somehow ends up being through the use of blackface). The conversations between the Wilsons and the Montgomerys take on a postracial tinge, and the main characters behave as if no one recognizes racial difference but without acknowledging that they have come into contact with very few if any Black characters up to this point in the series. Larry, Darrin's boss, is the first person to say anything that suggests he even notices racial differences when he announces that if they get the account, they will "really have a white Christmas"—which makes Keith jokingly respond, "Hey, watch that!" This moment is clearly played for laughs and is framed as what we might now term a microaggression—that is, it is a slight form of racism that the target is expected to shrug off without being offended.

In contrast to the adults, Tabitha and Lisa are constantly engaged in discussions of race once the girl at the park informs them of its importance. They seem to think of racial division and their inability to be sisters as a practical rather than metaphysical problem, and magic becomes its technical fix: we can't be sisters because we are different colors, so let's figure out how not to be different colors. When Samantha hears Tabitha announce that a girl from the park told her she and Lisa couldn't be sisters, her response is very slow, deliberate, and careful. At that moment, she is clearly trying to work out how best to handle this situation: should she just let it go, should she add critique, or should she explain the nuances of racism in America and is this a good time to bring up slavery? Eventually, she states that the girl in the park was wrong and that being sisters means that "you share something, usually the same parents. But if you share other things like good feelings, friendship, and love the way you two do, that makes you sisters in another way. Actually, all men are brothers, even if they are girls." By framing the problem of racism in terms of a general sense of universal sister- and brotherhood, the episode transforms the question of racial difference into a feminist, primarily gendered, concern. Not coincidentally, this is the general strategy for combating racism used by *Bewitched* and other fantastical sitcoms. And indeed, it is strategic, insofar as it attempts to make white people more comfortable with the fight for racial equality by equating it with the fight for gender equality—which they at least ostensibly supported.

Brockway's racism is clearly set up as the most egregious and in need of rebuke. A great deal of emphasis is put on his sin of noticing race at all and forthrightly acknowledging it both through his tacky gifts—a white doll for Tabitha, a Black doll for Lisa, and a panda for the child he hasn't seen yet—and his comments on how "gutsy" Darrin and Darlene are. Yet Brockway isn't exactly wrong to acknowledge that being in an interracial marriage in 1970 was gutsy. Fifty years later, as Kristen Warner has pointed out, it is now more problematic to ignore the power and importance of race than to confront it.[10] Through its laugh track and silences, "Sisters at Heart" suggests that Brockway's problem is less his noticing race than his putting far too much weight on that aspect of identity and judging people based on it.

Framing Brockway's racism as unintended and unconscious but very obvious allows the episode to address economic and structural racism in a relatively unaggressive way. It focuses on racism as an aspect of our subconscious, whose basis and effect on us are largely unknowable and unnoticed except in discrete moments. This way of imagining racism fits very nicely with the way VSEs more generally attempt to narrativize all social ills as caused by a lack of visibility: the television industry and scholars alike often imagine that by making a problem visible, they are one major step closer to solving it.[11] This framing also echoes the common liberal fantasy that racism is a hidden ideology that can be undone by making it visible and explicit. That fantasy largely discounts the possibility that racists may be aware of the effects of their actions and perform them anyway.

Racists thereby become less villainous and more childlike in their ignorance or innocence.

When we first meet Brockway, he asks for milk and cookies from his elderly and motherly secretary. This scene clearly infantilizes him and not only mocks his racism, but also makes it appear forgivable and easily remedied via education and a bit of self-reflection. Notably, this episode aired just weeks before the premiere of *All in the Family* (CBS, 1971–1979), a series known for its depiction of Archie Bunker, an endlessly redeemable and ostensibly well-meaning racist. But unlike Archie, Brockway needs only one lesson to cure his racism: he refers to the experience of seeing himself and everyone else as Black as a "realization" equivalent to "twenty years" of psychiatry.

Infantilization has its problems, especially since it ultimately lets Brockway off the hook not only for his current racist acts but also for all previous transgressions. Yet there is also something valuable in how it allows him to redeem and transform himself. I don't want to discount Brockway's experience as naïve, clichéd, or simply impossible. The epiphany is the guiding structure of both the VSE and the Christmas special, in which epiphanies and Christmas miracles go hand in hand. This makes sense, given the religious significance of the epiphany as a sudden and shocking manifestation of the divine and the celebration that surrounds it.[12] The description of Brockway's experience of seeing everyone including himself as Black as "equivalent to twenty years on a psychiatrist's couch" expresses the television industry's faith in the idea that the cure to any social ill, including racism, is to make it more visible.

While the audience, guided by the laugh track, is supposed to snicker at Brockway's ignorance of himself, one might also imagine that white liberal viewers may also have felt relieved to imagine their own racism as unconscious and easily solved by someone making them aware of it. In addition, I suspect that those viewers might have been relieved to see that such racism is easily forgiven, once forgiveness is asked for. Although simplistic, this way of tackling racism has the benefit of addressing racism without making everyone extremely defensive and anxious.

Indeed, this framing of racism as an innocent or unconscious error is important because it ends up privileging certain cures over others. Rather than shunning, shaming, or punishing Brockway and others for their racist acts, the cure for racism is presented here as generosity, patience, and education. This tactic problematically continues to place white people at the center of discussions of racial equity—thereby further disempowering people of color, who become simplistic props used to make white people better. And, of course, using blackface as a tool to fight racism is unconscionable from our contemporary vantage point. Now one cannot help but be amazed at the idea that blackface could somehow be viewed as a tool of cross-cultural solidarity and a cure-all for racism. One might argue that blackface was not as universally reviled in the 1970s as it is today, but that hardly ameliorates the situation. If anything, it just means that far too many people in that period were far too comfortable dehumanizing others. Eric Lott has perhaps most helpfully described how blackface is a theft of Black culture and bodies by whites who both love and fear them. Whatever admiration is expressed through blackface is mixed with a fear that Blacks might supersede whites (especially white men) and their culture and a desire to steal that culture for whites' economic gain. Blackface and minstrelsy typically present Blacks in a mocking, hypersexualized, dehumanized, and antebellum state, and Lott describes this representation as coming from a "pale gaze" interested in "projecting vulgar Black types as spectacular objects of white men's looking."[13] However, the fact that the script for the episode was written by Black students must complicate our evaluation of the tactic, even if the script was then staged by white producers.

Indeed, in many ways, this blackface is quite different from what Lott describes. First, the images of blackface are quite brief, with the camera focused only for one or two seconds on each character's face in makeup as they stand quite still. Given this brevity, there is certainly shock and spectacle, but little sense of cultural appropriation or theft. Nor is it a vulgar caricature of Blacks, as none of the characters take on a different persona or act in a different way. Brockway, the only person other than Samantha who can see everyone (including himself) in blackface, is simply shocked and confused and quickly leaves. This moment is played for ironic humor directed more at the absurdity of the situation than anything else—as Brockway sees himself and everyone around him as Black, the scene slows and gets quiet. The bits of laughter that do appear seem to be directed at Brockway rather than the Black bodies. Racism, apparently, is what is being laughed at. Indeed, this blackface is arguably less racially problematic than the recurring character of Dr. Bombay, who neither adopts the skin color or stereotyped mannerisms of Indians but does use the name Bombay and Orientalist fashion to appear more exotic.

Instead of a dehumanizing stereotype, the blackface parallels the depiction of Darlene and Keith, who are portrayed as bourgeois subjects who only passingly refer to their race through small quips. Darlene and Keith, along with all of the characters in blackface, are not minstrel figures but rather representations of what Herman Gray has called the "civil rights subject": "those Black, largely middle-class beneficiaries who gained the most visibility as well as material and status rewards from the struggles and opportunities generated by the civil rights movement. This cultural figure embodies complex codes of behavior and propriety that make it an exemplar of citizenship and responsibility—success, mobility, hard work, sacrifice, individualism."[14]

Darlene, Keith, and Lisa—as a nuclear family with elegant attire, a middle- or upper-class income, and seemingly complete integration into the Stephenses' community, if only for a brief episode—are subjects who no longer feel the need to fight for their rights: they have already won them. The Stephenses treat them as complete equals, making no mention of their race, nor do they react awkwardly when Keith briefly refers to it. When presented with Brockway's racism, they simply laugh it off as if he were a relic of a bygone and trivial past. Yet this Black family is contained within a VSE and never appears again in the series, suggesting that at this point, this subject formation is more fantasy than reality. Indeed, VSEs are generally replete with guest characters, like the drunk Uncle Ned (Tom Hanks) on *Family Ties* (NBC, 1982–1989) and the drunk-driving fatality Sandy (Mathew Perry) on *Growing Pains* (ABC, 1985–1992), whose brief appearances are used to teach a lesson to an assumed middle-class white audience. Notably, Gray suggests that representations of the civil rights subject do not start appearing until 1972, making "Sisters at Heart" an early model for the televisual representation of this new subject formation.[15] But the civil rights subject is not an entirely positive figure. As Gray and Bodroghkozy point out, the civil rights subject is damaging insofar as it seems to value only those middle- or upper-class Black subjects who were somehow able to prosper—with or without civil rights. In the process, the civil rights subject paradoxically helped present Blacks as equal to whites even as it suggested that civil rights were ultimately not necessary.

"Sisters at Heart" makes blackface an earnest if deeply problematic metaphor for the common hope—explicit in many VSEs—that by changing how viewers literally see something on their screen, television can change society more generally. In this way, the VSE also follows the "fake it till you make it" logic of postracial rhetoric, which suggests that if people simply state that all races are treated equally with enough conviction, we might eventually get there. Of course, central to the episode's postracial representation was its production backstory, presented both in the episode itself and in many syndicated newspaper stories. These stories focused on the benefits of the production to the students at Jefferson High School. In the process, the episode became a celebration of television's ostensible ability to appeal to people across racial, class, gender, and all of the other lines that divided America during this moment. This effort served to frame television as a mass medium that could appeal to everyone and, in so doing, unite them into a common audience. Ron Becker argues in chapter 9 of this anthology that the VSE has historically been a tool for shaping television as a mass medium for all audiences. But ironically and unfortunately, the reporting on "Sisters at Heart" uses this rhetoric at the expense of the students, who are diminished to make the accomplishments of Saunders and *Bewitched* appear even more impressive. At the same time, this effort follows the logic of the melting pot more generally and also echoes many of the themes and contradictions that appear within the episode about how best to be inclusive and antiracist.

Many articles describing the high schoolers go into detail, describing how they wrote the plot of Tabitha transforming her friend and the dilemma about whether to turn both children white or Black. Expecting that, either way, one or potentially all racial groups would be upset with their decision, the students chose instead to make the children polka-dotted, both to make it clear they were now each both white and Black and also to suggest that "they were giving something of themselves to each other."[16] One could argue that this image of a white girl and a Black girl becoming the same color is an image of integration in a melting-pot style. While this metaphor promises that integration will improve everyone within a community, it has also been roundly criticized as an attempt to erase the cultural differences that make us all unique. Ultimately, the melting pot has worked only to keep white American culture as the norm and force all others to assimilate into it. Yet the Jefferson High students also thought of their work as specifically empowering for their racialized community, as a way to "lighten the spirits of our students" and "say what we think in a nonviolent way."[17]

Asher liked the students' script and had the series writer, Barbara Avedon, help him revise and expand it to fit the show's half-hour length and format. In the process, a sense of the series' dominant white perspective was brought back in. All of the reporting and reviewing of this episode that I have found focuses narrowly on the plot of Tabitha's and Lisa's changing color and completely ignores Brockway, including his seeing everyone as Black. This could be due to a desire not to reveal the end of the episode, but it suggests that the Brockway plot was what Avedon ended up adding to make the episode the right length. At the same time, the working script was quite long, at forty pages, and much of what was cut during production and/or editing appears to be from Lisa's plot and her parents' dialogue. The result is that while Lisa is advertised as the reason to watch the episode, Brockway and the question of whether he will stop being so bigoted has just as much, if not more, narrative weight. This doesn't mean that the students were unaware of or did not agree with these changes and/or additions, but at the very least it shows the power dynamics implicit in any creative collaboration, especially when one side has all of the money and power. That said, the students continued to be involved all the way through production meetings, story conferences, rehearsals, and the filming of the episode. Asher reportedly marveled at their development, saying that "this is just one tiny example of what can happen when you reach out a hand and care." He hoped that this experiment might be a model for other businesses across the country that were serious about integration and making the world a "better place to live."[18] This belief was echoed by Saunders and her students, who used the money they earned through their scriptwriting and royalties to start a foundation at Jefferson High to support a mass media course and further creative efforts by students. What else could one ask for?

This story has everything: it's an assemblage of many of the central stories the television industry most fondly tells about itself—that it's timely, educational, a public good, and artistic. It is not just a mass medium; it is *the* mass medium. The story also illustrates how the VSE has helped television sell itself as such. Various newspaper articles about "Sisters at Heart" refer to television as a "teaching device" and use the episode to challenge the idea that television is a vast wasteland.[19] Spigel has remarked that fantastical sitcoms were often interested in challenging and reversing this wasteland depiction of television, with their focus on examining contemporary cultural dilemmas from a distanced perspective. Along with this trend, television producers have long relied on the VSE to suggest that they will at least occasionally center their efforts on education rather than just entertainment.[20] Furthermore, Saunders' use of television in class was praised for how she placed television on the same artistic level as literature and celebrated its ability to speak to current events and the lives of her students. While Brett Mills in chapter 12 of this anthology discusses the importance of liveness to the identity of television and the VSE, this episode of *Bewitched* celebrates how a sense of immediacy and closeness with audiences can be generated through the simpler act of commenting on current issues as a mediator speaking to all sides of an issue at once.

I discuss this production context not to suggest that we must read it positively and as well-meaning because it was created, in part, by Black teenagers. Rather, I think such a discussion is helpful for identifying the various competing meanings of this episode and for adding nuance to our evaluation of its antiracist messaging and use of blackface. It is indeed surprising that the students thought of racism in the innocent if not naïve way they did—that is what interested me in this episode in the first place. From their perspective, the blackface in this episode takes on a very different meaning from its dominant associations. While Lott argues that through blackface, white people have "ruthlessly disavowed [their] fleshly investments through ridicule and racist lampoon," these teenage writers at least imagined that blackface would instead disavow and ridicule racism itself.[21]

Like many ostensibly critical uses of blackface—from Linda Rondstadt's pimp persona to *Soul Man* (1986), Spike Lee's *Bamboozled* (2000), and *Tropic Thunder* (2008), not to mention the perennial college students who swear they are not being racist as they don blackface Halloween costumes—its use in *Bewitched* is perhaps simultaneously racist and antiracist. Just like Lott's blackface, the purpose of the magical transformations on *Bewitched* is fundamentally to entertain white audiences while also representing them as benevolent toward Black people. For Brockway, seeing everyone around him in blackface is a punishment, but for the audience, at least according to the laugh track, it is a moment of uneasy humor and momentary suspense about what Brockway will do.

Even with these important limitations, I can't help but see this moment as an attempt, however problematic, to argue that if white people could experience in an embodied way what it is like to be Black even for just a second, they would come to see Black people as equals and would thereby cease being racist. This moment is an attempt to place viewers in the embodied position of the Black teenage writers, for whom racism is less a topic for VSEs and holiday fables than it is a constant existential threat. For Samantha, this moment is magical vengeance for the disruption of her postracial fantasy; for Brockway, it is a Christmas miracle; but for the teenagers who wrote this episode, it is just another day.

But now, more than anything else, this episode—like many VSEs watched far after they were produced—generates an odd feeling of heartfelt cringing. It's hard to tell at times whether the episode is representing racism as sneaky, whether it is just sneakily being racist, or whether it is doing both at the same time. In the process, it illustrates many of the double binds that television puts itself in when it tries to tackle a divisive topic for a mass audience. While paying these students and giving them the opportunity to tell their story to a global audience were extremely admirable and constitute perhaps one of the most equitable and ethical experiments in mainstream television production history, it is also a shame that nothing further came of it. One can easily see in this episode why the criticism of the VSE has been so intense. Lisa, Tabitha's new best friend and sister, appears in this episode but never returns. Whatever hope was proffered for opening up more roles for people of color or having a more sustained focus on racial inequities on the series never materialized. Rather, the episode, like many VSEs, appears to solve racism so that the series never has to deal with it again.

Notes

1 For a more detailed explanation of how white flight was represented in these episodes, see Lynn Spigel, "From Domestic Space to Outer Space: The 1960's Fantastic Family Sit-Com," in *Close Encounters: Film, Feminism, and Science Fiction*, ed. Constance Penley, Elizabeth Lyon, Lynn Spigel, et al. (Minneapolis: University of Minnesota Press, 1991), 205–236.

2 Phoebe Bronstein, "On Feminism, Racism, and *Bewitched*'s Not-So-Magical Politics of Fun," *Flow*, February 27, 2017, https://www.flowjournal.org/2017/02/on-feminism-racism-and-bewitcheds-not-so-magical-politics-of-fun/.

3 Spigel, "From Domestic Space to Outer Space."

4 Steven D. Classen, *Watching Jim Crow: The Struggles over Mississippi TV, 1955–1969* (Durham, NC: Duke University Press, 2004); Aniko Bodroghkozy, *Groove Tube: Sixties Television and the Youth Rebellion* (Durham, NC: Duke University Press, 2001). See also Christine Acham, *Revolution Televised* (Minneapolis: University of Minnesota Press, 2005).

5 Aleene MacMinn, "Almost Like Magic," *Louisville Courier-Journal and Times*, December 13, 1970.

6 "'Bewitched' Yule Script Written by 10th Graders," *Norfolk Journal and Guide*, December 26, 1970.

7 Aleene MacMinn, "Class Bewitched into Achievement," *Los Angeles Times*, December 14, 1970.

8 Quoted in ibid.

9 Gabriel Lerner, "The Walkouts of 1968 and the Los Angeles Media," *Hispanic L.A.* (blog), February 15, 2019, https://hispanicla.com/the-walkouts-of-1968-and-the-los-angeles-media-31471.

10 Kristen J. Warner, *The Cultural Politics of Colorblind TV Casting* (New York: Routledge, 2015).

11 Monica J. Casper and Lisa Jean Moore, *Missing Bodies: The Politics of Visibility* (New York: New York University Press, 2009).

12 Georgia Petridou, *Divine Epiphany in Greek Literature and Culture* (New York: Oxford University Press, 2016).

13 Eric Lott, *Love and Theft: Blackface Minstrelsy and the American Working Class* (New York: Oxford University Press, 2013), 36.

14 Herman Gray, *Watching Race: Television and the Struggle for Blackness* (Minneapolis: University of Minnesota Press, 2004), 353.
15 Gray, *Watching Race*.
16 MacMinn, "Almost Like Magic."
17 Ibid.
18 Quoted in MacMinn, "Class Bewitched into Achievement."
19 "'Bewitched' Yule Script Written by 10th Graders"; MacMinn, "Class Bewitched into Achievement."
20 Spigel, "From Domestic Space to Outer Space."
21 Lott, 23.

3

Conspicuous Morality

Very Special Episodes, the War on Drugs, and Broadcast Deregulation

PHILIP SCEPANSKI

In 1983, President Ronald Reagan's favorite show, *Family Ties*, aired a very special episode (VSE) in which the main character illegally used prescription diet pills to help him study. Earlier that year, Nancy Reagan had appeared on *Diff'rent Strokes* after that show's main character uncovered drugs at his elementary school. As might be expected, both programs demonized drug use as an existential threat to young people, a lesson learned by characters and audiences alike. With a preponderance of episodes like these, the Reagan era has a decent claim to be the golden age of the VSE. At their most basic, VSEs deal with particularly serious social problems in ways that are unusual within the larger series. This frequently meant that these episodes' narratives and styles were also distinct. For instance, major character traits might be revealed, only to be ignored in the rest of the series.

The thin line between drug use and abuse was a major theme of these programs, appearing in many of the decade's iconic family sitcoms. During this period, the Reagan administration's war on drugs was kicking into high gear as the president and his wife labored to convince the American public that drugs were a significant threat. At the same time, the president's regulators were lifting requirements on broadcasters to perform certain kinds of public service. Although interventionist approaches to illegal drugs and laissez-faire economic policy seem to represent wildly different political philosophies, they proved complementary to the television industry. To broadcasters, supporting Reagan's drug policies helped justify deregulation. So when shows like *Family Ties* and *Diff'rent Strokes* produced antidrug episodes, it was part of a broader strategy by broadcasters to prove, by serving Reagan's social policies, that regulation was unnecessary.

In her classic study of television and Reaganism, Jane Feuer examines made-for-TV movies that dealt with significant social issues. She reads this cycle of movies as expressing a desire to resolve "the traumas of the American family in a rejuvenation of public institutions by the people, the same promise that got Reagan elected."[1] VSEs in this era do of much the same work. Especially in the episodes dealing with problems like drugs—issues framed as being most significant for young people—the narrative resolves threats to the family, though the extent to which public institutions come into play is variable. This chapter shares Feuer's concern with the interaction between television content and cultural politics. In Feuer's study, however, she consciously avoids engaging with the most notable Reaganite sitcoms in favor of analyzing a more general cultural politics, naming *Family Ties* along with *The Cosby Show* as archetypal examples that she explicitly avoids discussing in depth.[2] This study also differs from Feuer's in its engagement with electoral politics in the forms of presidential policy rhetoric and regulatory policy. But although this chapter uses Federal Communications Commission (FCC) documents and concerns FCC policy, it examines the way television programming reflected presidential policy rhetoric, arguing that television programming itself proved significant to Reagan's domestic programs. While there may not be a smoking gun to prove that broadcasters and regulators were meeting in back rooms to form alliances, there is a striking coincidence of discourses and interests between these parties in a relatively short period of deregulatory action. In the process of supporting Reagan's war on drugs, these VSEs also helped justify his deregulatory policy by using profitable, popular television to show how broadcasters could fulfill their public service obligations without being forced to do so by regulators.

Deregulation and Intervention: Reagan Policy, the FCC, and the War on Drugs

It is tempting to narrate the conservative revival of the 1980s purely as the politics of economic deregulation. To do so, however, is to ignore the many ways in which Reagan enacted interventionist, "big government" policies on issues like abortion, unions, military spending, and crime (including the war on drugs). While the television shows under examination in this chapter focus on drug abuse, the larger context of Reaganist politics demonstrates the complicated interactions of these different policies. VSEs supported the administration's rhetoric in the war on drugs to help build support for the economic deregulation of the television industry.

The United States experienced a moral panic over drug abuse in the 1980s. James E. Hawdon notes that, rather than simply responding to popular will, the administration built support for the war on drugs through pointed rhetoric.[3] Before addressing drug abuse with policy measures, both the president and first lady embarked on a rhetorical mission to create a popular desire for such policies. As the examples below demonstrate, however, rhetoric building support for a moral panic can come from many places, including family sitcoms. This fact evokes Horace Newcomb and Paul M. Hirsch's classic article, "Television as a Cultural Forum."[4] According to Newcomb and Hirsch, television has the power to set agendas for what people think about, even if it is not terribly effective at convincing them of anything. VSEs operating in the cultural forum could and did help the administration in this role. In tracing the larger strategy of the approaches to drugs of the administrations of Presidents Reagan and George H. W. Bush, Hawdon considers the early 1980s to be a period when presidential rhetoric aimed to convince people that drugs were an issue worth caring about. Later periods saw administrations suggest policy solutions to the problem after it had been put on the agenda. Because of their common cause and ability to bring attention to drugs as an issue worth thinking about, VSEs during the early 1980s dovetailed conveniently with the administration's goals.

While Reagan viewed the drug problem as an issue calling for intervention, his reputation at least on economic issues was as a deregulator. For media scholars, there is no clearer site of Reagan's economic deregulation than the FCC, headed by Mark Fowler. Under Fowler's supervision, the FCC enacted a number of far-reaching policies leading to, among other consequences, the rise of conservative talk radio, the creation of the Fox broadcast network, and various corporate mergers.[5] Fowler's FCC also weakened requirements for broadcasters to serve children with targeted educational programming. Toward the beginning of his tenure, Fowler and Daniel L. Brenner wrote a law journal article outlining his philosophy. Serving as a statement of purpose, "A Marketplace Approach to Broadcast Deregulation" rejected years of established regulatory policy, instead proposing that broadcasting should be regulated more or less like any other business.[6] Justifying their opinion on the grounds of increased competition for home entertainment and the First Amendment right to free speech, the authors ultimately redefined "public interest." While up to that point, the public interest had been satisfied by educational and public affairs programming, Fowler and Brenner argued that "the Commission should rely on the broadcasters' ability to determine the wants of their audience through the normal mechanisms of the marketplace. The public's interest, then, defines the public interest."[7] At the same time, the authors justified these actions in part by arguing that family programming, whose audience included children and adults, served the same purpose as more targeted educational programming for children only, while reaching a larger audience and being more profitable. Interviewed about the demise of *Captain Kangaroo,* which was a direct result of these policies, Fowler noted that shows like *Little House on the Prairie* and *The White Shadow* were "good wholesome programs" that served similar purposes (although *The White Shadow* had been canceled the previous season).[8]

In this environment, VSEs proved particularly valuable to broadcasters. By addressing issues that administration officials considered especially important, networks and producers could curry favor with them while also providing evidence that deregulated television served the public good as well as providing entertainment—an argument that they and the FCC would make explicit in further deregulatory policy by the end of 1983. According to the 1983 "Children's Television Programming and Advertising Practices Report and Order," ABC argued that "certain family-oriented program material, not designed for children, but nevertheless having special appeal for youthful viewers, should be recognized as reflective of a broadcaster's overall effort" to provide positive social and educational content for children.[9] Over the objections of researchers, special interest groups, and a dissenting member of the commission, the FCC agreed with broadcasters, decreasing the required hours per week of educational children's programming, which was less profitable than most other forms of programming.[10]

Broadcasters argued that they could accomplish their moral duty via more profitable prime-time family programming. At the same time, they managed to discuss and dismiss downer subjects like drug addiction in single episodes, effectively limiting their commitment to heavy issues to one or a handful of episodes per season. Antidrug VSEs clearly and usefully aped Reagan's rhetoric in the war on drugs, going so far as giving the first lady a platform in their fictional universe. Industry advocates and FCC officials were happy to use this type of programming as arguments in favor of their policies. In the lead-up to that 1983 report and order, television demonstrated its support for Reagan's policies in ways that were likely to gain the president's attention—for instance, by speaking through his favorite program or by inviting the first lady to appear as a guest star.

Family Ties: Drugs as a Threat to the Family

In 1986, Reagan delivered a speech promising in part that the federal government was taking an activist approach to strengthening the American family. Reflective of the Christian right's influence on his administration, the speech also demonstrated the extent to which small-government politics ceased where moral issues were concerned. Reagan also discussed *Family Ties* in this speech. "I draw even greater encouragement from the signs that the wider culture is once again beginning to respect, even to celebrate family life. It is no accident that *Family Ties* is my favorite TV show."[11] *Family Ties* centered on the Keatons, an upper-middle-class suburban family initially consisting of two parents and three children.[12] The show's humor frequently revolved around the political and cultural disagreements arising between parents and children. In this sitcom, the parents are progressive former hippies, and at least two of the children represent a rejection of their idealism: their daughter Mallory is a consumerist Valley girl, and their son Alex is a Reagan-loving young Republican. The character of Alex, played by Michael J. Fox, was the star of the show and frequently made cogent arguments in favor of Republican policy. However, Alex served as a bad example in at least one VSE.

About two and a half years before Reagan named the show his favorite, and about a month before the FCC's December 1983 deregulatory decision, *Family Ties* aired a VSE titled "Speed Trap." This was likely one of Reagan's favorite episodes. After all, it offered clear support to his antidrug policy rhetoric during the period when the president was building such support. In this episode, the show's main character, Alex, uses prescription diet pills illegally to help him study during a particularly challenging period in school. To secure this advantage, Alex asks Mallory to get the pills from her overweight friend, Effie. In repayment, Alex has to take Effie on a date. As would be expected for a VSE that aims to show the negative effects of drugs, the pills work well for a time, but they eventually take hold of Alex and cause negative consequences that far outweigh their benefits. Alex's behavior becomes erratic, and he begins to snap at his family members. After doing well on his midterms, Alex has one final hurdle: the state scholarship exam. But following a week of little rest, he oversleeps. Distraught, Alex hits rock bottom in full view of his parents as he desperately rummages through the garbage looking for additional pills. Alex admits his mistake and apologizes to his family, and the credits roll.

According to Hawdon's analysis, Reagan's antidrug policy rhetoric during this period was concerned with creating a moral panic to build support for harsh interventionist policies. To do this, the administration worked to convince the public that despite evidence of decreased usage, drugs remained a significant problem. While discourses on drugs had for a time portrayed them as the domain of people of color and the counterculture, policy rhetoric aimed to convince Americans that nobody was safe from drugs' nefarious grasp.[10] In one speech, for example, Nancy Reagan argued that "no one is safe from [drug and alcohol abuse]—not you, not me and certainly not our children. . . . Now you can see why drug abuse concerns every one of us, all the American family."[11] It is not clear that in "Speed Trap" the producers of *Family Ties* were responding directly to the concerns of regulators. Nevertheless, given that the Reagan administration wanted to convince Americans that everyone was at risk, a middle-class white suburban family could prove useful as a symbol of prototypical Americans. The middle-class white suburban Keaton family played a useful role in this regard. If this family, essentially an updated version of the Andersons of *Father Knows Best* in terms of race and class, was vulnerable to drug abuse, then certainly everyone could be. Moreover, Alex P. Keaton was the last character one would expect to use illegal drugs. A straitlaced, high-achieving, young Republican, he does not even use drugs recreationally—he needs them to get through his midterms on his way to the state scholarship exam. His more free-spirited and academically challenged sister, Mallory, might have been a candidate for drug abuse, but not Alex.

As generically American by virtue of their class and race, the Keatons were rhetorically useful to Reagan's pursuit of his policy goals. At the same time, their whiteness and Alex's use of diet pills as opposed to recreational drugs allowed the show to sidestep much of the racial and class politics associated with the war on drugs. The administration of President Richard Nixon had consciously worked to demonize drug use as a problem of Blacks and hippies as part of his race-baiting Southern strategy to flip the previously Democratic Southeast to the Republican party.[15] Reagan better hid the extent to which drugs operated as a racial wedge issue by painting drugs as a threat to everyone. At the same time, drug policies hit people of color the hardest, inflating the prison population of nonviolent drug offenders during the Reagan administration far above that of previous administrations.

The narrative of a young person heading down a dark path due to drug use is common not only in VSEs, but also in after-school specials, public service announcements, and educational films.[16] As a genre, the sitcom usually calls for some level of humor—even in VSEs, which tend to be more serious than typical episodes. Since Alex is a precocious young Republican, the primary source of humor from his character comes from the apparent disconnect between being a high schooler and identifying so closely with a septuagenarian president. In "Speed Trap," Alex's conservative tendencies approach absurd levels, as the pills amplify the character's quirks. After hearing that the family is playing Monopoly, Alex leaps across the banister from the second floor to reach the first—an expression of his love for the capitalistic game. His mind sharpened by the drugs, Alex overexplains his excitedness, "The precious hours spent in the familiar abode with loved ones playing a heartwarming game such as this are what make memories that one can treasure for all eternity." In a bizarre twist on the contradictions inherent in 1980s neoconservative ideology, Alex has used the free market to obtain drugs, which make him a more ideal free marketer. However, these contradictions cannot be held in tension for long. The comedy of exaggeration grows until Alex's application of law-and-order ethics causes him to lash out at his younger sister, Jennifer, when she asks for a do-over in the game. As Alex travels further down the dark path of pill abuse, he grows visibly aggravated at apparent violations of family values. Catching Jennifer and their mother, Elise, watching a sex ed documentary on PBS, Alex lashes out at them, angry that they are viewing "smut."

Although Alex's descent into speed-fueled economic and moral conservatism serves in some ways as a satire of 1980s Republicanism, it also reinforced a common talking point used to represent drugs as a threat to children and families. Alex represents youth in danger, but his predicament also evokes some of the rhetoric about how adult drug users can threaten children and families. In the scenes described above, Alex's treatment of his little sister seems especially cruel. He also snaps at his mother. He steals from and otherwise uses Mallory to secure pills. Although his actions are played for laughs, he also exploits Effie's crush and seemingly low self-esteem in pursuit of diet pills. Perhaps because doing so would be less likely to create pathos, Alex refrains from exploiting or attacking his father. Women apparently make for more effective victims in this morality tale.

Alex's mistreatment of the women in his life also serves the purpose of framing drug use as a moral issue. Hawdon divides political rhetoric about drugs into two primary categories: criminal and medical. The criminal model presumes that users are "in control of their behavior and willing participants in the lifestyle."[17] Under the medical model, users "cannot control their habits . . . [are] not accountable for their actions . . . [and] are victims deserving of sympathy, not punishment."[18] Certainly, the reality for most addicts involves some combination of both choice and physiology, and there are ways in which policy can respond to both models. However, the Reagan administration relied almost entirely on the criminal model, framing drug use as a choice and therefore a moral failing. The fact that Alex turns into a monster offers some support to this understanding of the drug problem. Of course, Alex is likable again by the end of the episode, allowing for the kind of sympathy that Hawdon associates with a medical understanding. But it is only because Alex quits that he becomes sympathetic again. Moreover, the ease with which Alex appears to kick the habit is not in line with medical understandings of addiction.

If the alternative to the choice model of drug use is one of medical addiction, then the episodic structure of this show's narrative offers stronger, if subtler, support for the criminal model. Like most VSEs, "Speed Trap" presents an issue and solves it over the course of a single episode. By the 1980s, most addiction experts from criminologists to clinicians had come to understand addiction recovery the way that their peers do today: as a long-term, often lifelong, process.[19] In the narrative universe of *Family Ties*, however, once Alex admits his mistake and apologizes—doing right by his moral obligations—he solves the problem.[20] There is no suggestion in later episodes that this is an ongoing issue. Alex never faces this particular temptation again, nor does he seek treatment or attend any Narcotics Anonymous meetings. If the narrative had played out differently, Alex could have gotten into trouble with the law, setting up a longer-term narrative responsibility to show the legal ramifications of drug use. By the strictest understanding, *Family Ties* does not make a very strong case for showing the criminal consequences of drug use either. In reality, however, although white suburban teenagers used illegal drugs at about the same rate as any of their peers, they faced far fewer legal consequences.[21] In that sense, this episode is inadvertently truthful about the lack of criminal consequences for people like Alex. However, it also serves as a rhetorical buttress for policies that would exacerbate the justice system's inequality by showing addiction as a moral failing that is easily overcome, all the while purporting to demonstrate the good moral character of television networks during a time when such displays were economically advantageous for broadcasters.

Diff'rent Strokes: Stunt Programming as Policy Rhetoric

If *Family Ties*'s didactic antidrug episode was designed to court favor with Reagan, *Diff'rent Strokes* blatantly demonstrated total cooperation with the administration in a 1983 VSE featuring Nancy Reagan. While the first lady's appearance in a fictional sitcom was unique, current or former first ladies had had a significant presence on television since the 1950s, when Mamie Eisenhower appeared in campaign ads and Eleanor Roosevelt hosted public affairs shows. However, the most significant precedent for this episode, was *A Tour of the White House with Mrs. John F. Kennedy*, which aired in 1962. In 1961, President Kennedy's FCC chair, Newton Minow, had called television a "vast wasteland," essentially threatening the television networks with regulatory consequences if they did not improve the quality of their programming.[22] According to Michael Curtin, this helped trigger the "golden age of television documentary," as networks aimed to demonstrate their value as a tool for public education and enlightenment.[23] In practice, Curtin notes, many of the documentaries from this era were on topics that explicitly repeated the Kennedy administration's Cold War rhetoric. However, the most famous of the documentaries gave Jacqueline Kennedy the opportunity to promote her most significant initiative as first lady, which was the preservation and restoration of the White House. The documentary was devoted mostly to showing the White House's design, art, and architecture, but it also contained pleas for additional funding for the project. All three networks carried the program, and although it was a popular success, its most significant role for the broadcasting industry was in garnering the FCC's sympathy. Twenty years later, broadcasters formulated a similar strategy, giving another first lady a platform for her primary initiative during an era of regulatory upheaval: the producers of *Diff'rent Strokes* invited Nancy Reagan to advocate for her agenda on television in 1983.[24]

In the episode titled "The Reporter," the main character, Arnold, enters a journalism contest in which a local newspaper will publish the best student-written news story. Arnold develops writer's block and stays up all night trying to think of a good piece. The next day, his lack of an idea and inability to stay awake in class frustrates Arnold. His friend Robbie offers him some pills that will help him stay awake and write the story. Unlike Alex Keaton, Arnold resists the temptation to use drugs to study. Instead, he senses a journalistic opportunity. Robbie sets up a meeting between Arnold and his dealer, who is also in elementary school, securing Arnold's scoop. Before the piece can be entered in the contest, however, the school's principal intercepts it and accuses Arnold of making up the sensational story for the contest. Undeterred, Arnold sends the story directly to the newspaper, which reports on it and the principal's incredulity. Reading the story on a trip to New York, where the show is set, Nancy Reagan makes a surprise visit, going first to Arnold's home and then to his school. She believes Arnold and convinces the principal that drugs are in fact a problem in elementary schools, saving Arnold from punishment and teaching everyone a valuable lesson in the process.

VSEs can deal with racial politics, as television shows ranging from *That's So Raven* to *Family Guy* demonstrate. Like the upper-middle-class white families it represented, *Family Ties* had the luxury to ignore the structural racism inherent in the war on drugs. *Diff'rent Strokes* relied upon on a different family situation that inadvertently underscored the intersectionality of class and race, though it still sidestepped a direct discussion of these issues. In the program, Philip Drummond, a white widower and wealthy businessman, adopts Arnold and Willis, the two sons of his Black maid, when she dies. The boys—two street-smart, but ultimately family-friendly, young Blacks—are contrasted to Drummond's biological daughter, Kimberly. At one level, the humor frequently arises as the young boys, now fish out of water, adjust to life in the penthouse set. Especially in early episodes, and as might be expected from a Tandem Productions series (the company was also responsible for *All in the Family*, which holds a notable place in television history as a sitcom that boldly engaged controversial topics from 1971 to 1979), racism was a frequent topic of this show. When Arnold and Willis apply to an exclusive prep school, the headmaster conspires to make them fail the entrance exam. When Arnold is supposed to share a hospital room with a white girl, her father forbids it. However, although race seems to have been on the mind of the casting director, it does not serve as a major theme in the politics of "The Reporter."

The episode does not explicitly discuss race as a significant issue in the war on drugs. However, it casts against stereotype, pitting antidrug people of color against white drug-pushing students. In denying the obvious racial politics of the war on drugs, it serves President Reagan's goal of making drugs appear to be a threat to all Americans and countering possible accusations of racism in drug policy. Besides Arnold, four students play significant roles in this episode. Robbie and Dudley are Arnold's good friends, Lisa is Arnold's goody-two-shoes nemesis, and Sidney is the drug dealer. Of the Black students, Arnold, Dudley, and Lisa express antidrug messages. Although Arnold's journalistic crusade is based more on a search for glory than opposition to drugs, he expresses a general fear of and opposition to them and dealers. When the dealer prices a pill that will "keep [Arnold] happy" at twelve dollars, Arnold replies, "That will make you a lot happier than it will make me." Dudley offers more antidrug comic relief. After his friend Robbie says that the drug dealer is "trying to make a few extra bucks," Dudley quips, "If he gets caught, he's going to be making a few extra license plates." Even Lisa expresses her opposition to drug abuse. "I think drugs are disgusting, and I would never take them," she tells Nancy Reagan. In contrast, white students are responsible for most of the drug problem at Arnold's school. As noted above, after Arnold's long night of struggle with writer's block, his white friend Robbie offers him an "upper" to help him overcome his tiredness and kick-start his creativity. These examples serve as subtle repudiations of stereotypes. However, the show uses some humor to highlight the contrast between common imaginings of drug dealers and the character that plays that role in this episode. While waiting for the pusher, Arnold asks Dudley what a dealer looks like. "Probably a big mean-looking dude with a scar," his friend replies. Although they do not explicitly mention race, this creates an expectation about drug dealers to be subverted. An innocent-looking white child with a high-pitched voice approaches. "Look, what kind of pills do you want? I haven't got a lot of time," he says, setting up the sense that he is nefariously pushy in his salesmanship before concluding, "I gotta go to the bathroom." Inasmuch as this child represents a rejection of drug dealer stereotypes except for gender, his whiteness implies that the expected dealer would be Black or brown. Presumably well-meaning in its attempt to subvert racial stereotypes about drug use, this effort also supports the rhetoric that drugs are a ubiquitous threat in much the same way that *Family Ties* did. If even white children are using and distributing drugs, there must be a problem. At the same time, this effort disguises the biased racial politics inherent in the actual war on drugs.

While the adults in this episode are more unified than the children in their opposition to drugs, there is an additional distinction between those who believe drugs to be a problem and those who deny that there could be drugs in an elementary school. Arnold's principal, who is Black, refuses to believe Arnold's story. Eventually, he admits his mistake as a number of children tell Nancy Reagan that they have been offered and/or tried drugs. The principal of *Diff'rent Strokes* represents an inversion of Morgan Freeman's iconic character in *Lean on Me*. In this film, a streetwise principal turns around a failing inner-city high school by expelling every suspected drug dealer and gang member and lovingly terrorizing the halls of his school with a baseball bat. A Reagan-era fantasy microcosm of how heavy-handed law and order could clean up America's problems, the film principal's Blackness is key in the sense that only he has the street smarts to understand the problems. Moreover, he realizes that the only things criminals understand are power and violence. On *Diff'rent Strokes*, however, the Black principal's street smarts are deficient. And if even the Black principal of a New York City public school is ignorant of the drug problem, then certainly all of America needs to wake up.

Like *A Tour of the White House*, *Diff'rent Strokes* presents a first lady in a flattering, personable light to support her initiative. Nancy Reagan arrives at the penthouse where Arnold and his family live, graciously dealing with the family's awkwardness as they adjust to the shock of her presence. She also demonstrates that she is a down-to-earth and caring person by her friendly relationship with the housekeeper and her relatively casual engagement with the children. There is also a moment of levity that reveals a personal side to the first couple. Calling her husband, she tells him that she loves him. After a brief pause, she gently scolds him, "Now if I can say it in front of strangers, you can say it in front of [Democratic Speaker of the House] Tip O'Neill."

Arriving at Arnold's school, the first lady switches into a more didactic mode, addressing the class and, by extension, the television audience. Treating the class meeting like a town hall discussion, she begins asking questions: "How many of you have heard about the drug problem in our schools? How do you feel about drugs? . . . Has anyone tried to sell you children drugs?" The children respond appropriately to the first two questions but look around nervously at the third. Reagan understands their hesitation but persists: "You know nothing could be more important than for you to speak up right now. This is something that could really affect your whole future." About a quarter of the children on-screen (three white and one East Asian) raise their hands. Reagan then asks the children if any of them have experimented with drugs. Understandably, no one volunteers such information, so she gently prods once again: "You know, I've spent many hours with children who've gotten involved with drugs. They start [at] your age. Even younger. And they're all tragic stories of kids with great potential whose lives were ruined." Arnold's friend Robbie asks if some drugs like marijuana are okay. "Let me tell you a true story about a boy we'll call Charlie," Reagan responds. "He was only fourteen and he was burned out on marijuana. He was in a stupor—a permanent daze. And one day when his little sister wouldn't steal some money for him to go and buy some more drugs he brutally beat her. The real truth is there's no such thing as soft drugs or hard drugs. All drugs are dumb and if you're involved in them, please talk to your parents, your teacher, whoever. But don't end up another Charlie." At this, Robbie admits that he has used drugs. The first lady warmly thanks him and praises his bravery in admitting his mistake. With some urging from the caring first lady, a few more students, two white and one Black, admit to experimenting with drugs. Adults and children in the room heave visible sighs of relief at this catharsis. The principal apologizes to Arnold for "closing [his] eyes to something [he] didn't want to see." Drummond, Arnold's father, sums up the overall message: "Maybe we should all open our eyes a little wider. . . . This has certainly been a revelation to me, Mrs. Reagan. I think it would be a good idea to let all the parents know what's going on." As the episode ends, the children rush to the front of the classroom to shake Reagan's hand—proof of her good nature.

This scene demonstrates the ways in which television supported Reagan policy rhetoric in the early 1980s by promoting increased concern about drug abuse despite a statistical decline in use.[25] Moreover, the first lady's remarks to children and Drummond's expanding of her comments to adults make explicit the dual address to children and adults that policy makers and television industry advocates would highlight in their arguments for deregulation. But more than that, "The Reporter" offered Nancy Reagan an ideal platform to show that the war on

FIG. 3.1 First Lady Nancy Reagan uncovers a drug ring at Arnold's elementary school.

drugs was not an example of the cruelty of a faceless bureaucracy but the policy of a kind, mother-like figure (a point made more relevant by the conspicuous lack of biological mothers in *Diff'rent Strokes*). Indeed, the Reagans' warm façade and friendliness with mass media would prove key to much of their policy rhetoric, as was the case with the Kennedys two decades earlier. "The Reporter" provided a controlled environment by way of fiction in which the first lady could promote her message, which certainly garnered favor with the administration overall.

This episode aims at many of the same goals as the episode of *Family Ties* did. The primary purpose of "The Reporter" was to convince Americans that drugs are a pernicious threat to children. It buried the racial politics of the war on drugs and also contained a didactic element to scare young people away from trying drugs. Like *Family Ties*, *Diff'rent Strokes* denied the racial politics of the war on drugs. However, the two differ in their takes on this concern based on the episodes' specifics—including the programs' racial representation and the presence or absence of the first lady within the narrative.

Conclusion: Deregulating Broadcasting and Demonizing Drug Use

Both of these episodes aired in 1983. By the end of that year, the FCC had decided to further deregulate television by eliminating requirements for educational children's programming.[26] While shows like these, and VSEs in particular, were certainly not the only factor in the television deregulatory decisions of the

Reagan era, the 1983 report and order demonstrates that such programming was an explicit part of broadcasters' attempt to demonstrate that they could serve the public interest without government regulation.[27] As noted above, ABC argued that "certain family-oriented program material, not primarily designed for children, but nevertheless having special appeal to youthful viewers, should be recognized as reflective of a broadcaster's overall effort in this area."[28] The FCC's official decision went further, arguing that because family programming was viewed by more children than programming focused on children alone, family programming could be more effective at delivering positive social messages. As evidence, the FCC noted that "when the Fonz, the central *Happy Days* character, obtained a library card, many child viewers did likewise."[29] The same report inadvertently also reveals why such changes were so valuable to broadcasters. In a section arguing that overcommercialization of children's programming is not a danger, the FCC explained: "Advertisers desire the largest possible audience of potential buyers for their advertised products, but young children have an influence to buy only a relatively few advertised products. Thus, the amount of money spent on children's advertising appears to be small relative to the amount spent [on] advertising to adults."[30] In other words, broadcasters preferred to satisfy any requirements for children's programming with shows that attracted adult consumers. Family programming like *Diff'rent Strokes* and *Family Ties* could appear to address children, while advertisers could feel assured that grown-ups were in the room to see their commercials.

Although the Reagan administration took a small-government approach to economic policy, it was much more interventionist on social issues. In their attempts to demonstrate good corporate citizenship in pursuit of deregulation, television shows from this era became a tool in the administration's larger strategy to cause a moral panic over drug use. Although it is not clear that the FCC and broadcasters specifically agreed to cooperate in this way, the timing, alignment of interests, and arguments made in FCC documents suggest that at the very least, players in the television industry were conscious of VSEs' ability to garner support among administration officials. By the end of the 1980s, the public had been convinced enough of this threat that zero tolerance became the ruling philosophy for the war on drugs. The neat endings and laugh tracks of these VSEs belied the devastating effects these policies had on America's most vulnerable populations, but they worked well in service of the interests of anti-drug politicians and broadcasters.

Notes

1 Jane Feuer, *Seeing through the Eighties: Television and Reaganism* (Durham, NC: Duke University Press, 1995), 19.

2 Ibid., 12.

3 James E. Hawdon, "The Role of Presidential Rhetoric in the Creation of a Moral Panic: Reagan, Bush, and the War on Drugs," *Deviant Behavior* 22, no. 5 (2001): 419–445.
4 Horace Newcomb and Paul M. Hirsch, "Television as a Cultural Forum," in *Television: The Critical View*, ed. Horace Newcomb, 5th ed. (New York: Oxford University Press, 1994), 503–515.
5 Juanita "Frankie" Clogston, "The Repeal of the Fairness Doctrine and the Irony of Talk Radio: A Story of Political Entrepreneurship, Risk, and Cover," *Journal of Policy History* 28, no. 2 (April 2016): 375–396; Jennifer Holt, *Empires of Entertainment: Media Industries and the Politics of Deregulation, 1980–1996* (New Brunswick, NJ: Rutgers University Press, 2011).
6 Mark S. Fowler and Daniel L. Brenner, "A Marketplace Approach to Broadcast Regulation," *Texas Law Review* 60 (1982): 207–257.
7 Ibid., 210.
8 Ernest Holsendolph, "Are Children No Longer in the Programming Picture?," *New York Times*, July 25, 1982.
9 Quoted in United States Federal Communications Commission, "Children's Television Programming and Advertising Practices Report and Order," in *Federal Communications Commission Reports: Decisions and Reports of the Federal Communications Commission of the United States*, 2nd series, vol. 96 (Washington, D.C.: U.S. Government Printing Office, 1984), 639.
10 Ibid., 644.
11 Quoted in "President Reagan, Saying the Sitcom 'Family Ties' Is His . . . ," UPI Archives, June 23, 1986, https://www.upi.com/Archives/1986/06/23/President-Reagan-saying-the-sitcom-Family-ties-is-his/7373519883200/.
12 A fourth child was added in later episodes.
13 See Ronald Reagan, *Public Papers of the Presidents of the United States, Ronald Reagan: 1981–1988–89*, ed. J. E. Byrne and Frank G. Burke (Washington, D.C.: U.S. Government Printing Office, 1986), 1984: 226; Ronald Reagan, *Ronald Reagan's Weekly Radio Addresses: The President Speaks to America*, ed. Fred L. Israel (Wilmington, DE: Scholarly Resources, 1987), 222.
14 Quoted in "Excerpts from Speech on Halting Drug Abuse," *New York Times*, September 15, 1986.
15 Katherine Beckett, *Making Crime Pay: Law and Order in Contemporary American Politics* (New York: Oxford University Press, 2000).
16 Dave Quinn, "*Saved by the Bell*'s Jessie Spano Was Originally 'So Excited' on Speed, Not Caffeine Pills," *People*, May 22, 2018, https://people.com/tv/saved-by-the-bell-jessie-spano-speed/. Spano is perhaps the most famous imitator of Alex Keaton's drug use, and as her VSE was written, she as well as Alex was supposed to have been using speed. The network's standards and practices department switched her to caffeine pills.
17 Hawdon, "The Role of Presidential Rhetoric in the Creation of a Moral Panic," 424.
18 Ibid..
19 Robert L. Bogomolny, "Drug Abuse and the Criminal Justice System," *Journal of Drug Issues* 6, no. 4 (October 1976): 380–389; Frank A. Seixas, "Alcoholism Treatment . . . A Descriptive Guide," *Psychiatric Annals* 12, no. 4 (April 1982): 375–376 and 381–385.
20 The tension between issues that require longer-term solutions and episodic television's desire for discrete narrative closure haunts VSEs. In *The Fresh Prince of Bel-Air*, Will commits to rebuilding a neighborhood in South Central Los Angeles

after the 1992 riots, but the show never revisits the topic. In *Saved by the Bell*, Zach Morris and his mother agree to take in a homeless family until they get back on their feet, but no one from the family appears after that episode.

21 Jamie Fellner, "Race, Drugs, and Law Enforcement in the United States," *Stanford Law and Policy Review* 20, no. 2 (Spring 2009): 257–291; Elizabeth Kai Hinton, *From the War on Poverty to the War on Crime: The Making of Mass Incarceration in America* (Cambridge, MA: Harvard University Press, 2016).

22 Newton N. Minow, "Television and Public Interest," May 9, 1961, American Rhetoric Speech Online Speech Bank, http://www.americanrhetoric.com/speeches/newtonminow.htm.

23 Michael Curtin, *Redeeming the Wasteland: Television Documentary and Cold War Politics* (New Brunswick, NJ: Rutgers University Press, 1995).

24 Seth Abramovitch, "Former Addict Todd Bridges Recalls How Nancy Reagan on 'Diff'rent Strokes' Helped Change His Life," *Hollywood Reporter*, March 6, 2016, https://www.hollywoodreporter.com/news/nancy-reagans-diffrent-strokes-visit-873052. According to one of the stars, Todd Bridges, it was the idea of a producer to invite her.

25 Beckett, *Making Crime Pay*.

26 United States Federal Communications Commission, "Children's Television Programming and Advertising Practices Report and Order." While not terribly specific in terms of hourly requirements, the 1974 report and order required, for instance, that broadcasters show educational children's programming throughout the week as opposed to only on weekdays and that such programming needed to be directed at various age groups—particularly young children, whose early development was deemed paramount. See Federal Communications Commission, *Children's Television Report and Policy Statement* (Washington: ERIC Clearinghouse, 1974). By 1979, the FCC had concluded that broadcasters had not complied with these requirements and proposed a number of solutions. See Susan C. Greene and United States Federal Communications Commission Children's Television Task Force, *Television Programming for Children: A Report of the Children's Television Task Force* (Washington, D.C.: Federal Communications Commission, 1979). The FCC weighed these options and in 1983 decided against imposing new requirements, effectively eliminating the proposals in the 1974 report and order and the 1979 recommendations.

27 United States Federal Communications Commission, "Children's Television Programming and Advertising Practices Report and Order," in *Federal Communications Commission Reports: Decisions and Reports of the Federal Communications Commission of the United States*, 2nd series, vol. 96 (Washington: U.S. Government Printing Office, 1984), 639.

28 Quoted in United States Federal Communications Commission, "Children's Television Programming and Advertising Practices Report and Order," 639.

29 Ibid., 650.

30 Ibid., 636.

4

"Due to Its Subject Matter"

Creating the Very Special Teen Sex Talk in 1980s Sitcoms

BARBARA SELZNICK

As this volume demonstrates, very special episodes (VSEs) take on a range of topics. However, only some series that deal with important or sensitive issues are considered VSEs. Episodes about date rape or drug use may constitute VSEs for some dramas or comedies while being familiar parts of story lines on others. Factors that contribute to making a topic special for one show but not for another include the show's intended audience (adults, families, or children), genre (sitcom or drama), and purpose (a realistic take on contemporary society or a family show intended to entertain a mass audience). In a circular fashion, these considerations impact what audiences expect from any given program's take on a significant contemporary issue and, therefore, how the show addresses this issue. Thus, a topic that is special for one show may not be for another simply because of what's expected of the programs, based on their places within the television industry.

Writing in 2003 and lamenting the end of the VSE, Emily Nussbaum observed that the genre "requires innocence of a degree hard to imagine for today's wisecracking characters."[1] This attribution of cynicism to contemporary television overlooks a number of television shows from previous decades that also eschewed innocence to focus on what is sometimes called social relevance. This chapter will explore how two sitcoms in the 1980s—one with a seeming position of innocence and one with a stronger bent toward social relevance—approached the very special topic of teenage sex. More specifically, this chapter will home in on the conversations between mothers and their teenage children as the teens decide if they are ready to have sex. Conversations about sex and readiness for it bring to the foreground what television may say to its viewers, as programs attempt to deal with weighty yet everyday issues. The importance of sitcoms stems from the idea that they often explore conflicts within the nuclear family that expose contradictions.[2] By raising serious issues, sitcoms open up space for viewers to think about these issues in a reflective way even if, as Lauren Rabinovitz argues, they use the issue as a "hook or lure of relevancy" that is "rerouted once it is introduced."[3]

This chapter will focus on two episodes from the mid-1980s that included conversations between mothers and teens about sex.[4] "Jennie and Jason" (November 3, 1986) is an episode of *Kate & Allie* (CBS, 1984–1989), a show about two divorced women who live together in Manhattan as they raise their children. This episode highlights the relationship between Allie and her daughter, Jennie, as the teen contemplates having sex with her boyfriend, Jason. "Bad Timing" (February 8, 1987) is an episode of *Valerie* (NBC, 1986–1990; CBS, 1990–1991), a sitcom starring Valerie Harper about a nuclear family in Illinois. In this episode, the oldest of the family's three sons is considering having sex with the teenage daughter of a visiting family. As discussed below, both "Bad Timing" and "Jennie and Jason" can be read as VSEs. They address a relevant social issue in somewhat simplistic terms and aim to provoke discussion while avoiding controversy. "Jennie and Jason" is a bit different in that it takes some of the focus off the issue and emphasizes the mother-daughter communication necessary to navigate it. This episode also avoids a clear resolution to the question of teen sex. While both episodes deal with the same general topic in some of the same ways, the differences between them—and what led to the episode of *Valerie* being discussed as a VSE more than the episode of *Kate & Allie*—can be understood by examining the sociocultural context of the episodes and the industrial goals that led to the programs approaching the issue of teenage sex in different ways. By addressing the industrial positions of these programs along with the sociocultural context of the 1980s, this chapter explores how these factors came together to create messages for both parents and teens or younger children about sex, gender, and responsibility.

"How Come Nobody Got Pregnant?": Television in Context

Within the industrial ecosystem of the 1980s, network executives recognized and reacted to many changes, including the value ascribed to different audiences, the growth in the number of television networks and other forms of competition,

FIG. 4.1 Kate and Allie have a heart to heart.

shifts in viewing habits, and the fragmentation of the audience. Starting in the 1960s, advertisers and network executives looked toward young, urban, educated viewers who were seen both to be in the market for consumer goods and to have disposable income.[5] The resulting socially relevant comedies of the 1970s later softened in the 1980s as they negotiated the family values popularized by the neoconservative movement.[6] At the same time, cable television and home video pulled audiences away from mainstream, broadcast television. Network television program producers were faced with two options: target quality demographic groups that had value for advertisers or appeal to a mass audience and achieve high ratings. Additionally, as discussed below, the syndication market continued to be seen as an important source of revenue for sitcom producers. Programs that appealed to children had more value in this market than did quality comedies.[7] So while quality shows may have attracted critical attention and buzz, programs such as *Punky Brewster* (NBC, 1984–1986; syndication, 1987–1988) and *Silver Spoons* (NBC, 1982–1986; syndication, 1986–1987) had a higher potential in syndication. Not surprisingly, then, although family sitcoms seemed to be disappearing in the early 1980s,[8] they reemerged around 1984 reflecting alterations shaped by the women's movement, the rise of the two-income family, and the neoliberal agenda of the Reagan era. Many sitcoms demonstrated a return to innocence. Nussbaum observed that, in fact, the VSE can be seen as a "safer mutation" of the 1970s socially relevant shows, in which the contemporary social issue is shoehorned into a single episode.[9]

The neoconservative focus on the return to traditional families clashed with the new conception of gender roles that emerged from the feminist movement of the 1960s and 1970s. In the 1980s, even though more women joined the workforce and more families were headed by single parents, "the momentum of the women's liberation movement had slowed."[10] Public discourse in the 1980s—including mainstream television—reconfigured and reinforced old-fashioned gender roles that highlighted traditional family values.[11] Additionally, while the depictions of mothers on television in the 1970s may have highlighted their humanity, offering complex characters such as Ann Romano on *One Day at a Time* (CBS, 1974–1984) or Maude Findlay on *Maude* (CBS, 1972–1978), the 1980s returned to the ideal of the perfect mother who rarely doubted her own parenting skills and accepted ultimate responsibility for the fate of her children.[12] Viewers were presented with images of mothers who, although placed in situations that may have challenged their strength, were self-assured and confident in their parenting. Discourses of the 1980s also identified a crisis of masculinity resulting from the tension that existed between the sensitive so-called new man of the 1970s and the hegemonic masculinity of the Reagan era.[13] Books and articles in the 1980s noted that "American men are increasingly bumping up against the limits of traditional concepts of masculinity, attempting to push beyond the rigid role prescriptions that constrain male behavior."[14] Looking specifically at changing conceptions of fatherhood, Victor Seidler observed that as men were expected to be more involved in fatherhood, they found that the traditional tools they used to succeed at work did not transfer well into the home, leading to frustrations.[15] Sitcoms, in their depictions of men, reconceptualized masculinity to balance conventional stereotypes of it—"will and determination"—with sensitivity and vulnerability.[16]

Shifts regarding gender roles generated fear among some people, who believed that the increased autonomy available to women (due to factors such as financial independence, birth control, and legalized abortion), as well as the decrease in male hegemonic power, contributed to the decline of U.S. society and the traditional family in particular. Concerns about moral decline, the increase in teen pregnancy, and the developing AIDS epidemic resulted in an emphasis among people in the New Right on chastity and morality as the way to keep children safe in this changing world. The right applied its neoliberal ideal of personal responsibility to the promotion of abstinence.[17] Despite constant criticism for their loose morals, television networks and production companies often joined the New Right to focus on traditional values. In addition to the sitcoms that featured nuclear families and strong moral messages, television networks banned the airing of ads for contraceptives. One *Boston Globe* columnist decried the lack of the "2 Cs" on television: contraception and consequences.[18] A spokesman for NBC explained that "we avoid broadcasting material we believe would offend the moral or religious sensitivities of substantial segments of the audience."[19] Regarding the ban on contraception commercials, George Schweitzer, CBS's vice president for communications, stated: "We believe they would intrude on the moral and religious beliefs of many members of our audience. We agree that issues such as unintended pregnancies are important social issues, and they are not ignored in our broadcasts. They are covered in news and public affairs and in some entertainment programming, in a balanced context."[20] Fourteen years earlier the network had aired an episode of *Maude* in which the lead character discussed and had an abortion, but CBS had clearly been impacted by the social and cultural atmosphere of the Reagan era.

However, the Christian right was not alone in pressuring television networks and producers. In 1986 Planned Parenthood launched an ad campaign focused on the prevention of teen pregnancy that targeted teenagers, parents, lawmakers, and television networks.[21] One Planned Parenthood ad in the *Los Angeles Times* asked: "They did it 9,000 times on television last year. How come nobody got pregnant?" This print ad came along with cut-outs for readers to fill in with their names and addresses and mail to each of the television networks (at the time, ABC, NBC, and CBS), saying that the "T.V. industry censorship of birth control is making a bad problem worse. Please reverse your policy. Permit programs *and* advertising to discuss birth control."[22]

Additionally, television networks and producers acknowledged the impact of AIDS on programming. A *New York Times* article from March 1987 discussed impending changes to television shows that were going to limit "promiscuity."[23] The producers of several shows—particularly those making "serious dramas that deal with contemporary issues . . . are concluding that given AIDS and the return to more conservative values regarding fidelity and commitment, it is no longer credible to write plots that include a lot of casual sex."[24] Notably, the reality of AIDS led to the depiction of monogamy rather than protection, suggesting that the AIDS crisis was not the only factor influencing these representations. George Dessart, then head of program practices at CBS, explained: "For a lot of reasons, marriage is back in style. It's partly because of AIDS and herpes, but it also reflects some thinking about the nature of commitment and traditional values."[25]

Shows that acknowledged the controversial issue of teen sex in the 1980s waded into the topic in the midst of the rise of AIDS, the strengthening of the New Right and the Christian right, the increasing number of teen pregnancies, and the reshaping of the U.S. family. The industrial ecosystem of the 1980s that included increased competition from cable and home video, a focus on audience demographics, and a resurgence of family sitcoms influenced how television comedies navigated the sociocultural minefields of the 1980s. The remainder of this chapter focuses on the episodes from *Kate & Allie* and *Valerie* that depicted teenagers facing their first sexual experiences and the industrial standing of the programs that influenced how they addressed this very special topic.

"But She's a Child!": "Jennie and Jason" (*Kate & Allie*)

Kate & Allie walked a tightrope in its representation of family and gender in the 1980s that is better understood by looking at its industrial position. As discussed above, sitcoms in the early 1980s were struggling to find their place. When *Kate & Allie* began airing in March 1984, the family sitcom had not yet made its full resurgence (*The Cosby Show* [NBC, 1984–1992] would first air in September of that year), and the show—the only comedy in the top ten Nielsen ratings in its first season—was designed to target quality adult viewers, not families.[26] The show's lack of appeal to children was demonstrated in 1986 when, despite *Kate & Allie*'s success in the ratings and with critics, it flailed in the syndication market precisely because it didn't do well enough with children.[27] *Kate & Allie* was seen as a comedy for adults at a time when audience fragmentation began to justify this type of partitioning.[28]

As a result of CBS' chasing of the quality, adult audience, *Kate & Allie* reflects the culture wars of the 1980s in interesting ways. Seen as a descendant of the socially relevant shows of the 1970s,[29] *Kate & Allie* approached the topic of parenting from the perspective of the women's movement, yet the show's treatment of the topic was watered down by the traditional family discourse of the 1980s and the network's reluctance to anger viewers or alienate advertisers. The anxiety surrounding the roles of women in the 1980s is reflected in analyses of the show that both celebrate and criticize it for its representation of women. Portraying two divorced women who lived together and shared household responsibilities, *Kate & Allie* was praised for its representations of a strong female friendship as well as the characters' personal and economic struggles. At the same time, however, the show was disparaged for re-creating a traditional family: the more conservative Allie served as the stay-at-home mom, taking care of household chores and child care, while Kate, depicted as "the cool mom,"[30] worked as a travel agent and performed more "fatherly" duties (such as teaching Allie's young son to defend himself against bullies).[31] The program allows for women's autonomy but still reaffirms some traditional ideas about how families operate.

The resulting show features complicated characters who are explored as single women, mothers, and even daughters. Rabinovitz observes that it is actually the mother-daughter relationships seen on sitcoms that have the potential to highlight feminist possibilities within the shows, as it is there that we see "the adult female's uncertain familial position and the adolescent female's vacillating obedience to cultural authorities."[32] "Jennie and Jason" opens not with the story line about teen sex but with Kate and Allie discussing Allie's problems with her mother. Allie describes her mother as overly critical, and the women talk about how they hope to have better relationships with their own children. Mother-daughter communication is thus set up as a main theme of the episode. "Jennie and Jason" approached the topic of teen sex with an eye toward the adult female audience whose members faced the somewhat muddled expectations for women and mothers in the 1980s. As a result, the episode focuses less on Jennie's decision about sex and more on how Allie reacts to finding out that her daughter is contemplating having sex. Neither network executives nor viewers expected the show to have a large family audience that would be influenced by its depiction of teen sex. As a result, this episode of *Kate & Allie* was never promoted or discussed as a VSE.

Within the episode, seventeen-year-old Jennie is considering having sex with Jason, a boy that she has been dating for "a couple of months" and whom Allie really likes.[33] Jennie confides in Emma—Kate's seventeen-year-old daughter, with whom she shares a bedroom—who has no advice for Jennie but serves as a sounding board for her. After weighing the pros and cons (which include that she loves Jason, but also the recognition that it may not be actual love), and without any consideration of the consequences of sleeping with him or any discussion of birth control, Jennie decides she will have sex with Jason, who (like her) is a virgin. After an awkward dinner, Jennie and Jason end up on a sofa-bed in Jason's living room where, while they are simply holding hands and have all their clothes on except their shoes, they are interrupted by Jason's mother who has come home unexpectedly. After Jennie leaves in an embarrassed rush, Jason's mother calls Allie and tells her what she interrupted. The episode now decisively shifts to focus on Allie, who immediately calls Kate to get advice on how to handle Jennie. Allie is clearly concerned and confused. Her uncertainty, however, is not about what she thinks Jennie should do but about how she should talk to Jennie about it.

When Allie appears in her bedroom, Jennie acknowledges that Allie knows that she almost had sex. Allie responds, "I'm glad you're not denying it." This discursive reference to sex as something that might guiltily be denied immediately sets up an adversarial tone to the conversation that never quite goes away. Jennie gets ready for a lecture with a huffy, "here we go." After a brief conversation, Allie storms out of the room and describes the conversation to Kate as round one: "She was defensive, I was hurt. She was accusatory; I was defensive." Allie then returns to Jennie's room for round two. In this show, intended for adults and designed to appeal to the mothers in the audience more than to teens, the conversation about sex is set up as a battle full of accusations, defensiveness, and hurt. The exchange between Allie and Jennie takes up most of the rest of the episode.[34] Allie attempts to treat Jennie in a more mature manner but urges her to "wait until it's right," focusing on the emotional impact of sex and the importance of its being "special." In the end, Jennie agrees to think about what her mother said, but we don't get a resolution to Jennie's dilemma. Rather, the episode ends with Allie walking away from Jennie's room with a smile, indicating that she feels satisfied with her handling of the situation.

This conversation between Allie and Jennie demonstrates how the show balanced its sociocultural context with its appeal to a specific audience. Significantly, it is the daughter of the more traditional Allie, not the daughter of Kate, who is thinking about having sex. As mentioned above, Allie does not waver in her belief that Jennie is too young to have sex, but she is confused about how to communicate with Jennie. One of the first things Allie says to Kate when she learns that Jennie was found on a bed with her boyfriend is: "But she's a child!" Throughout the episode, Allie struggles to transform the way she sees her daughter. As they begin round two of their discussion, Allie proposes to Jennie, "I won't think of you as a child if you don't think of me as a stranger." As discussed below, other VSEs about teen sex in the 1980s emphasized the importance of treating teens as young adults, with most parents simply acknowledging that their teens are old enough to make these mature choices. However, Allie grapples with accepting her teen as a young adult, and the basis of her argument really is that Jennie is just not mature enough for this kind of relationship (she tells Jennie, "You have to have a certain amount of maturity to have an intimate relationship"). Allie ultimately concedes that the choice is Jennie's, but she does so in a way that unambiguously presents her opinion:

JENNIE You want me to wait.
ALLIE Definitely, yes.
JENNIE But you do agree that the choice is mine.
ALLIE Unfortunately, yes.

Then, in a refreshing move for 1980s television, Allie advises Jennie that if she does decide to have sex, she should do so "responsibly" by first seeing a doctor and getting birth control. Allie never utters the words "pregnancy," "sexually transmitted disease," or "AIDS," even though AIDS was a serious concern by 1986. The discussion of the pill (not condoms) puts the responsibility for birth control squarely on Jennie's shoulders and ignores the necessity of other forms of protection. In a show that is perhaps less interested in courting teen viewers than adults, the emphasis is less on educating teens to allow them to make healthy and responsible choices than on the difficulty of allowing teens the freedom to make these choices. The fact that Allie may be right about Jennie's maturity is supported within the episode as Jennie and Jason declare their love for each other, clumsily prepare to have sex, but don't seem to consider any of the potential consequences. Throughout the episode, Jennie acts more like a petulant child—retreating to her bedroom and sniping at her mother—than a mature young adult ready for an intimate relationship. Allie's insistence that Jennie should not have sex is based on her belief that Jennie isn't emotionally prepared rather than any religious or value-laden convictions. *Kate & Allie* then is able to move through the cultural debates of the 1980s by supporting abstinence without relying on the moral panic of the neoconservative movement and by broaching the idea of birth control while not condoning its use. Furthermore, the episode acknowledges women's autonomy to make decisions about their bodies while also questioning the emotional consequences of the sexual freedoms afforded by the 1970s feminist movement.

The negotiation of issues surrounding teen sex on *Kate & Allie* reflects the show's industrial and cultural position in the 1980s. As a quality show on a broadcast network that sought an adult audience, it was expected to address socially relevant topics regularly but to do so in a way that would not alienate viewers or advertisers. The result was an episode that raises some questions—about the relationships between mothers and daughters and the benefits of abstinence—but presents them within a discourse that reaffirms traditional family values. Comparing this to a similar episode of *One Day at a Time* in the 1970s, Rabinovitz explains, that unlike Ann Romano's very ambivalent and neurotic reaction to finding out that her daughter was thinking of having sex, Allie embraces her moral authority, demonstrating the difficulties of communicating her values to teens.[35] The emphasis throughout "Jennie and Jason" is on abstinence, though with the recognition that if teens don't abstain, they should be responsible. What this episode says, then, about teen sex is that it's the responsibility of the mother (or another parent) to discuss sex with a daughter (though "cool mom" Kate avoids such a conversation with her own daughter) so that teens—who are still children—recognize that sex is a big decision with emotional consequences, even if these consequences are not explained.

"Please Take That Seriously": "Bad Timing" (*Valerie*)

Three months later, *Valerie* offered another approach to talking about teen sex when the main character's oldest son, David, considers having his first sexual experience. Unlike *Kate & Allie* very little has been written about *Valerie* except to document the dispute between the star, Valerie Harper, and Lorimar Productions, the show's producers, that led to her being fired from the show just before the start of the third season in 1987.[36] One of Harper's problems with the show was her desire for it to be more realistic. Reacting to an accusation made by Lorimar Productions, Harper explained: "I said I thought all the episodes were getting to look cookie cutter-ed: Mom in the kitchen with a morality segment in the second part of every show. I never said, 'I don't want to stand in the kitchen giving advice.' What I said was, 'I don't *just* want to stand in the kitchen giving advice.'"[37] Despite Harper's hopes for the show, *Valerie* was designed to capitalize on the mid-1980s boom in nuclear family sitcoms. Valerie had a job that rarely took her away from her family, and her attention was squarely focused on raising her three boys. Her husband, Mike, was an airline pilot who was frequently away but present enough to be a constant figure in the boys' lives. Many episodes often ended with a vague moral lesson. The show, which found success after moving to an 8:30 (Eastern Standard Time) slot following the hit *ALF*, was clearly designed to appeal to a family audience.

Not surprisingly, *Valerie*'s take on teen sex epitomized the VSE. "Bad Timing" was aired with a disclaimer before it ("Due to its subject matter, parents may wish to view tonight's episode with their children"), highlighting the important social issue of the episode. In a move that foregrounded the potential for controversy, one NBC affiliate in Albany, New York, refused to air the episode at all, and three others aired it out of prime time (at least one aired it at midnight).[38] Articles in popular periodicals encouraged—and warned—viewers to expect something serious. All of these examples demonstrate ways that "Bad Timing," independent of its actual content, was marked as unusual sitcom fare, setting up viewers to think of the episode as special.

In this episode, seventeen-year-old David is propositioned by Laurie, the daughter of family friends staying with the Hogan family. Laurie and David had known each other as children, and this created a connection between them that leads to flirting and kissing. Laurie later crawls into David's bed and asks him to "make love" to her.[39] David is clearly nervous and somewhat reluctant but agrees, with mannerisms that tell the audience that his discomfort is overwhelmed by hormones. As they kiss on the bed, David eventually asks, "What are you using?" Laurie, who is in Chicago for college interviews, doesn't even understand the question until David clarifies it: "I mean birth control. Are you on the pill or something?" When it's established that she's not on the pill—and intends to have sex without contraception (saying "I'm pretty sure it's safe"), David is the one who insists that they wait until the next day when he can get "protection." He specifically cites a concern about Laurie getting pregnant (again, discounting any worries about sexually transmitted diseases), but the two do specifically talk about condoms. Press coverage of this episode repeatedly notes that this was the first time the word "condom" was used on a television sitcom, demonstrating the importance of the episode. According to Chip Keyes, one of the writers of the episode, NBC executives had no problem with mentioning the pill, but they were uncomfortable with the reference to condoms—though they did eventually approve it.[40] The episode can be commended for acknowledging the use of condoms, even though it doesn't acknowledge some of the risks that necessitate their use, and for showing a teenage boy taking responsibility for birth control.[41]

The purchase of the condoms instigates the mother-son interaction about sex. The next day, David goes to the store and among other things, buys condoms for himself (in one bag) and cough drops for Valerie (in another bag). In true sitcom fashion, the packages get switched, and Valerie ends up opening the bag with the condoms. The two unload groceries while Valerie literally "stand[s] in the kitchen giving advice." Here, the differences between *Kate & Allie*'s episode (in which Allie struggles with the idea of her child growing up) and *Valerie*'s VSE (designed to teach families about an issue) become clear. After looking at the condoms, Valerie commends David for being mature and responsible. She does not offer him any real direction, only motherly advice on how to think about the relationship. They don't have a conversation in which David's thoughts and feelings are heard (in fact at some point Valerie says that she doesn't want to know about David's previous sexual experience). Throughout the conversation, David says very little, as he stands in the kitchen looking at his mother. Here, it seems, is the lecture that Jennie didn't want to hear, but without any concrete advice from Valerie or hostility from David. Valerie tells David: "I know that you have a lot of choices that, gee, I never even had to confront when I was your age. I just hope that you try to remember stuff that Dad and I tried to teach about, well, about everything. And about sex, David. There is nothing, nothing wrong with the feelings you have but a sexual relationship is just that—a relationship. There's responsibility attached to the other person and yourself. Please take that seriously."

Valerie goes on to tell David that when he does decide to have sex, he should "make sure, whatever you do, it's the right time in your life and the right time in your relationship." David thanks his mother for not treating him like a kid, and she replies, "well, you're not." Unlike Allie, Valerie has no problem telling David that he's not a child. Speaking about the episode, Harper explained that she "expects the show to draw some critical mail because the mother does not tell her 17-year-old son, David . . . not to have sex. Instead, she awkwardly congratulates him for being responsible enough to use protection."[42] Yet in many ways, Valerie does treat David like a child, failing to ask him pertinent questions that would give authority to his ideas and feelings. Valerie doesn't speak to David about the emotional side of a sexual relationship or about maturity or feeling special. Rather, she cautions him to take responsibility for the other person and himself and to do what's "right." While Jennie is asked to consider her feelings (while also being responsible), David's feelings about Laurie and sex are assumed to be only physical (and normal), reinforcing traditional appeals to men about sexual relationships that assume boys will, of course, want to have sex but must take responsibility for their actions.

Interestingly, and perhaps dictated by the format of the show and its focus on its star, we don't see Valerie ask her husband (who we know is in town for this episode) for advice about David's buying condoms (in the way we see Allie immediately call Kate for help), nor does she suggest that David may want or prefer to talk to his father. The father's absence in this discussion is particularly noteworthy because, unlike in many other episodes with conversations about teen sex (including "Jennie and Jason"), this is a conversation between mother and son. Throughout the 1980s, teenage boys were presented with different, and often conflicting, ideas about their responsibilities in sexual relationships. Additionally, there's no indication that Valerie plans to mention to Laurie's mother what is happening. In contrast to the situation on *Kate & Allie*, when Jason's mother immediately phones Allie (whom she didn't know and had to find by calling information), Valerie is friends with Laurie's mother and, after seeing the condoms, spends the entire day with her at a football game. While this may have been too much for a thirty-minute sitcom episode to handle, the lack of concern about Laurie may signal to viewers the insignificance of teen girls who are already sexually active.

And in contrast to the episode in *Kate & Allie*, in "Bad Timing" we eventually get a clear resolution to the teen-sex story line. When David and Laurie are alone in the house, they are rushed and clumsy. The scene foregrounds physical comedy, so it is not surprising when David—explaining that he's never had sex before and wants it to be special—follows his mother's advice and decides that it's not the right time. Laurie simply responds, "So we'll wait; it's not the end of the world." They kiss and hug, and the episode ends. The message of abstinence prevails again, this time more forcefully as the teens decide not to have sex (or, at least, David decides to wait). Harper, expecting criticism of the episode, said in an interview: "The show is really not about running out to buy condoms. . . . It's about saying 'no'—but if you are saying 'yes,' then for heaven's sake, use something."[43] Unlike *Kate & Allie*, however, while *Valerie* may come down strongly in favor of teen abstinence, the message of morality comes more from the teens' actions than from clear motherly guidance. Nevertheless, Valerie is depicted as the stronger mother, who is confident in communicating with her teen. While Allie struggles to connect with her daughter, Valerie has her advice ready to go. She needs no support from friends or family members. Instead, she offers the audience an image of a mother who knows what she wants to say and says it clearly, and whose words then lovingly guide her child to make good choices. As a family show with a star focus, *Valerie* centers on the expert motherly advice that was being dispensed in many 1980s family sitcoms and provides a family-friendly resolution to a complicated topic. *Kate & Allie*, in contrast, is a more complex series that targeted a quality, adult audience. Allie gives her daughter clear advice that is discussed in a nuanced manner, foregrounding the difficulties and awkwardness for both parents and teens.

Both programs had to negotiate a complicated sociocultural period when ideas about gender and sex were shaped by the culture wars. The two episodes both promoted abstinence, and neither approached contraception with profundity, assuming that the mention of protection was enough. Furthermore, the episodes sidestepped questions of morality that often undergirded the neoconservative focus on abstinence by redirecting the argument, proposing that the value of abstinence lay in its benefits for teens who were not yet responsible or mature enough for sexual relationships. This type of argument allowed the episodes to avoid alienating audiences and advertisers along the political and social spectrum. These similarities between "Jennie and Jason" and "Bad Timing" indicate that both episodes could be read as VSEs. However, only "Bad Timing" was treated this way by the industry, press, and viewers. "Jennie and Jason," in its examination of Jennie and Allie's communication about sex as an eventuality of raising teens, highlights *Kate & Allie*'s standing as a quality, adult comedy. *Valerie*, in contrast, was a family sitcom that was seen as disrupting its focus on generally innocent issues of miscommunication and adolescent misbehavior to tackle an important social issue. Along with actual episode content, these programs' sociocultural contexts, industrial goals, distribution platforms, and target audiences all contributed to the ways that they presented the issues as they worked through conversations about teen sex. We can see, then, that a program's position within the ecosystem of television not only shapes how it presents complicated social topics but also whether these depictions will be understood as very special.

Notes

1 Emily Nussbaum, "When Episodes Could Still Be Very Special," *New York Times*, April 13, 2003.
2 George Lipsitz, *Time Passages: Collective Memory and American Popular Culture* (Minneapolis: University of Minnesota Press, 2001), 57.
3 Lauren Rabinovitz, "Sitcoms and Single Moms: Representations of Feminism on American T.V.," *Cinema Journal* 29, no. 1 (1989): 12.
4 Two episodes of *Family Ties* (NBC, 1982–1989) also featured direct conversations between parents and teens about sex: in "Summer of '82" (October 27, 1982), Steven Keaton speaks to his son, Alex, after Alex loses his virginity, and in "Ready or Not" (February 9, 1984), Elyse Keaton and her daughter Mallory talk after Mallory tentatively decides not to sleep with her boyfriend.
5 Mark Alvey, "'Too Many Kids and Old Ladies:' Quality Demographics and 1960s U.S. Television," *Screen* 45, no. 1 (2004): 48.
6 Alice Leppert, "Solving the Day-Care Crisis, One Episode at a Time: Family Sitcoms and Privatized Child Care in the 1980s," *Cinema Journal* 56, no. 2 (2017): 72.
7 "Lack of Kid Appeal Affecting 'Kate & Allie' Syndie Prospects," *Variety*, June 4, 1986.
8 Ella Taylor, "From the Nelsons to the Huxtables: Genre and Family Imagery in American Network Television," *Qualitative Sociology* 12, no. 1 (1989): 22.
9 Nussbaum, "When Episodes Could Still Be Very Special."
10 Shari Thurer, *The Myths of Motherhood: How Culture Reinvents the Good Mother* (Boston: Houghton Mifflin, 1994), 253.
11 Leppert, "Solving the Day-Care Crisis, One Episode at a Time," 68.
12 Susan Douglas and Meredith W. Michaels, *The Mommy Myth: The Idealization of Motherhood and How It Has Undermined All Women* (New York: Free Press, 2004), 7.
13 Michael Kimmel, "The Contemporary 'Crisis' of Masculinity in Historical Perspective," in *The Making of Masculinities: The New Men's Studies*, ed. Harry Brod (New York: Routledge, 1987), 121.
14 Ibid.
15 Victor Seidler, "Fathering, Authority and Masculinity," in *Male Order: Unwrapping Masculinity*, ed. Rowena Chapman and Jonathan Rutherford (London: Lawrence and Wishart, 1988), 290.
16 Ibid.
17 This emphasis was highlighted by the Adolescent Family Life Act of 1981, which directed government funding for sexual education programs to abstinence-only curricula.
18 Ellen Goodman, "Telling Junior the Facts of Life—on T.V.," *Boston Globe*, December 4, 1986.

19 Quoted in Beverly Beyette, "Teen Sex-Education Campaign Launched," *Los Angeles Times*, October 17, 1986.

20 Quoted in ibid.

21 Ibid.

22 See *Los Angeles Times*, November 25, 1986.

23 Tamar Lewin, "New Sex Mores Are Chilling T.V. Ardor," *New York Times*, March 8, 1987. For example, *Cagney and Lacey* (CBS, 1982–1988), which had previously worked to "dispel the myths about women's lack of sexual curiosity," planned to make the single Chris Cagney "relatively monogamous" in the upcoming season due to concerns about responsible and realistic representations of sex during the AIDS crisis in the age of AIDS (ibid.).

24 Ibid.

25 Quoted in ibid.

26 According to David Poltrack, the vice president of research for CBS, in the 1980s upscale women ages 25–54 were seen as the primary target audience for advertisers. See Rabinovitz, "Sitcoms and Single Moms," 7.

27 "Lack of Kid Appeal."

28 Ella Taylor argues that eventually *Kate & Allie* shifted its focus to children and away from the "witty comedy of divorce manners and single life" ("From the Nelsons to the Huxtables," 23–24).

29 Vincent Stephens, "Odd Family Out: Closely Reading *Kate & Allie*'s 'New Women' Household," *Journal of Popular Culture* 45, no. 4 (2013): 890.

30 Leppert, "Solving the Day-Care Crisis, One Episode at a Time," 79.

31 Ibid., 77.

32 Rabinovitz, "Sitcoms and Single Moms," 9.

33 Allie sings Jason's praises: he fixes things around Kate and Allie's house, he makes sure that Jennie does her homework, and he's been accepted to Yale.

34 There is a brief scene in which Kate and Emma awkwardly agree to avoid talking about sex until "later."

35 Rabinovitz, "Sitcoms and Single Moms,"15. In contrast, in the two episodes of *Family Ties* mentioned above, Elyse and Steven Keaton demonstrate an almost hands-off approach to parenting their children through their first sexual experiences.

36 At this time the show was renamed first *Valerie's Family* and then *The Hogan Family*. The firing also resulted in Harper's winning a lawsuit against the production company for wrongful termination. She and her husband (a producer on the show) received approximately $1.8 million in damages.

37 Quoted in Michael Kubasik, "Valerie Harper Talks of Suit, Series," *Newsday*, September 22, 1988.

38 One affiliate replaced the episode with a rerun of an episode from Valerie Harper's previous sitcom, *Rhoda*. See "Albany TV Station Cancels NBC Show over Condom Issue," *New York Times*, February 8, 1987.

39 Interestingly, while Laurie's family is visiting, David is sleeping on a sofa-bed in the living room, similar to the one on which Jennie and Jason planned to have sex—perhaps hinting at the attempt on the part of television producers to keep teenage sex out of bedrooms.

40 Greg Dawson, "T.V. Sex Ventures into Real World," *Orlando Sentinel*, February 8, 1987.

41 Laurie's complete disregard of the need for birth control is a bit implausible, especially since the episode confirms that she is not a virgin. The network, according to Keyes,

was adamant that "we stress that it was not simply a sexual relationship . . . that the girl did not appear morally loose or sleazy" (ibid.). This demand on the part of the network helps explain the character of Laurie, who is weakly conceived as she wavers between being sexually provocative and innocent, in an attempt to both depict the relationship as something real and allow David to shine as the responsible partner.

42 Quoted in Kathryn Baker, "'Valerie' Episode Expects Criticism,'" *Great Fall Tribune,* February 8, 1987.

43 Quoted in ibid. Of course, the character who is actually sexually active does not indicate that she will use protection in the future, and it's only the character who chooses to abstain who now has condoms.

5

"Thanksgiving Orphans"

Cheers and Very Special Holiday Episodes of Television

JENNIFER PORST

Cheers (NBC, 1982–1993) is one of the most beloved and critically acclaimed U.S. television series of all time. Even though the show was a sitcom, over the course of its eleven seasons, the characters dealt with a range of serious topics that could easily fit on a list of stereotypical very special episode (VSE) plots. For example, in the first season, the series won critical acclaim for an episode whose title, "The Boys in the Bar," referred to the play and movie *The Boys in the Band*. In that episode, Sam's friend and former teammate writes an autobiography in which he comes out as gay. Some of the regulars in the bar pressure Sam to make sure that Cheers does not become a gay bar, and the episode serves as a cultural forum on antigay prejudices. In the second season, a murderer attempts to rob the bar and tries to kill Diane. In the third, a man whose wife slept with Sam confronts Sam and shoots him in the leg, and Norm has a scare when a chest x-ray comes back with suspicious results. In the seventh season episode "Call Me Irresponsible," Woody developed a gambling problem. In the eighth season, the show made Carla a widow. Despite these serious topics, the critic Vikram Murthi observed about "Endless Slumper," an episode in the first season in which Sam, an alcoholic, struggles to avoid a relapse, the show "never falls into maudlin very-special-episode territory, but remains grounded and simple."[1] The show's writers' also explicitly objected to the idea of *Cheers* ever fitting a VSE mold, which make it a useful space to consider the fundamental characteristics of the sitcom and the VSE. In this chapter, I turn first to the changing depiction of the family in sitcoms in the second half of the twentieth century and the sitcom's depiction of the most family-centric of American holidays, Thanksgiving. I then chart the parallel rise of Thanksgiving and television to better understand how the two have influenced each other, and finally I take a closer look at the "Thanksgiving Orphans" (November 27, 1986) episode of *Cheers* to define very special holiday episodes of television and their place in television history.

Situation comedies, or sitcoms like *Cheers*, feature weekly situations that were resolved by the end of the episode every week. The situations themselves may or may not have been funny, but the process of resolving them, and the fact that they were resolved by the characters' coming together at the end rather than in death or expulsion from society, provided the comedy. As the media scholar Jane Feuer has pointed out in her work on the genre, "the TV sitcom is by nature a conservative and static form" because the resolution of the situation most often returns the characters to the story world's status quo.[2] Practically speaking, this is the case because sitcoms are meant to carry on endlessly (or at least until enough episodes have been produced to earn a lucrative run in syndication), so their characters have only a limited capacity for change. As a result, some topics often seem too complex for this format to address adequately. For instance, the producers of *Mr. Belvedere* (ABC, 1985–1990) debated but eventually decided not to make Heather Owens, an eighteen-year-old character, the victim of a date rape. As an article in *TV Guide* explained, "What the show will deal with instead is Heather's trauma after fending off an attempted assault by her date. 'We did consider having her raped,' says co-executive producer Liz Sage, 'but you would forever change the character and 22 minutes is not adequate to deal with such absolutes.'"[3] But the show had previously dealt with other serious topics such as AIDS and child molestation, so its choice in this instance illustrates the fact that the line between what can and what cannot be addressed in a half hour is highly elastic.

Although all sitcoms share many characteristics, the sitcom, like all genres,[4] has developed and changed over time. Those changes have often occurred in response to changing social and cultural norms and values. When in the late 1960s television shifted away from rural sitcoms like *The Andy Griffith Show* (CBS, 1960–1968) and *Green Acres* (CBS, 1965–1971) to the more socially relevant sitcoms like those produced by Norman Lear's Tandem Productions and Mary Tyler Moore's MTM Enterprises, many sitcom families began dealing with social and political issues on a weekly basis. The Bunkers in *All in the Family* (CBS, 1971–1979), for example, dealt with situations involving everything from racism, homosexuality, and feminism to cancer and the Vietnam War. After that, it became almost necessary for sitcoms to deal with the serious issues of the day, to avoid appearing out of touch. That was particularly true for series that sought critical acclaim and awards along with higher ratings. Sitcoms shifted back to a more conservative focus on the family in the 1980s, but television still tackled challenging subjects. However, they were often relegated to stereotypical VSEs about drug abuse or illiteracy and what those problems could teach us about life. These shifts in the ways in which sitcoms dealt with the serious issues of their time raises a question: particularly after television's turn toward relevance in the sitcom, how are we to distinguish between relevant TV and VSEs? If all or most of a series' episodes deal with significant and relevant issues of the time, what makes any one of the episodes rise to the level of very special?

VSEs are meant to somehow stand out from the diegetic world of the series, distinguishing themselves from the series' narrative and stylistic world. In sitcoms, that distinction is often attained by the introduction of different characters and locations that function to help the central characters, and the audience, learn something about an important topic. Holiday episodes are particularly adept at this, since holidays like Thanksgiving stand out from the ordinary flow of life in American culture and typically involve travel and the coming together of family members who may not be a part of people's regular lives. While television plays a hegemonic role as a site of negotiation for society's ideological beliefs,[5] in VSEs that role is heightened by virtue of the fact that the episodes take on some of the more significant issues of the day. In so doing, VSEs can help audiences address or contain those difficult issues, often by framing them as personal dilemmas faced by the show's characters and resolvable within an episode.

In the 1980s, one of the important issues facing American culture was the transformation of the nuclear family. From 1960 to 1980, the divorce rate more than doubled, more women entered the workforce, and more children were born to single parents and blended families.[6] Some sitcoms in the 1980s, like *The Cosby Show* (NBC, 1984–1992), returned to the traditional nuclear family, while others, like *Roseanne* (ABC, 1988–1997 and 2018), featured a nuclear family that deviated from the typical middle-class sitcom family. Still others, like *Cheers*, featured a workplace family composed of people who are related through work and their workplace. All of these sitcoms featured special Thanksgiving episodes. To more clearly conceptualize what it means to be a VSE, this chapter looks at Thanksgiving special episodes in general, and the "Thanksgiving Orphans" episode of *Cheers* in particular. This analysis demonstrates the important relationship between Thanksgiving and television, the role of Thanksgiving and television in maintaining a normative ideological conception of the family, and the ways in which a show like *Cheers* gave American audiences an opportunity to negotiate the changing notions of family and what it was to be American in the 1980s.

The Rise of the Thanksgiving Holiday

Thanksgiving, like many holidays, is an invented tradition, and it has become a domestic occasion in the United States when families gather in someone's home and pay homage to the ideal of the affectionate family. That family has been idealized as a privatized nuclear one, with a nurturing mother who creates the proper home atmosphere. Even though the conception of the ideal family was a nuclear one, the celebration often included extended family. Some families would invite neighbors or strangers to join them, so that those people would not be left alone on a day of family gathering. The holiday was originally celebrated by the upper and middle classes, whose members could afford the relative luxury of a traditional Thanksgiving feast. But, much like broadcasting, it spread throughout society in the twentieth century. It developed as both an expression and a result of the middle-class ideology of the affectionate family.

But, as the scholar Leigh Eric Schmidt has argued, "the history of popular culture, especially the history of popular festivals, is full of reform-minded stratagems to purify, streamline, or correct the perceived excesses and deficiencies of plebeian celebrations."[7] Thanksgiving serves as a clear example of one of those reform-minded strategems, and started out as a very different kind of celebration than the one we have today. Originally, it was a "communal celebration, often raucous, usually outdoors, which involved lower-class males demanding treats from the wealthy."[8] It was a "masculine escape from the family, a day of rule breaking, and spontaneous mirth."[9] Boys and men, called Fantastics or Fantasticals, wore costumes and paraded in rural and urban areas in the Northeast, often demanded treats or money along the way, and even committed physical assaults on Thanksgiving as well as Christmas. In the mid-nineteenth century, there was a push to make the holiday more safe, sane, and sober,[10] and Sarah Josepha Hale, the editor of *Godey's* magazine, published yearly editorials encouraging people to celebrate Thanksgiving, reprinted recipes for the feast, and published stories of prodigal sons returning home. Just as Thanksgiving episodes of television shows do today, Hale "showed how Thanksgiving should be celebrated and explained its meaning."[11] When Abraham Lincoln formally proclaimed Thanksgiving to be an annual national holiday in November 1863, the country was in the middle of the Civil War, and he hoped that the holiday would help bring the nation together.[12]

Then, in the late nineteenth century, there was a push to acculturate and assimilate the rising number of immigrants into American life, and the holiday became a way of expressing the more abstract values of nation and home. As the Progressive era refashioned Thanksgiving into a domestic occasion that indoctrinated newcomers into American customs, the tradition of wearing costumes and demanding treats shifted to Halloween.[13] By that time, most states had passed legislation making Thanksgiving a legal holiday, and teachers in schools throughout the nation began to teach their pupils the story of the Pilgrims. This instruction provided children with a dominant set of symbols such as turkeys, ears of corn, and Pilgrims.[14] Schools especially encouraged immigrant families to demonstrate their acceptance of American customs and their knowledge of American history by celebrating the holiday at home.[15] Thanksgiving became even more important in American culture in the late nineteenth and early twentieth centuries, when industrialization and urbanization caused more people to move away from home for work and increased the number of hours worked per week. For people who were away from home more often, the holiday introduced a scheduled event that provided a time when people returned to their homes.[16]

At that same time, broadcasting was on the rise, and many people conceived of the medium as a means of educating the public and improving culture and society. From its earliest years, broadcasting was supported by advertising and consumer culture, which spread along with the middle-class notion that "the 'innocent' amusements of holiday gift giving within the 'domestic circle' represented 'the progress of refinement.'"[17] Trade journals encouraged merchants to take advantage of the commercial potential of holidays by "conjur[ing] up 'the spirit of hearty celebration' for the purposes of merchandising and consumption."[18] Merchants and the trades who supplied them realized that "holidays were a great store attraction, and merchants should take the lead in hearty commemoration. In carefully staging holiday celebrations from one year to the next, merchants helped lift certain observances and symbols into national prominence."[19]

One of the merchants that used the holidays to increase its sales was Macy's. The company introduced the Macy's Thanksgiving Day Parade in 1924 as a prelude to the Christmas shopping season. Santa appeared at the end of the parade to symbolize "the bounty of Christmas and the desire to shower children with presents. So clear was the connection between the two holidays that Macy's at first called its November spectacle a 'Christmas parade.'"[20] However, the Macy's Thanksgiving Day Parade was not the first parade to take place on Thanksgiving. The Fantastics paraded through town in their costumes, and football fans paraded to the field of play. Thanksgiving Day football games started in 1876 when the Intercollegiate Football Association, a group run by college students, scheduled their first championship game on Thanksgiving. Only twenty years later, "the *Chicago Tribune* estimated that about 10,000 high school and college teams, and those of athletic clubs were playing football on Thanksgiving Day."[21]

To avoid competing with football games, which were played in the afternoon, Macy's parade took place in the morning. In the 1920s, football moved into the home thanks to radio, so that "the family might dine and then listen to a football game on the radio as a form of after-dinner entertainment." Once television had penetrated most American homes in the mid-1950s, football moved to television. Men "quickly came to regard listening to the game as traditional, part of what made the [Thanksgiving] ritual authentic and meaningful," and families often scheduled their dinner so that it would not interfere with watching the game.[22] By the mid-twentieth century, for many families, the ritual of Thanksgiving involved watching the Macy's Thanksgiving Day Parade in the morning, while in the afternoon, the men watched football in the living room while the women labored in the kitchen to prepare the feast.

By 2018, the Macy's parade was the third-most-watched entertainment program of the year, with an average of 23.68 million viewers over its three-hour running time. The three National Football League (NFL) football games broadcast that year earned 26.5 million viewers, 30.48 million viewers, and 21.73 million viewers, respectively.[23] This relationship between the television schedule and the schedule of Thanksgiving rituals is an example of the ways that Nick Browne conceived of television as a "supertext," which "helps produce and render 'natural' the logic and rhythm of the social order."[24] The two schedules evolved together, and each affected the other to the point that most people take for granted that the contemporary rituals of the holiday, and the television programs that audiences watch as part of those rituals, are simply how the day is celebrated. This brief history also shows how the "popularity of modern holidays is to be understood through the dense interplay of cultural production and consumption, in the powerful dynamism of 'cultural creation and cultural reception.'"[25]

The Very Special Thanksgiving Episode

While there have been one-off holiday specials (perhaps the most famous are *A Charlie Brown Thanksgiving* [CBS, November 20, 1973] and its more successful relative, *A Charlie Brown Christmas* [CBS, December 9, 1965]), sitcoms throughout television history have featured Thanksgiving episodes. One of the earliest examples was "Thanksgiving" (November 22, 1951), an episode of *The Burns and Allen Show* (CBS, 1950–1958). Since then, shows including *Adventures of Ozzie and Harriet* (ABC, 1962–1966), *Father Knows Best* (CBS, 1954–1955 and 1958–1960, NBC, 1955–1958), *The Donna Reed Show* (ABC, 1958–1966), *The Munsters* (CBS, 1964–1966), *The Brady Bunch* (ABC, 1969–1974), *WKRP in Cincinnati* (CBS, 1978–1982), and *All in the Family* (CBS, 1971–1979) have featured episodes in which their characters celebrate the holiday. Often, these episodes fulfill what the scholars John Fiske and John Hartley described as the "bardic function" of television, which enfolds each member of the culture into that culture's dominant value system and mythologies.[26] The episodes often do so by featuring a family celebrating the holiday, and the situation the characters encounter is related to some obstacle that threatens to prevent an idyllic celebration from occurring. For example, in *That Girl*'s (ABC, 1966–1971) Thanksgiving episode (November 23, 1967), "Thanksgiving Comes but Once a Year, Thankfully," the eponymous "that girl," Ann Marie, and her boyfriend, Donald, cannot decide which family to spend Thanksgiving with, so they invite their parents to celebrate with them in Ann Marie's apartment. Hilarity ensues when the families argue over whose Thanksgiving traditions are the correct ones—for example, one family advocates cooking a turkey, while the other has traditionally cooked a goose. In these cases, the debate and the ultimate resolution of the conflict about the rituals of the holiday serve as a reminder to the audience of the nature of the holiday and the ways it should be celebrated.

The fact that *That Girl* featured a single working woman who had a long-term boyfriend but did not, at least in the show's diegesis, get married, reflected the changing roles of women and the family in American society during the second wave of feminism in the 1960s and 1970s. *The Mary Tyler Moore Show* (CBS, 1970–1977) also featured a single working woman, but *The Mary Tyler Moore Show* spent more time with Mary's "work family" than it did with her life outside of work. Although *The Mary Tyler Moore Show* never aired an episode explicitly about Thanksgiving, it produced many episodes that aired in mid-November and in which Mary would host a dinner party that threatened disaster. For example, in "The Dinner Party" (November 17, 1973), Mary threw a last-minute dinner party for a congresswoman. Mary had only six dining-room chairs and enough food for six people, but unexpected guests and food timing issues threatened to ruin the evening. In the episode "Not a Christmas Story" (November 9, 1974), Mary and the newsroom gang were trapped in the office during a snowstorm and ended up sharing the Christmas meal prepared by Sue Anne for the Christmas special she had taped earlier that day. The meals symbolized the Thanksgiving feast, and the situations resolved themselves with the characters putting aside their differences, at least momentarily, and coming together at the dinner table. All of these cases serve as examples of the way in which anxieties about changing norms of gender and family were negotiated in the cultural forum of television. The shows created a space where shared beliefs and values were negotiated to maintain the social order and help audiences adapt to economic and social transformations.[27]

In the 1980s, *Cheers* took another step in the evolution of the sitcom by focusing almost exclusively on a workplace family. *Cheers* was one of the highest rated and most critically acclaimed shows of its time. It aired during the last gasp of the network era of broadcasting, just before cable took a serious bite out of the networks' ratings and when television was still dominated by the big three networks (NBC, ABC, and CBS). As the historian Michele Hilmes has described, by the early 1980s, "network programming strategy itself had reached a crisis. . . . Increased competition from cable and videocassette recorders had resulted in a 12% drop in network share between 1979 and 1982, tending to draw away 'upscale' viewers whose tastes—and pocketbooks—ran to theatrical films and 'narrowcasted' cable services of a 'high culture' variety."[28] She continued: "When Grant Tinker took charge of NBC in 1981, he brought the MTM image of 'quality TV' to the third place network—along with MTM 'quality' demographics: 'a liberal, sophisticated group of upwardly mobile professionals' . . . ; 'upscale urbanites whose status as active consumers rendered them a desirable "target market" for TV advertisers.' . . . But this appeal to an 'upscale' audience had to be made without alienating TV's 'mass' audience; 'high culture' viewers had to be entertained, but not at the expense of 'low culture' fans."[29] *Cheers* was almost exclusively set in the bar from which the show took its name, and much like the other shows on the résumés of James Burrows (*Cheers*'s co-creator and principle director) and Les and Glen Charles (*Cheers*'s co-creators and writers), it featured a workplace family. Although exceedingly white, the cast of characters was otherwise eclectic, which allowed many audience members to identify with any number of the people and stories on the show.

Although *Cheers* eventually became a huge success for NBC, initially it had a difficult time catching on with audiences. But when *The Cosby Show* debuted in 1984, during *Cheers*'s third season, those shows—along with *Family Ties* (NBC, 1982–1989) and *Night Court* (NBC, 1984–1992)—allowed NBC to build a Thursday night ratings juggernaut. As Warren Littlefield, who was vice president of comedy programming at NBC and later became president of the network, recalled, *Cheers*'s "audience was huge and reliable (for both original episodes and repeats) and was divided almost evenly between men and women. That's rare enough in the TV business to approach unique. Better still, *Cheers* was a bull's-eye show for advertisers' dream demographic, the coveted eighteen- to forty-nine-year-old urban viewer with disposable income. It was also an Emmy magnet of unquestioned quality and pedigree."[30] The show eventually became a Thursday night tent pole for the network, and Thursday generated more advertising revenue for NBC than the other six nights of the week combined.[31] The amount of advertising revenue a network like NBC can earn is based on its programs' ratings, and in the 1980s there were four key times (known as "sweeps") in a given year when ratings held extra importance. Sweeps happened in February, May, July, and November, when Nielsen ratings information was "swept" up and used by the networks to sell ad time to sponsors. During sweeps weeks, as one journalist described it, "networks inundate the TV-viewing public with a veritable flood of plot-twisting, cringe-inducing, shark-jumping moments in the hopes they'll tune in."[32] Today, digital technologies allow Nielsen to continuously record detailed information about its households' viewing data, and the ubiquity of data collection among streaming services and cable and internet providers has lessened the emphasis on sweeps weeks. During the 1980s, however, the importance of sweeps weeks in determining ad revenue was still intense, and networks would do just about anything to make sure that audiences tuned in during those periods.

Due to the holiday season, December was often a month of reruns, but November, a sweeps month, still featured new episodes. Earning high ratings throughout that month was extremely important because those ratings set the ad rates for the three following months. Thanksgiving complicated matters, because ratings on Thanksgiving and the day after were traditionally off by 10–15 percent because of the many holiday distractions competing for viewers' attention. *Variety* referred to it as the "low sets-in-use Thanksgiving night."[33] In 1989, some stations were so desperate to raise their Thanksgiving ratings that they attempted to skew the numbers by "throwing out shows with low ratings on those two days by slapping different titles on them and then claiming they didn't count against the monthly averages."[34] As a result, Arbitron, one of the leading audience measurement companies at the time, had to take an "unusual action" and "deleted all of the ratings for Thanksgiving Day (November 23) and Friday (November 24), from its November-sweeps averages."[35]

Today, the most reliably high ratings on Thanksgiving are for NFL football games. Although the networks now broadcast three NFL games on Thanksgiving, with the last one airing during prime-time, in the 1980s NFL games were broadcast during the day, with the last game played at 3:00 P.M. Central Standard Time.[36] With no prime-time football game competing for viewers, *Cheers* almost always aired a new episode on Thanksgiving, which helped NBC regularly claim a ratings win for that evening. For example, when NBC won the ratings for the week in 1985, *Broadcasting* reported that "the NBC victory also came despite the normal ease of the post-turkey television blahs across the country on Thanksgiving Thursday."[37] Since the Thursday night lineup was NBC's ratings juggernaut, even if *The Cosby Show* or other Thursday night shows scheduled reruns, *Cheers* ran a new episode. Despite that, the series aired only two episodes on Thanksgiving night during the entire course of its run that explicitly referred to Thanksgiving. One of those was "Thanksgiving Orphans," an episode that makes it to the top not only of "best of" lists of special Thanksgiving episodes of television, but also of the lists of best television episodes of all time.

"I Don't Think Watching Television Was the Pilgrims' Original Intent"

"Thanksgiving Orphans" originally aired as the ninth episode of season five. The episode stood out from the rest of the series in part because it took place primarily in a setting outside of the bar, with the characters gathering for Thanksgiving at Carla's house. As one of the episode's writers, Cheri Steinkellner, recalled: "We always thought of the people at *Cheers* as a family. In the sense of, no matter whether you like 'em or don't like 'em, you still have to see them tomorrow. So I think it's the idea of putting them in the ultimate family situation, which is, Let's have our family Thanksgiving."[38] With *Cheers*, the bar family was what the scholar Hamid Naficy has termed the "paradigmatic media family," in that it was "both a metaphor for the nuclear family and a metonym for American cultural values and mores."[39] Even though the *Cheers* family was not a nuclear one, the episode ultimately serves as a validation of family and the importance of celebrating Thanksgiving together.

The episode starts in the bar with everyone discussing their plans, or lack thereof, for the holiday. Diane takes the holiday very seriously and has planned to spend the day at her professor's home, where they would re-create the first Thanksgiving. Sam has a date. Carla's husband and kids are in Atlantic City. It is Woody's first Thanksgiving on his own. Norm is supposed to go to his mother-in-law's house. With everyone facing a lonely or dispiriting holiday, Diane twists Carla's arm to host everyone at her house for the day. Steinkellner explained:

"The idea was to give everybody a Thanksgiving issue, whether it's food-related, game-related, parade-related, other people–related. To just make a giant list of all the things about Thanksgiving that have the potential to make you crazy. Because the expectation is so high that we're all gonna have this wonderful day together. Of course, you just want to punch holes in that."[40] Once at Carla's house, Woody, Cliff, Norm (who ended up at Carla's after fighting with his wife about skipping her mother's that year), Sam (whose date canceled on him), and Frasier sit around the television watching the Macy's Thanksgiving Day Parade, football games, and professional wrestling. Norm has brought the turkey, which he throws in the oven to cook while they watch television. Diane shows up dressed as a Pilgrim after realizing that she was invited to her professor's home only to serve drinks and food to the real guests.

There is the normal *Cheers* bickering and banter, and Diane works to reinforce the central traditions of the holiday by reminding the others about important elements of the holiday. For example, "I don't think watching television was the Pilgrims' original intent when they created the holiday." On Carla's walls hang her children's drawings of turkeys and Pilgrims. Ironically, Thanksgiving was invented far after the Pilgrims, but the set design and Diane's pronouncements help frame the holiday as ahistorical and fundamentally ideological. While during the 1980s American culture and families were changing in ways that made it harder to celebrate holidays with a nuclear or even extended family, this episode works to maintain the value of family as a concept. For example, Frasier, the other character representing the upper-class elite, tells those he is celebrating with both on-screen and at home, "Family is not necessarily limited to blood relations." Later, Diane makes everyone stand up and take turns toasting that for which they are thankful. Everyone grumbles but takes a turn. Woody is thankful that he is an American, for the upbringing his parents gave him, and for the friends he has made in Boston, but he ends by expressing thanks for the facial contortions he can do. As the others begin to demonstrate their own idiosyncratic abilities, Diane yells: "We are not here to be thankful for the strange things we can do with our bodies!" Eventually, everyone is starving and impatient, but it is revealed that (spoilers ahead!) Norm managed to mess up cooking the turkey. Playful bickering escalated to more pointed barbs, which then progressed to throwing food. As Bill Steinkellner, another of the show's writers, recalled: "*Cheers* was supposed to be a classy show, and this is about as unclassy as you can get, to have a food fight. But I think that's part of what makes it work."[41]

After the food fight, the episode fulfilled what Feuer has argued is the conservative role of the sitcom, with a sentimental scene in which the "family" eats and drinks and laughs together and toasts their loved ones who are not with them. As a good comedy, however, that sentimentality was ultimately diffused by one of the other moments that makes this episode stand out from the rest of the series: the fact that we get to see Norm's wife. For those who have not seen the episode, I will not spoil this classic moment by revealing exactly why, but the

FIG. 5.1 The *Cheers* gang celebrates in the true spirit of Thanksgiving.

audience is still denied a look at her face. This episode, like so many other special Thanksgiving episodes of television, ultimately reinforces the importance of family and country and demonstrates over and over again the correct way to celebrate this very American tradition. But it manages to escape the stereotypical conception of the VSE, in part through its lack of sentimentality. The characters display emotion, but the acting is restrained, and the sincerity ultimately diffused with humor.

As a VSE, this episode stands out from the rest of the series by placing its action in a setting outside the bar and featuring the appearance of a special character who is legendary for being much discussed but never seen in the rest of the series. Moreover, it fits the definition of a VSE by dealing with the nature of family during a time when the definition of the American family was changing. In so doing, the episode serves to reinforce dominant ideological values about America in the form of the celebration of Thanksgiving. Even though it fits so much of the core definition of a VSE, it has never been described as one. Cheri Steinkellner even went out of her way to deny its status as a VSE when she said that *Cheers* didn't do holiday episodes often because it was "a little bit against policy, to have a Very Special blah blah blah."[42] Unlike in stereotypical VSEs, and as part of a sitcom that conceived of itself as high quality, the characters in "Thanksgiving Orphans" treated themselves and the situations in which they found themselves with only limited seriousness. The show was set in a bar, after all.

The fact that the episode avoided stereotypical VSE status may also be related to the function of the problem in the episode. In this case, and throughout the rest of the series, the problem serves as a device for plot or character development rather than as a focus in and of itself. In "Thanksgiving Orphans," the problem of conflicting ideals about the holiday and the possibility that the characters' dinner might be ruined is the central conflict, but the characters, more than the conflict, remain the focus of the episode. This and other episodes in the series also avoid clumsy attempts at conveying some larger moral lesson. Diane moralizes about the true meaning of Thanksgiving, but the rest of the characters groan and consistently undermine her seriousness. As the television journalist Bill Carter observed, "On 'Cheers,' the lessons are incidental, and its subtext will have to be unearthed or imagined by the sociologists of the future. Rather, what the show's creators aimed to do was deliver pure comedy that was sophisticated but not pretentious, 'I Love Lucy' as told by Noel Coward."[43] Burrows also argued that "we're not an issue show at all. We write adult stuff."[44] That stuff, however, was often more challenging than the typical sitcom fare produced for family audiences. But, as scholar Michele Hilmes has pointed out, "The program's success in drawing and keeping audiences suggests an ability to address topics, attitudes and situations relevant in some way to millions of people."[45] The realistic and humorous ways that "Thanksgiving Orphans" represented family and Thanksgiving resonated, and still resonates, with audiences.

In one way or another, VSEs are meant to rise above what Raymond Williams described as televisual flow[46] through some combination of stylistic or narrative elements that make the episodes distinct from the rest of their series and other television programming. Just as Thanksgiving stands out as distinct from the normal flow of days in a year, so do very special Thanksgiving episodes of television. In the same way that commercial institutions like Macy's helped standardize a set of Thanksgiving symbols out of a mishmash of local, regional, and ethnic traditions, so did the great mediator of broadcasting. While the traditions of Thanksgiving as a domestic holiday on which men watched football while women worked in the kitchen to prepare dinner were formed, in part, by the television schedule, Thanksgiving episodes like "Thanksgiving Orphans" played a significant ideological role in cultivating American norms about men, women, and the family. Reconceptualizing holiday episodes of television shows as VSEs can help us understand what a VSE is and can be. Television and its commercial, ad-supported roots have influenced the ways that Americans celebrate holidays like Thanksgiving, just as the ritual celebration of such American holidays have influenced television. Even though the importance of the Thanksgiving holiday in the understanding of America and the powerful myth of the heterosexual nuclear family as the eternal foundation of society are conceived of as natural and given, in actuality they are myths that have been constructed and reinforced over time with the assistance of television—and Thanksgiving VSEs in particular. But as this analysis has shown, looking at Thanksgiving VSEs at different points in time can help us understand the evolution of television, Thanksgiving, and the American family.

Notes

1 Vikram Murthi, "When *Cheers* Became *Cheers*: An Appreciation of 'Endless Slumper,'" *Vulture*, December 6, 2017, https://www.vulture.com/2017/12/cheers-an-appreciation-of-the-endless-slumper-episode.html.
2 Jane Feuer, "Genre Study and Television," in *Channels of Discourse, Reassembled: Television and Contemporary Criticism*, 2nd ed., ed. Robert C. Allen (Chapel Hill: University of North Carolina Press, 1992), 148.
3 "Date Rape Is Target of TV-Movies, Series," *TV Guide*, October 28, 1989, 34.
4 Rick Altman, *Film/Genre* (London: British Film Institute, 1999).
5 Ron Becker, "Ideology," in *The Craft of Criticism: Critical Media Studies in Practice*, ed. Mary Celeste Kearney and Michael Kackman (New York: Routledge, 2018), 11–22.
6 Pew Research Center, "Parenting in America," December 17, 2015, https://www.pewsocialtrends.org/2015/12/17/1-the-american-family-today/.
7 Leigh Eric Schmidt, *Consumer Rites: The Buying and Selling of American Holidays* (Princeton, NJ: Princeton University Press, 1995), 9.
8 Elizabeth Pleck, "The Making of the Domestic Occasion: The History of Thanksgiving in the United States," *Journal of Social History* 32, no. 4 (Summer 1999): 773.
9 Ibid., 776.
10 Schmidt, *Consumer Rites*, 30.
11 Pleck, "The Making of the Domestic Occasion," 775–776.
12 Ibid., 776.
13 Ibid., 776–778.
14 Ibid., 779.
15 Ibid., 780.
16 Ibid., 773–774.
17 Schmidt, *Consumer Rites*, 32.
18 Ibid., 18.
19 Ibid., 34.
20 Pleck, "The Making of the Domestic Occasion," 781–782.
21 Ibid., 777.
22 Ibid., 782.
23 Rick Porter, "Thanksgiving TV Viewers Feast on Macy's Parade, NFL," *The Hollywood Reporter*, November 26, 2018.
24 Nick Browne, "The Political Economy of the Television (Super) Text," *Quarterly Review of Film Studies* 9 (Summer 1984): 176.
25 Schmidt, *Consumer Rites*, 10.
26 John Fiske and John Hartley, *Reading Television* (New York: Methuen, 1978), 88–89.
27 Horace Newcomb and Paul M. Hirsch, "Television as a Cultural Forum: Implications for Research," *Quarterly Review of Film Studies* 8, no. 3 (1983): 45–55.
28 Michele Hilmes, "Where Everybody Knows Your Name: *Cheers* and the Mediation of Cultures," *Wide Angle* 12, no. 2 (April 1990): 67.
29 Ibid., 68.
30 Warren Littlefield, *Top of the Rock: Inside the Rise and Fall of Must See TV* (New York: Doubleday, 2012), 4.
31 Ibid., 6–7.

32 Dan Fletcher, "A Brief History of Sweeps Week," *Time*, October 29, 2009, http://content.time.com/time/arts/article/0,8599,1883157,00.html.

33 Bob Knight, "'Cosby' & ABC Football Go thru Roof," *Variety*, December 11, 1985, 147.

34 "November Sweeps Roundup—ARB Sweeps Exclude Holiday Ratings," *Variety*, December 6, 1989, 123.

35 Ibid.

36 Fletcher, "A Brief History of Sweeps Week."

37 "NBC Claims Thanksgiving Victory with Return of Perry Mason," *Broadcasting*, December 9, 1985, 58.

38 Quoted in Dave Nemetz, "Food Fight! The Messy True Story behind the Classic 'Cheers' Episode, 'Thanksgiving Orphans.'" *Yahoo! Entertainment*, November 24, 2015, https://www.yahoo.com/entertainment/news/cheers-thanksgiving-orphans-episode-true-story-054056375.html.

39 Hamid Naficy, "Television Intertextuality and the Discourse of the Nuclear Family," *Journal of Film and Video* 41, no. 4 (Winter 1989): 50.

40 Quoted in Nemetz, "Food Fight!"

41 Quoted in ibid.

42 Quoted in ibid.

43 Bill Carter, "Why 'Cheers' Proved So Intoxicating," *New York Times*, May 9, 1993.

44 Ibid.

45 Hilmes, "Where Everybody Knows Your Name," 65.

46 Raymond Williams, *Television: Technology and Cultural Form* (New York: Routledge, 2003).

6

Very Spooky Episodes

Roseanne, Working-Class Monsters, and the Playful Perversions of Halloween TV

DAVID SCOTT DIFFRIENT

The annual celebration popularly known as Halloween—a contraction of All Hallows' Eve (referring to the night before All Saints' Day)—has been a recurring theme in U.S. television programming since the medium's earliest days as a form of mass entertainment. Although the once-religious but now-secular festival dates back to the ancient Celtic celebration of Samhain,[1] not until the final years of the Great Depression and the early postwar era did its various modern-day connotations (for example, trick-or-treating, costume parties, and haunted houses) begin to circulate in newspaper articles and via radio broadcasts. In the 1950s, they achieved audiovisual expression through the next major form of American popular culture, television. It was during the first half of that decade when such disparate TV sketch comedies and sitcoms as *The Jackie Gleason Show* (DuMont, 1949–1952; CBS, 1952–1957) and *The Adventures of Ozzie and Harriet* (ABC, 1952–1966) crystalized some of the many activities that make Halloween unique as a time of potentially transgressive merriment, thus distinguishing it from less taboo-shattering holidays (including the medium's other two seasonal mainstays, Christmas and Thanksgiving). Typically framed as a temporary relaxation of social inhibitions, whereby revelers are able to cross lines of decorum through costuming and other forms of camp performance, Halloween can be seen as a kind of release valve for the culture at large. It is therefore akin to TV comedy and other forms of humorous discourse insofar as it gives people the chance to satirically mock certain institutions and traditions (religious and otherwise) while "blowing off steam" or relieving the pressures of everyday life (that is, "pent-up aggressions, anxieties and repressed desires").[2] Though far removed from one another in terms of their settings and class stratifications and couched within ostensibly conservative or restrictive generic frameworks (overseen by network executives, regulators, and sponsors), *The Jackie Gleason Show*'s "Halloween Party for the Boss" (October 25, 1952) and *The Adventures of Ozzie and Harriet*'s "Halloween Party" (October 31, 1952) gesture toward this holiday's playful "perversions" and set the template for future depictions of what the cultural historian David Skal refers to as a yearly event that "turns the world upside down."[3]

In *Death Makes a Holiday*, Skal writes that Halloween has historically been the one day when "permission would be granted to mortals to peer into the future, divine their fates, communicate with supernatural entities, and otherwise enjoy a degree of license and liberty unimaginable—or simply unattainable—the rest of the year."[4] Nothing so elaborate or paranormal takes place in *The Jackie Gleason Show* and *The Adventures of Ozzie and Harriet*, but in their own small way these programs demonstrate the ease with which a simple change in physical appearance (such as Ozzie Nelson's choice of a devil costume) can alter one's perception of their main characters as personifications of the presumed threat posed by monstrous others to mainstream society. In the case of the former show, Ralph Kramden (the character played by the star and host of *The Jackie Gleason Show*, who is a forerunner of his more famous sitcom character in *The Honeymooners* [CBS, 1955–1956]), destroys an old tuxedo so as to create the look of a homeless bum, which he dresses up as in preparation for a Halloween party. After his neighbors Ed and Trixie Norton—cross-dressing as a flapper girl and a sailor boy, respectively—enter the Kramdens' tiny one-bedroom apartment in Brooklyn, Ralph rips his tux jacket and puts it on, covering the embarrassing Zulu chief costume that his wife, Alice, has made for him. Ralph's layered costuming, in which a caricatured image of a white working-class hobo or Chaplinesque tramp rests atop an equally stereotypical representation of racialized otherness (the Black Zulu chief), hints at the artificiality of monstrous alterity, or its status as a cultural construct. The meagerly paid bus driver, whose financial woes are frequently the cause of blustery outbursts and domestic spats with Alice, is able to dress the part of someone lower on the socioeconomic scale by ruining a piece of clothing that, if left intact, would otherwise signify power and wealth. The fact that this early representation of Halloween costuming on American TV leans heavily on the visual coding of social class is relevant. So is the inclusion of Ed and Trixie's drag performances, a gender flip that could be permitted only within the liberating constraints of this most pagan of holidays, which, as Skal argues, allows for the temporary reversal of "roles and fortunes."[5]

A decade after these episodes of *The Jackie Gleason Show* and *The Adventures of Ozzie and Harriet* aired, Halloween was already becoming something of a televisual touchstone, an annual event paradoxically made more singular yet commonplace by virtue of the increased attention given to it in seasonally themed installments of classic domestic sitcoms such as *Leave It to Beaver* (CBS, 1957–1958; ABC, 1958–1963), *Dennis the Menace* (CBS, 1959–1963), and *My Three Sons* (ABC, 1960–1965; CBS, 1965–1972). Each of these latter three network programs, like countless others that aired before and after their initial broadcasts, mined the cultural imaginary of mid-century monsterdom and made Halloween an increasingly "special" part of the fall television season. For example, the precocious middle-class protagonist Dennis Mitchell and his neighbor, Tommy Anderson, primed for a night of trick-or-treating, don grotesque masks in "Haunted House" (October 29, 1961), an episode from the third season of *Dennis the Menace*, as the preteen pranksters Chip Douglas and Sudsy Pfeiffer do in "The Ghost Next Door" (October 25, 1962), an episode from the third season of *My Three Sons*. In these and other domestic sitcoms, characters and audiences alike are spooked by the presumed presence of otherworldly beings (hideously deformed monsters, spectral apparitions, and so on) that would not be out of place in that era's science fiction and fantasy programming (for example, *The Twilight Zone* [CBS, 1959–1964], *The Outer Limits* [ABC, 1963–1965], *The Addams Family* [ABC, 1964–1966], and *The Munsters* [CBS, 1964–1966]). Such representations, while comparatively tame, are exceptional in their break from normality—the veneer of middle-class sameness that masks potentially dangerous or perverse ideas and that is prominently displayed in other, non-Halloween-themed episodes of these series. Additionally, these early representations paved the way for more egregious displays of small-screen, Halloween-themed horrors in the years to come, a historical trajectory that ultimately leads to the one American sitcom that arguably did more than any other—with the obvious exception of *The Simpsons* (Fox, 1989–present)—to domesticate that most macabre, death-fixated of holidays, in the process transforming it into the "second-largest seasonal marketing event after Christmas" around the turn of the century.[6]

That television show, *Roseanne* (ABC, 1988–1997), is famous for many things besides its annual Halloween installments. At once conservative and progressive, this critically lauded multicamera sitcom, created by the veteran TV producers Marcy Carsey and Tom Werner, was initially touted as a reflexive (if not radical) reworking of traditional representations of middle- and working-class America, foregrounding a closely knit yet raucously fractured family that was "beset by financial hardships and emotional pain."[7] Taking its title from the name of its unconventional star (Roseanne Barr), this series broke from earlier depictions of domestic bliss—as seen, for instance, in episodes of *The Donna Reed Show*

(ABC, 1958–1966)—by focusing on an "overweight, loud, and domineering" mom who frequently challenged her husband's and male bosses' patriarchal authority, brashly lashing out at systems of gendered oppression that remain at least partially intact today.[8] In stark contrast to the doting maternal figures on view in *Leave It to Beaver, Dennis the Menace*, and other 1950s and 1960s sitcoms, Roseanne Conner (Barr's character) embodied a new form of prime-time feminism during the 1980s and 1990s.[9] However, from a contemporary perspective, she might also be seen as a reactionary throwback to old-fashioned, red-state "family values." This became especially pronounced when both the race-baiting star and her unruly character threw their support behind President Donald Trump after his November 2016 election. Tellingly, the much-anticipated relaunch of *Roseanne* in the spring of 2018, coinciding with the rise of a Trump-era social-media politics of xenophobic exclusion and othering, was soon overshadowed by the show's sudden cancellation in May of that year—an about-face (initiated by ABC's president, Channing Dungey) that denied longtime viewers of the program an opportunity to indulge their Halloween fantasies one last time with the Conners.

And what led to that cancellation? In the wake of Barr's racist comment about Valerie Jarrett (formerly a senior advisor to President Barack Obama), which she posted on Twitter on May 29, 2018, the controversial actress-comedian was publicly brought to task for her inflammatory rhetoric and was forced to step away from the recently revived television series that bears her name. Within hours of the tweet, Dungey announced that Barr's remark was "abhorrent, repugnant and inconsistent with [the network's] values" and the reason why *Roseanne*—a sitcom once celebrated for its social consciousness and commitment to working-class values, but now scorned as a hideously deformed mouthpiece for Trump's "Make America Great Again"–style nativism—was dropped from ABC's prime-time lineup and consigned to an early grave.[10] The latter metaphor, which is perhaps more suggestive of cemetery-filled horror films, is an apt description not only of *Roseanne*'s precipitous cancellation but also of the star's figurative demise in the public eye, one that echoes the rhetorical maneuvers of her most vocal online critics. Indeed, if one word sums up the moral outrage engendered by Barr's racially insensitive barb directed at a Black woman, not to mention the questionable comportment of this iconoclastic figure within the overlapping spheres of popular culture and political communication, it is "monster."

From the many journalists who called *Roseanne* a "monster hit" (that is, a show boasting "monster TV ratings") in the days following its March 27 relaunch to fellow cast and crew members (in addition to other industry spokespeople) who have weighed in on her bad behavior (which, in the words of one writer, had already succeeded in "scaring away liberal viewers" from her program),[11] one term more than any other has become so synonymous with Barr that the star's on-air hosting of an earlier reality TV series—the tellingly titled *Momsters: When Moms Go Bad* (Discovery, 2014–2015)—should not come as a surprise. Critical recourse to the word "monster" is not unusual when it comes to the discursive framing of working-class characters on American television, a medium that has long treated blue-collar laborers and economically struggling families as freakish miscreants whose otherness is the source of often-dehumanizing humor.[12] As Richard Butsch has argued in his historical overview of social hierarchies in U.S. sitcoms, the relative "prestige and privilege" with which middle-class lifestyles are associated in TV programming remain beyond the reach of low-wage workers—especially in *Roseanne*, in which the monstrous eponymous character appears to be "content with and unapologetic about" her low standing and laughably bad taste but also expresses anger, sarcasm, and volatility toward those who would deprive her of the respect that she ironically believes her family deserves.[13]

Significantly, Barr's much discussed "monstrosity" had been anticipated by her character Roseanne Conner's fondness for dressing the part in Halloween-themed episodes of the series—a "very special" annual event (occurring every fall during the show's original run, except in its first season) in which various creatures were allowed to come out of the proverbial closet and give voice to otherwise-repressed elements in the culture at large. Whether playing the "Wicked Witch of the Midwest" (in "Boo" from season two) or donning a bloodied shirt as a knife-wielding homicidal maniac (in "Trick Me Up, Trick Me Down" from season four), the comedian habitually literalized the metaphor of monstrosity that has long haunted her on- and offscreen personas as a self-described "domestic goddess." Those episodes, in which faked disembowelings, eye gougings, and other kinds of body horror are performed with devilish glee for neighborhood trick-or-treaters and in-studio audiences, laid the foundation for subsequent television series that use Halloween as an excuse for staging similarly grisly scenes inside cluttered suburban spaces and working-class homes. Since *Roseanne* debuted in the late 1980s, several live-action and animated sitcoms, ranging from *Home Improvement* (ABC, 1991–1999) and *Family Matters* (ABC, 1989–1997) to *Family Guy* (Fox, 1999–present) and *Bob's Burgers* (Fox, 2011–present), have incorporated such horrifying, holiday-based iconography in their own "very spooky episodes," further perpetuating the idea of socially disenfranchised or downwardly mobile Americans as monstrous others.

In this chapter, I explore two specific episodes of *Roseanne*—"Trick or Treat" from season three and "Skeleton in the Closet" from season seven—both of which depart from the traditionally moralizing tone of more typical "very special episodes" (for example, *Diff'rent Strokes*' "The Bicycle Man" [NBC, February 5, 1983] and *Saved by the Bell*'s "Jessie's Song" [NBC, November 3, 1990]) but nevertheless adopt the same teacherly principles of other U.S. sitcoms, instilling valuable lessons about inclusivity, tolerance, and the benefits of celebrating cultural differences across class lines. As contradictory as the "festival of death and life" that inspired them,[14] these episodes are doubly instructive case studies, laying bare the otherwise hidden "horrors" of America's most venerated of institutions—the traditional nuclear family—while masking the outspoken star's more reactionary leanings (only recently brought to light) behind her progressive political stands on issues related to women's rights and workers' rights. To varying degrees, "Trick or Treat" and "Skeleton in the Closet" reveal the radically denaturalizing potential of Halloween as well as the inherent limitations of network television programming (at least that driven by commercial interests and advertiser dollars) in fully representing historically marginalized individuals and groups. The latter includes members of the LGBTQ community who, ironically, look to Halloween as a kind of counter-Christmas: a potentially subversive, prank-filled corrective to more conservative holidays. Before returning to these case studies, let us first explore some of the underlying themes as well as narrative elements at play in many if not all of the "very spooky episodes" devoted to the holiday.

Playing with Gender and Queering Halloween

"Play," it turns out, is the operative word. In addition to humor, it is one of the two "dominant tropes of Halloween," according to Nicholas Rogers, a cultural historian who notes the importance of this transitory moment of carnivalesque potential in "promoting different ways of seeing the world" and giving people the opportunity to test the "limits of permissiveness" each year, if only fleetingly.[15] Like an actual carnival, especially one aimed at marginalized youth or other subcultures, Halloween provides "a public space for social inversion or transgression" that unsettles older generations of Americans.[16] But, as Rogers is quick to acknowledge, Halloween in its most commercial manifestations also exhibits hegemonic and "homogenizing" tendencies, "as the epitome of [a] North American mass culture" that continues to be exported globally and that feeds multiple revenue streams across different industries.[17] Given his and other scholars' emphasis on humor and play, it is not too big a leap to suggest that the sitcom genre, which is likewise snagged between contrasting polarities (as a comfortably discomforting cultural form that pleases and perturbs in equal measure), is a natural fit for Halloween, and vice versa. That is, the yearly festival has found a home in the sitcom, an ostensibly conservative genre of highly contrived or ritualized rhetorical figures and morally circumscribed domestic settings that is nevertheless playful and even progressive in its disarming use of humor to "parody power and mock its pretensions."[18] With that in mind, let us turn to some of the distinguishing features of Halloween TV.

One of the most fascinating, if also frustrating, aspects of Halloween TV is its tendency to use the holiday as an excuse to approach gender dynamics, sexual orientation, and other issues related to identity in a seemingly progressive way, only to retreat to a glib, rigid definition of what men and women are or should be. The sheer number of references to "slutty" costumes alone (references made by characters in *Friends* [NBC, 1994–2004], *How I Met Your Mother* [CBS, 2005–2014], *Last Man Standing* [ABC, 2011–2017; Fox, 2018–present], and *The*

Goldbergs [ABC, 2013–present], among many other shows) is enough to make one question the supposedly enlightened worldview of Hollywood screenwriters or the emancipatory function of a seasonal event that is so frequently handcuffed to images of scantily clad and sexually promiscuous nurses and other women.[19] Additionally, this ultimately regressive perspective, on view in contemporary sitcoms like *According to Jim* (ABC, 2001–2009) and *The King of Queens* (CBS, 1998–2007), typically results in the male protagonist or some other adamantly heterosexual character defensively asserting his masculinity in the presence of gay men or liberal-minded straight metrosexuals whose Halloween costuming (for example, the clothing of camp cinematic icons, such as Dorothy from *The Wizard of Oz* [1939] or Faye Dunaway as Joan Crawford in *Mommie Dearest* [1981]) hints at the possibility of a holiday inspired queering of the text.

For example, in "Dana Dates Jim," an episode of *According to Jim*, Andy (a plus-size supporting character whose dating woes are a running gag in the series) attends a costume party in the guise of a generic superhero, complete with red cape, gold boots, and a chintzy headband in the shape of a winged eagle. Spotting a fellow reveler dressed as Raggedy Ann across the room, he approaches and says, "You know, I may be a superhero, but I still like to play with dolls," to which the recipient of this cheesy pickup line responds, "You know I'm a guy, right?" Awkward tension results, and the momentary silence between the two is plastered over with the eruption of the in-studio audience's laughter. Soon, though, Andy exchanges a firm handshake with the man, falsely telling him that his name is Jim and that this is his house before quickly turning on his heels and leaving the scene.

Similarly, in the episode "Ticker Treat," from the blue-collar comedy *The King of Queens*, another superhero—this time a young boy dressed up as one of the Powerpuff Girls (Blossom, whose bright pink uniform codes that character as outwardly feminine)—is the subject of nervous talk concerning his sexual orientation. Specifically, Doug Heffernan, the main character, tries to ease the mounting anxieties of his best friend and fellow delivery driver, Deacon Palmer, who worries that his young son might be gay (given the latter's choice in Halloween costuming). Telling Doug that he is afraid to go home at night, for fear that he might walk in on Kirby "wearing a girdle," Deacon reminds us that a more pernicious moral panic beyond the largely unfounded trepidation over candy tampering (a topic of public safety debates during the 1970s and 1980s, when the catchphrase "stranger danger" gained cultural currency) haunts this holiday,[20] a time when so-called transgressions or violations of social decorum give opponents an excuse for the worst kind of fear mongering. "Take it easy," Doug says to his friend, noting that "just because [the boy] wants to be a girl superhero doesn't mean he's gay." His concluding statement on this matter—"You know they say that most drag queens are actually straight"—does little to allay Deacon's doubts about his son's heterosexuality and even less to correct this episode's tone-deaf approach to a subject that has become increasingly central to Halloween TV's rhetorical moves and representational modes.

Consider, as well, the "Halloween Story" episode of *Ned and Stacey* (Fox, 1995–1997), which features a masquerade party that brings together two men who must negotiate each other's sexual orientation as a result of their gender-coded costuming. Here, a supporting character named Rico, who has been forced to attend the party in the guise of a female nurse, must contend with the grabby advances of a bisexual man dressed as a surgeon, especially after Rico tells him, "I'm a *guy*." Similar same-sex encounters, always played for laughs, occur in other Halloween-themed episodes (especially those of less-than-progressive sitcoms such as *The Norm Show* [ABC, 1999–2001] and *Good Morning, Miami* [NBC, 2002–2004]), perpetuating stereotypes not only about female impersonators, transvestites, and drag-queen culture but also about genderqueer people who ironically might look to Halloween as an opportunity for cross-class solidarity and self-expression. The questionable sentiment that "Halloween is to gays what St. Patrick's is the Irish," familiar to anyone who has studied this most subcultural, yet strangely domesticated, of holidays, has solidified into a kind of "truth" for those commentators who either celebrate or castigate its queering potential.[21]

Funnily enough, an earlier scene in *Ned and Stacey*'s "Halloween Story," showing the female member of the eponymous duo bingeing on junk food while watching a scary movie on TV (a way for this freelance journalist to feed her emotional hunger after having an article turned down), makes direct reference to a sitcom that not only made "very spooky episodes" a much-anticipated yearly event but also pioneered more progressive forms of nonbinary and queerly transgressive representations. The television series to which I am referring is the one that I mentioned at the beginning of this chapter and focus on throughout its second half: a working-class classic that is mentioned by title, or rather by name, when Stacey's sister, Amanda (who is dressed as Glinda the Good Witch from *The Wizard of Oz*), asks the sweatpants-wearing consumer of junk food if she is going to the upcoming costume party "as Roseanne."

"Trick or Treat," a third-season episode of *Roseanne* that was written by Chuck Lorre and that originally aired on October 30, 1990, stands in stark contrast to the shows cited above, mainly because it disrupts their outmoded representations while also thematically unpacking the discomfort that one character—Roseanne's husband, Dan—experiences when it comes to the subject of homosexuality and "any incipient sign" of his preteen son's "effeminacy."[22] As Tison Pugh argues in *The Queer Fantasies of the American Family Sitcom*, the holidays—including Christmas and Thanksgiving—provide a backdrop for some of this series' most revealing signs of that discomfort, which manifests itself paradoxically at the moments when lesbianism and other forms of queer desire are expressed—either directly (via the physical attraction between two supporting characters, Nancy and Marla, who were introduced in the fourth and fifth seasons, respectively), or indirectly (via cutaways to Dan, for instance, just as Nancy and Marla lean in for a mistletoe kiss). But it is Halloween, more than any other celebratory event in the Conners' working-class lives, that most emphatically propels Dan and his more open-minded partner toward a resolution that is truly cathartic, making this "very spooky episode" very special indeed.

Like every other *Roseanne* episode, "Trick or Treat" begins with an opening-credits sequence that in a single shot (accompanied by the show's bluesy, harmonica- and saxophone-driven theme music) encircles the Conner family as they sit around the kitchen table—starting with the main character and then showing her husband, Dan; son, D. J.; daughters, Darlene and Becky; and sister, Jackie Harris. The setting of this sequence stayed roughly the same for the nine years during which the series was broadcast, although the family's activities changed each season. As an episode from the third season, "Trick or Treat" highlights the Conners' togetherness by way of a "high stakes" card game, with a pot of pretzels, cookies, and candy in the middle of the table that the eponymous star scoops up to the tune of her trademark cackling laugh. Tellingly, the first scene, which immediately follows the opening sequence, is likewise set around the kitchen table, only this time the characters are an all-male group of poker players—Dan and his belching, beer-guzzling friends—whose bubble of hypermasculinity is breached once Roseanne and Jackie enter the scene, breaking up the men's sexist fraternizing. Soon, young D. J. swoops in wearing his Halloween costume, a black witch's outfit—"complete with broom, long pointy nose, and red sparkly shoes"[23]—that draws a look of concern on Dan's face. After sending his son upstairs to his bedroom, Dan informs his wife that "witches are girls," not boys. "Witches are *women*," Roseanne corrects him, and then explains to her husband that D. J. got to pick his own costume this year. Clearly agitated, Dan wishes that his child had picked something "normal" (that is, less "sissy") to wear as a trick-or-treater who will be seen by their neighbors—"like a vampire or a nice ax murderer."

The excessiveness of Dan's remark is accentuated by the next scene, which begins with a phone conversation between Becky and her offscreen mother, who is now at work. While speaking on the phone, the young girl, shown from her left side, turns to reveal the right side of her body, which is covered in fake blood. One of her eyeballs also appears to have popped out, a bit of prop humor that might remind viewers of other instances of body horror on the small screen: from the obviously plastic axe blade that has settled into the torso of Alex, the female lead in the short-lived sitcom *In-Laws* (NBC, 2002–2003), to the large knife that is lodged in the blood-spurting chest of Hakeem, a teenage character who pretends to be the victim of a stabbing and plays dead in a Halloween-themed episode of *Moesha* (UPN, 1996–2001). These examples, like so many other "very spooky episodes" on prime-time TV, can be said to push the boundaries of what is permissible on network television (at the time of their original broadcast, if not today). With only one side stained with viscera, Becky's prom dress (which is almost as gross as her sister's *Alien* inspired stomach-bursting costume) connotes the two-sided nature of the main conflict that drives a wedge between

FIG. 6.1 *Roseanne* uses the queering potential of Halloween to challenge gender expectations.

husband and wife in "Trick or Treat." Eventually, Roseanne and Dan resolve their differences of opinion about D. J.'s clothing and come together as a stronger married unit—husband and wife, or rather husband and husband—during the episode's final scenes.

Set in an old-fashioned, wood-paneled bar, those concluding moments show Roseanne in cross-dressing mode, decked out in a lumberjack's camouflage hat, a plaid shirt, and a khaki jacket. She and Jackie have taken shelter in the dive after her car has broken down, and she is nervous because she is "the only person here in a costume"—a statement that is particularly ironic given that the female protagonist, in traditional male truck driver's garb, looks like most of the men in the bar (hinting at the fact that their own masculinity is a put-on or a performance). Later, after she has insulted and drawn the ire of a group of braggarts playing pool, Dan arrives and rescues her from "a fight with an aggressive boor."[24] When that person asks Dan why he is sticking his nose in their business, Dan steps closer to Roseanne and responds chivalrously, saying, "He's my *husband*. . . . Anyone that messes with him messes with me." This transgressive moment is capped with a final exclamation point: the sight of the seemingly same-sex couple kissing. Although this gender-bending scene from *Roseanne* is something of a ruse, a "mask" like the one worn by the bearded, burly title character (insofar as it covers up the reality of a heterosexual, rather than homosexual, embrace), it nevertheless proves both "the perversity of heterosexuality and the fundamental normativity of homosexuality," at least as much as that is possible "within the protocols of network television and its ostensible family hour."[25] Thus, "Trick or Treat"—and, to a certain extent, the star of the series as whole—serves as a "privileged site of homoerotic presence," according to Pugh, one that would have been much less apparent or explicitly visible were it not for the playful "perversions" unique to Halloween TV.[26]

Not surprisingly, the series returned in season seven to the queering potential of the holiday in another Halloween-themed episode, the tellingly titled "Skeleton in the Closet." Once again, cross-dressing revelers come to the fore in scenes showcasing the performativity of gender, with Roseanne dressed up as the stubble-faced musical legend Prince (whose all-purple outfit is mistaken for that of Barney the Dinosaur) opposite Dan's more rigidly masculine emulation of the Western film icon John Wayne. This admittedly odd couple descends on the Lanford Lunch Box, a sandwich spot that Roseanne and Jackie own with their business partner, Leon Carp, who is throwing a Halloween party there. As a proudly gay man, Leon labels himself the "Queen of Halloween" (which "everyone knows . . . is *our* holiday") and has made every attempt not to turn this queer-friendly soiree into one of Roseanne's "lame little lodge parties." But because Leon has invited many members of this small though apparently liberal-minded town's LGBTQ community to the gathering, Jackie's husband, Fred, shows up in a state of duress, fearful—like Dan, who is imitating Wayne—that gay men will spend the night hitting on him. Leon tries to calm Fred, reassuring him that "we don't bite," but he fails, and the Batman-suited straight man leaves the party prematurely. Partly because "Fred doth protest too much" (to borrow the words of Nancy, Roseanne's bisexual friend), but also because one of his friends, a drag queen, informs Roseanne that her brother-in-law has been living a lie this whole time, she soon believes that he is "gay, gay, gay, gay, gay" (or, as she sums up, the "gayest"). Fred's homosexuality would appear to be confirmed in the episode's penultimate scene, in which Roseanne and Jackie find their husbands in bed together, interrupting what looks to be a lovers' tryst. However, in keeping with the Conners' knack for outlandish Halloween tricks, this moment of coitus interruptus is simply the culmination of everyone's "long con," or what Dan, now beaming, calls the "all-time greatest prank in the history of the universe." The truth is revealed when Jackie begins giggling uncontrollably and Leon and Nancy (dressed as Hillary Rodham Clinton and Marilyn Monroe, respectively) burst out of the bedroom closet to declare, "We're everywhere!"

As Lynne Joyrich notes in her brief assessment of "Skeleton in the Closet," *Roseanne* was "at the forefront of queer representation throughout its network run," perhaps never more so than in this episode. However, Joyrich points out that this seemingly progressive installment highlights "the way in which U.S. television both impedes and constructs, exposes and buries, a particular knowledge of sexuality."[27] This is made more evident if one takes into consideration the second of the two pranks played on Roseanne in this episode, which concludes with a shot of her overbearing mother, Bev (who will eventually come out as a lesbian during the show's ninth season), removing her wig to reveal a nearly bald head, with only a few wisps of tangled hair left. As one beauty salon stylist had informed Roseanne earlier in the episode, children tend to inherit their mothers' hair (or lack thereof), and this brazen display of maternal baldness in the final scene cuts the main character to her core. Throughout much of this episode—and at various points throughout the series—Roseanne has grappled with the prospect of her elderly mother's passing away as well as with her own anxieties about aging. Thus, "the uncertainties of sexual bodies" (those of actual and pretend queer people in this episode) merge with "the uncertainties of aging bodies," and it is clear that the extended Conner family (including Darlene's former boyfriend, David, and Becky's husband, Mark) is eager to "mock both fears" with devilish glee.[28]

Indeed, "Skeleton in the Closet" ends with a literal unmasking that complements its metaphorical one, showing Dan, Jackie, and the other family members joining Bev in her baldness by removing their own wigs and leaving Roseanne in a state of shock. Refusing to go down without a fight, and never one to be beaten in a game of one-upmanship, she resorts to an even greater prank than the ones they have pulled on her and promptly blows up their house with dynamite that she had stashed away beneath the kitchen sink. In the words of Joyrich, "discovering that Dan is gay," which overlaps with Roseanne's discovery that her mother is bald, "would be tantamount to exploding the familiar and familial TV diegesis," and "bringing what typically exists outside TV's representational space into its core creates an epistemological crisis that threatens, both literally and figuratively, to blow this space up."[29] In this way, "Skeleton in the Closet" exemplifies the problematic tendency in Halloween-themed episodes to dangle the prospect of queer desire and nonheteronormative subject positions, only to erase or annihilate those representations by treating the image of same-sex couples as a sight gag or as the punch line to an elaborate prank or juvenile joke. This—one of the paradoxes of Halloween TV more generally—serves as a reminder that, for all that *Roseanne* did to give "voice to those pushing back against a socioeconomic system that demanded greater sacrifices and offered fewer rewards for working families,"[30] the show was not the fully inclusive one about marginalized communities that its makers might have intended it to be. And though its Halloween-themed episodes boldly go where few other programs before or since have ventured, the show's naked (dare I say "bald") disregard for the niceties of more tastefully appointed holidays proves to be something of a ruse in hindsight: a "long con" prank pulled on former fans of the show by a politically reactionary star who has since used a different form of mass communication—social media—to explode her own myth and reveal the "monster" beneath the mask.

Conclusion: The Paradoxical Meanings of (*Roseanne*'s) Halloween

Privileging tricks over treats, *Roseanne* embraces the orderly disorder or carefully structured chaos of Halloween, never more so than in the trippy episode in season eight that is misleadingly titled "Halloween: The Final Chapter" (October 31, 1995; followed by season nine's equally scattershot "Satan, Darling" broadcast one year later). Lacking a central plot and structured as a series of tangential mini-episodes, including encounters with unusual trick-or-treaters (such as the former *Tonight Show* sidekick Ed McMahon, who shows up at the door toting an oversize Publishers Clearing House jackpot check), this hallucinatory installment of the series plays out like a stream-of-consciousness dream narrative, jumping from (1) a spooky family séance at the kitchen table, in which Dan is overtaken by the spirit of Elvis; to (2) an extended scene of Roseanne and Jackie battling one another with flashlights and syrup bottles, while dressed as a gypsy woman and wicked witch, respectively; (3) another stab at otherworldly communion by way of a Ouija board; (4) a suite of flashbacks to previous Halloween episodes, rendered as Roseanne's memory of better times while lying in a hospital bed; and (5) a concluding tie-dye costumed dance and musical number in the hospital's delivery room, where Roseanne gives birth to a baby boy she christens Jerry Garcia (in honor of the Grateful Dead's lead guitarist, who somehow spoke to her from the beyond when she was in a Demerol-induced haze). Sprinkled between these bizarre segments are now-dated jokes about the O. J. Simpson trial (in which a verdict had been reached three weeks before the airing of "Halloween: The Final Chapter") and still-relevant debates about the best kind of goodies to hand out to neighborhood children. Although Dan and Roseanne, childish as ever, contend that sugar-filled sweets are the proper treats, young David, wise beyond his years, insists on filling the kids' Halloween bags with apples, nectarines, and other fresh fruit—a seemingly sensible yet risible thing to do that leads the peeved trick-or-treaters to hurl those healthy yet unenticing snacks back at him. Notably, this is one of several moments in *Roseanne* when the adult members of the Conner clan use Halloween as an excuse to indulge their most juvenile fantasies, as suggested by Roseanne's fond reminiscence (in "Trick Me Up, Trick Me Down") of throwing flaming bags of dog doo-doo onto the next-door neighbor's lawn and Dan's plan (in "Halloween IV") to moon the town's retirement home and stuff dead fish through people's mail slots (which, he sheepishly admits, is a "childish" activity).

One sign of this series' cultural impact is the prevalence of the theme of adults acting like kids in more recent sitcoms, in which neighborhood competitiveness or friendly familial infighting leads characters—many of whom are stuck in arrested development—to do things that they would normally refrain from doing at any other time of the year.[31] As Roseanne tells David at one point, "This is *Halloween*. It's the one night of the year where you're *supposed* to break all the rules"—words of advice that are meant to prevent the teenage boy from sitting at home all evening being "good and nice and well-behaved." For the most part (and with few exceptions), before *Roseanne*'s premiere on October 18, 1988, U.S. sitcoms tended to play by the rules as "good and nice and well-behaved" cultural productions, with Halloween episodes giving showrunners, writers, and performers the rare opportunity to "cut loose" or "let their hair down" (only to return to more conventional representations of domestic and workplace relations in non-holiday-themed installments). In a way, the kitschy clutter and narrative chaos of "Halloween: The Final Chapter" and the seven other "very spooky episodes" starring Barr are merely intensified—more fantastical and grotesque—versions of what plays out in her show's 223 non-Halloween-themed installments, which likewise derive their humor from "the incongruity between the Conners' life and that of other families in sitcoms past and present."[32] Ironically, in the years since the airing of *Roseanne*'s two-part series finale "Into That Good Night" (which pulled one last prank on its audience by revealing that the ninth season—and many of the events leading up to it—was a lie, only to upend that claim with yet another revelation at the beginning of its 2018 relaunch), several U.S. sitcoms have demonstrated its lasting influence, especially around the end of each October. From the relatively comforting depictions of blue-collar life in *The Middle* (ABC, 2009–2018) and *Raising Hope* (Fox, 2010–2014) to the more extreme visions of working-class squalor and monstrous behavior seen in *It's Always Sunny in Philadelphia* (FX, 2005–2012; FXX, 2013–present), today's television programming is more populated than ever by characters who dress the part of the downwardly mobile or disenfranchised (or what Roseanne herself has called "poor white trash"), and who view Halloween as she did: an opportunity for potentially enfranchising forms of role-playing, including that which blurs the line between genders.

As I have highlighted in this chapter, more than one of *Roseanne*'s Halloween-themed episodes hinges upon the uncanny effects of cross-dressing, which the star herself performs in season three's "Trick or Treat" (in which she pretends to be a burly, bearded truck driver) and season seven's "Skeleton in the Closet" (in which she dresses up as Prince). In these and other installments of her eponymous series, Roseanne is there but not there, a "monster" hiding in plain sight beneath layers of clothing that a drag king might wear on any given night besides All Hallows' Eve. But nothing is ever as it seems in these "very spooky episodes," and looks can be doubly deceiving.

This is especially apparent in "Halloween V," from the show's sixth season. Most of this episode's humor derives from the one-upmanship between Roseanne and Dan, her more-than-game husband who is happy to compete against her for the honor of pulling off the most audacious prank. As any fan of the original series knows, a running gag in this annual celebration is the married couple's back-and-forth battle for Halloween supremacy, something that can be achieved only when one completely fools the other. This element was initiated in *Roseanne*'s first Halloween episode ("Boo," from season two), which shows Dan rushing into the kitchen after a terrible woodworking accident, with blood spurting from his apparently severed fingers. By the time "Halloween V" aired on October 25, 1993, audiences would have witnessed even more shocking displays of Grand Guignol–style tomfoolery, making one seriously question Jackie's remark that Dan's bloody hand trick from four years earlier was "the sickest thing [she had] ever seen."[33] In fact, during the opening scene of "Halloween IV," which aired one year before this episode, Dan one-ups himself by sticking his hand into the kitchen sink's garbage disposal only to have it cut into shreds by the whirling blades. Unfazed by the fleshy shrapnel shooting out from the sink, Roseanne knows better than to take him seriously and sees through her husband's sanguinary charade. Yet even she is duped by episode's end, following a series of escalating pranks that culminates with her next-door neighbor's apparent decapitation at the hands of Darlene (who, like the rest of the family, is in on the twisted joke). Significantly, besides alluding to Nancy's plan for Dan to cross-dress as *Leave It to Beaver*'s matriarch, June Cleaver, (despite his discomfort at having to wear high heels) and suggesting that—in nearly shocking his wife to death with the sight of a teenage girl's decapitation—Dan has gone too far as a prankster this year, "Halloween V" draws attention to the multiple layers of deception or masquerade that make it difficult to locate the real Roseanne. It does this through a speech she delivers to her husband in a moment of ironically misleading candor, or truthful trickery: "You never tell people that you like that you like 'em. The only people that you ever tell that you like are the people that you actually *don't like*."

In closing, it is important to note that Halloween traditions such as the ones cited above offer more than a release valve for the Conners and other working-class TV families. The holiday's paradoxical appeals—as a largely harmless invitation to confront physical pain and death through the horrifying yet humorously deployed iconography of "rotting corpses, mutilated body parts . . . and skeletons of all sizes"[34]—is one matter worth considering, but the yearly rituals enacted by Roseanne and her cohort should also be seen as a means of bringing stability and predictability to a family unit that often copes with financial instabilities. Living paycheck to paycheck and moving from one pink-collar service-sector job to another (for example, shampoo girl in a beauty parlor, home-based telemarketer, secretary at a meat-packing plant, waitress at a shopping mall café, and assembly line worker at a factory) in search of the security that seems to have eluded her since before her marriage to Dan,[35] Roseanne justifiably looks to Halloween as a source of perverse pleasure, thumbing her nose at institutions that have exploited her. Yet it is also a way for Roseanne to ironically reduce the unpredictability that has largely defined her life up to that point. Halloween, as we have seen, is a way to satirically mock traditions, but it is a tradition in its own right: one that, steeped in odd rituals, has relied upon the repeated cultural enactment of certain tropes to challenge the primacy of other holidays likewise noted for bringing families together. One trope in particular—the act of dressing up as someone else, so central to the holiday's (and the television medium's) appeal as a form of escapism—has shifted from its initial connotations in 1950s sitcoms such as *The Jackie Gleason Show* and *The Adventures of Ozzie and Harriet* toward more progressive and potentially transgressive notions of gender fluidity in recent years' Halloween celebrations. And, for better or worse, we have Roseanne Barr, the always controversial TV star, to thank for that.

Notes

1 For information about Samhain, a combined New Year's Day for the Celts as well as a Day of the Dead that vaguely anticipates some contemporary Halloween practices and iconography, see Jack Santino, "Introduction: Festivals and Death and Life," in *Halloween and Other Festivals of Death and Life*, ed. Jack Santino (Knoxville: University of Tennessee Press, 1994), xiv–xvi.

2 Craig Semon, "Halloween, Horror: Harmless Fun or a Step Too Far?," *Associated Press*, October 17, 2015, https://www.apnews.com/42f2a6be8aa2491c89a294156fa29002.

3 David Skal, *Death Makes a Holiday: A Cultural History of Halloween* (New York: Bloomsbury, 2002), 17.

4 Ibid.

5 Ibid., 9.

6 Dina Khapaeva, *The Celebration of Death in Contemporary Culture* (Ann Arbor: University of Michigan Press, 2017), 57.

7 Joanne Morreale, *The Donna Reed Show* (Detroit, MI: Wayne State University Press, 2012), 125.

8 Ibid. See also Janet Lee, "Subversive Sitcoms: *Roseanne* as Inspiration for Feminist Resistance," *Women's Studies* 21, no. 1 (1992): 87–101; Sujata Moorti, "Brown Girls Who Don't Need Saving: Social Media and the Role of 'Possessive Investment' in *The Mindy Project* and *The Good Wife*," in *Television for Women: New Directions*, ed. Rachel Moseley, Helen Wheatley, and Helen Wood (New York: Routledge, 2017), 101.

9 Bonnie J. Dow, *Prime-Time Feminism: Television, Media Culture, and the Women's Movement since 1970* (Philadelphia: University of Pennsylvania Press, 1996), 99–100.

10 Quoted in Lesley Goldberg, "*Roseanne* Canceled at ABC Following Racist Tweet," *Hollywood Reporter*, May 29, 2018), https://www.hollywoodreporter.com/live-feed/roseanne-canceled-at-abc-racist-tweet-1115412.

11 Jonathan Berr, "Is ABC's Monster Hit *Roseanne* Scaring away Liberal Viewers?," *Forbes*, April 14, 2018.

12 In the words of William Douglass, working-class characters—husbands, in particular—are commonly portrayed as "inept, immature, stupid, lacking in good sense, and emotional," in contrast to "their middle-class counterparts" ("Subversion of the American Television Family," in *Television and the American Family*, ed. Jennings Bryant and J. Alison Bryant (Mahway, NJ: Lawrence Erlbaum Associates, 2001)232. This othering of low-wage male workers (epitomized by slump-shouldered, beer-bellied protagonists in such prime-time cartoons as *The Flintstones* [ABC, 1960–1966] and *The Simpsons* [Fox, 1989–present]) is distinct from the way in which their working-class wives are typically depicted ("as relatively intelligent, rational, and

responsible" women who nevertheless lack the power or monetary means to escape their fate as domestic "servants" [ibid.]). For a different, non-TV-specific take on widespread cultural attitudes toward working-class women, see Ruth Sidel, "The Enemy Within: The Demonization of Poor Women," *Journal of Sociology and Social Welfare* 27, no. 1 (March 2000): 73–84.

13 Richard Butsch, "Six Decades of Social Class in American Sitcoms," in *Social Class on British and American Screens: Essays on Cinema and Television*, ed. Nicole Cloarec, David Haigron, and Delphine Letort (Jefferson, NC: McFarland and Company, 2016), 27.

14 Santino, "Introduction," xiv–xvi.

15 Nicholas Rogers, *Halloween: From Pagan Ritual to Party Night* (New York: Oxford University Press, 2002), 165 and 172.

16 Ibid., 9.

17 Ibid., 163–164.

18 Ibid., 172.

19 "Ronnie's Party," an episode in season two of the Canadian sitcom *Schitt's Creek* (CBC, 2015–present), features dialogue between a brother and sister (David and Alexis Rose) that refers to the long-entrenched stereotype of the slutty nurse within the holiday's more salacious traditions. Noting the unusually designed scrubs that Alexis has put on in preparation for her new job at a veterinarian's clinic, David tells her, "I don't think sex appeal is the guiding principle behind nursing uniforms." In defense of her clothing choice, Alexis responds, "Obviously, you've never been out for Halloween."

20 Throughout the 1970s and 1980s, reputable publications (including the *New York Times*) encouraged adults to check trick-or-treaters' candy for hidden sewing needles, razor blades, and shards of glass. As the "high holy day of candy," to borrow the words of Samira Kawash, Halloween has been a source of consternation for many parents and other adults concerned not only with the physical health of young people (whose hearts, kidneys, livers, and teeth are put to the test by this "annual sugar-fueled ritual") but also about the possibility that kids might come into contact with "bad apples" (figuratively and literally) when unleashed on suburban and city streets as trick-or-treaters (*Candy: A Century of Panic and Pleasure* [New York: Farrar, Straus and Giroux, 2013], 9).

21 Lisa Morton, *The Halloween Encyclopedia*, 2nd ed. (Jefferson, NC: McFarland and Company, 2011), 85.

22 Tison Pugh, *The Queer Fantasies of the American Family Sitcom* (New Brunswick, NJ: Rutgers University Press, 2018), 124.

23 Saniya Lee Ghanoui, "Mediated Bodies: The Construction of a Wife, Mother, and the Female Body in Television Sitcoms: Roseanne," *Proceedings of the New York State Communication Association* 2012, article 5, http://docs.rwu.edu/nyscaproceedings/vol2012/iss1/5.

24 Pugh, *The Queer Fantasies of the American Family Sitcom*, 125.

25 Ibid.

26 Ibid.

27 Lynne Joyrich, "Epistemology of the Console," in *Queer TV: Theories, Histories, Politics*, ed. Glyn Davis and Gary Needham (New York: Routledge, 2009), 20.

28 Ibid., 38.

29 Ibid., 20.

30 Michael Grabowski, "Resignation and Positive Thinking in the Working-Class Family Sitcom," *Atlantic Journal of Communication* 22, no. 2 (2014): 125.

31 The short-lived sitcom *In-Laws* (NBC, 2002–2003) demonstrates suburban dwellers' tendency to let the holiday's built-in competitiveness (to outscare or outdecorate one's neighbors) get the best of them. In the episode "Halloween: Resurrection," an already combative Italian American family informs its most recent member—the young Jewish-American man who has married into it—that past years' celebrations have nearly brought about the ruin of their neighborhood, owing to the destructive vandalism that sometimes creeps into the proceedings. Regardless, the Pellets (led by the tellingly named patriarch, Victor) succumb to the pressure of competing against their neighbors once more, installing a giant crypt on their front lawn that, despite costing a fortune, might be "the difference between [their] winning and losing."

32 Julie Bettie, "Class Dismissed? *Roseanne* and the Changing Face of Working-Class Iconography," *Social Text* 14, no. 4 (Winter, 1995): 135.

33 For example, the scene before the credits in season four's "Trick Me Up, Trick Me Down" shows an undead version of Dan tricking his neighbor into believing that he is the latest victim of his homicidal wife, who appears to have stabbed him in the stomach with a knife. As his guts spill out from the bloody wound onto the kitchen floor, the neighbor, shocked beyond belief, rushes toward the front door, gasping, "That was a horrible, horrible, *horrible* thing to do!"

34 Khapaeva, *The Celebration of Death in Contemporary Culture*, 56.

35 Melissa Williams, "'Excuse the Mess, But We Live Here': Roseanne Barr's Stardom and the Politics of Class," in *Film and Television Stardom*, ed. Kylo-Patrick R. Hart (Newcastle upon Tyne, UK: Cambridge Scholars Publishing, 2008), 193; Bettie, "Class Dismissed?," 130 and 133; Michael Grabowski, "Resignation and Positive Thinking in the Working-Class Family Sitcom," *Atlantic Journal of Communication* 22, no. 2 (2014): 127.

7

A Very Special Visit to the "Old Neighborhood"

Containing the Los Angeles Uprising on *The Fresh Prince of Bel-Air*

LINDSAY GIGGEY

In June 2020, *Time* reported that "a black person is killed by a police officer in America at the rate of more than one every other day."[1] On May 25, 2020, George Floyd became part of those statistics when a white police officer in Minneapolis, Minnesota pushed his knee into Floyd's neck until he stopped breathing. However, if a bystander had not captured video footage of the event, the officer's conduct would never have attracted national attention. It also served as the breaking point for Black Americans and their allies, as they took to the streets to protest the ways in which systemic racism continues to kill people of color. Although the protests started in Minneapolis, they quickly spread to cities and towns across the United States. Although most of the protests were peaceful, the media focused incessantly on instances of violence and looting. Whether prompted by righteous anger or racist instigators, scenes of looting evoked memories of civil unrest not seen since 1992, when a nearly all-white jury acquitted four white officers for beating Rodney King in Los Angeles. In both the Floyd and King cases, bystander video provided irrefutable evidence of racial violence perpetrated by the police, and those videos were repurposed in countless television news stories which provoked a national dialogue about race, racism, and policing in the United States. Moreover, both uprisings represented breaking points after prolonged periods of seeming inaction on the part of those in power. Although the civil unrest in the wake of Floyd's murder happened almost immediately, his death was the latest incident in a series of widely documented Black deaths at the hands of police throughout the United States. While the Los Angeles Uprising occurred from late April to early May 1992, tension over racially motivated violence had been building for over a year. In a two-week period in March 1991, the public was confronted with irrefutable visible evidence of racially motivated violence in the videotaped beating of King and the surveillance video showing Soon Ja Du, the Korean owner of a shop, shooting the Black teenager Latasha Harlins in the back of the head after arguing over a bottle of orange juice. The King video became "the most widely replayed video of the year," while the security footage of Du and Harlins was extensively shown throughout Los Angeles.[2] Both events and the resulting trials of Du and Los Angeles Police Department (LAPD) officers Stacey Koon, Theodore Briseno, Laurence Powell, and Timothy Wind were closely followed, especially in Los Angeles, and the resulting lack of punishment for both sets of perpetrators suggested how little Black lives mattered in the eyes of the justice system.

Both videos as well as the resulting trials became media events in their own right, especially as the verdicts in both cases served as the tipping point after which anger could no longer be contained. Using John Fiske's definition of a media event as "not a mere representation of what happened, but [something that] has its own reality, which gathers up into itself the reality of the event that may or may not have preceded it," provides a helpful framework in thinking about not just the 1992 uprising but also the circulation of the videos, the discourse that preceded their circulation, and the television programming that followed.[3] Despite news media's posture of objectivity, the television apparatus (encompassing the technology to distribute and circulate messages as well as the content creators and network executives responsible for determining what is broadcast) was not a neutral actor in meaning making. Fiske further explains how television discourse, especially about media events, ultimately serves dominant power structures and institutions: "To make sense of the world is to exert power over it, and to circulate that sense socially is to exert power over those who use that sense as a way of coping with their daily lives."[4] As this chapter discusses, television in the early 1990s acted as a mechanism to spread awareness of racial injustice while also anointing itself as a space to work through the resulting trauma its exposure caused. Even as the uprising was happening, sitcoms were called upon to mediate issues of race. In the midst of wall-to-wall broadcast news coverage of the violence, Tom Bradley, the mayor of Los Angeles, urged citizens to go home and watch the series finale of *The Cosby Show*, suggesting the power that sitcoms had to encourage empathy among audiences of all races.

One of the mechanisms used to ultimately reestablish order was a series of scripted very special television episodes dealing with the uprising in an attempt to model racial harmony in their aftermath. The uprising occurred in late April and early May (the time when scripted television wraps up its seasons), so when the 1992–1993 television season kicked off in the fall, several shows addressed the uprising with very special episodes (VSEs). The shows included *Doogie Howser, MD* (ABC, 1989–1993), *Beverly Hills, 90210* (Fox, 1990–2000), *Melrose Place* (Fox, 1992–1999), *Knots Landing* (CBS, 1979–1993), and *L.A. Law* (NBC, 1986–1995). They used secondary, tertiary, or guest characters of color to teach their white protagonists about racial inequality but offered no substantial interrogation of the larger social structures that had caused Angelenos to rise up in the first place. These episodes remapped societal issues onto individuals, allowing the problem to be solved within the closed narrative structure of the episode. While white characters feel momentary discomfort within an episode, that discomfort is limited to that episode. All conflict is neatly resolved, resetting the narrative and characters by the episode's conclusion.

Rather than consider how racial inequality affects white people, shows featuring primarily all-Black casts had an opportunity to use their familiar characters to articulate nonwhite perspectives on the uprising and perhaps engender a different level of empathy. Two prominent shows featuring all-Black casts with crossover appeal at the time were *A Different World* (NBC, 1987–1993) and *The Fresh Prince of Bel-Air* (*FPBA*; NBC, 1990–1996). In its two-part premiere for the 1992–1993 season, *A Different World* used its large ensemble cast to complicate an assumed monolithic Black perspective and generate a nuanced and impassioned conversation about the uprising, done in part by placing the newlywed protagonists Dwayne (Kadeem Hardison) and Whitley (Jasmine Guy) directly into the events as they honeymooned in Los Angeles. This episode is frequently lauded as an example of the deft ways in which *A Different World* tackled difficult issues facing young Black people, but I focus instead on *FPBA*'s far messier attempt to address the uprising. Even though the second episode of *FPBA*'s third season, "Will Gets Committed" (September 12, 1992), is an effort to offer a Black perspective on the uprising, it does so at a distance. *FPBA*'s upper-middle-class Black protagonists help clean up a neighborhood that was decimated during the uprising, but they never actually discuss any specifics about the uprising, let alone its root causes. The ways in which *FPBA* addressed the larger issues facing Black Americans encapsulates the uneasy way in which television programming at the time struggled to portray Blackness for what had been conceptualized as a predominantly white audience. Moreover, this VSE is also representative of television's larger attempts to reestablish social order in the wake of the Los Angeles Uprising. Repositioning racial injustice in the sitcom formula dictates that problems be addressed and solved within the confines of the episode rather than engaging in long-term structural overhaul to address sources of injustice. In this chapter, I consider the ways in which television, sitcoms, and this VSE work to mediate significant questions around race and racial violence without interrogating the role of whiteness in perpetrating that violence. While *FPBA* showcases Black experiences, there is an underlying industrial and institutional push to do so without alienating white audiences or upending the normativity of white privilege at the center of American culture.

"Very Special" Ruptures to Television Time

Before addressing how specific episodes functioned in the aftermath of the Los Angeles Uprising, it is worth considering what VSEs are and how they function to point out the exceptional. From its inception, television has been predicated on the management and articulation of time: instituting live programming was a means of differentiating television from film and radio, and the feeling of liveness and immediacy is central to how we conceive of television. Networks sell the viewing time of their audiences to advertisers, and advertisements serve as a steady stream of information that promotes new products and services.[5] Although for the most part, programming outside of news and sports is no longer broadcast live, the proximity of programming to live material as well as the consistent introduction of new episodes over a calendar year creates the feeling of timeliness. Similarly, the construction of time on television from the idea of flow, according to Raymond Williams, as the organization of the continual succession of programs, advertisements, and so on—as well as Nick Browne's assertion that the organization of television programming is further organized and segmented based on the time of day—underscores the way in which television norms are ingrained through the structuring of time.[6] Within the constant flow of programming, VSEs call attention to themselves as something out of the ordinary and thus items that audiences should schedule their time around to view. The episodes disrupt the normal flow of television by calling attention to time.

On a very basic level, "VSE" is essentially a marketing term: highlighting any particular episode as "special" is designed to isolate it and promote it as significant. Depending on the show and when in the season the VSE airs (season premieres, finales, and sweeps episodes are other examples of extraordinary content used to encourage additional viewers to watch), its specialness can be attributed to featuring a special guest star or dealing with an exceptional plot line. For example, lighthearted sitcoms may shift their tone to engage with a serious issue. Given the content of those plotlines, it is clear that VSEs are instances of television programs' taking advantage of television's immediacy as a medium and its pervasiveness in people's homes as a means of addressing a contemporaneous social issue and delivering social commentary within the familiar confines of the sitcom genre. Calling attention to these specific episodes underscores their exceptionally important content, whether it's used to drive ratings or serve a cultural purpose.

Considering the existence and effect of these particular VSEs requires contextualizing them in both historical time and television time. The episode of *FPBA* in response to the Los Angeles Uprising calls attention to its specialness on two levels, each applying a different interpretation of Mary Ann Doane's theorization of television catastrophe as an "unexpected discontinuity in an otherwise continuous system."[7] The first is the VSE's inclusion in the way in which television structured the uprising as both a concentrated incident and a months-long media event. In thinking about the constant stream of programming, Doane argues that there is a structuring logic that television uses in covering media events: television "fills time by ensuring that something happens—it organizes itself around that event."[8] If we think about the uprising in this way, as a media event it occurred over two timelines: the five-day period from April 29 to May 4, 1992, (or from the announcement of the officers' verdicts in the King trial to Mayor Bradley's lifting of the city-wide curfew) and the period between March 3, 1991 and the September 1992 fall television premieres (which included the initial airing of the King videotape, its consistent reviewing in the lead-up to the April 1992 trials, the uprising, and its aftermath). Within the latter period, although the VSE of *FPBA* may have been unique in the context of the series, it was in line with the saturation of programming about the larger media event that focused on racial injustice.

To understand how this and other VSEs fit into this media event as a means of reinstating discursive control of dominant power structures and institutions, it is worth thinking about the coverage of King's beating, the subsequent trials of the officers, and the resulting uprising. The existence and circulation of the videotape of the beating ruptured the status quo (read: predominantly white) perspectives on the LAPD and its treatment of the poor and members of minority groups. The LAPD systematically used excessive force without being punished for doing so, while also ignoring racism and sexism within its ranks.[9] What made King's ordeal different was that his beating was recorded. The video made it to news stations before it could be confiscated or covered up, so within forty-eight hours of the beating, the LAPD's long history of systemic racism had been exposed. The tape eliminated law enforcement institutions' ability to spin what viewers saw and constituted a powerful piece of visible evidence. In the months that followed, the video ended the country's silence about racial violence. This consciousness about police brutality against people of color continued in the lead-up to the trial, the release of the verdict, and the uprising that occurred in its aftermath. The uprising was a catastrophic event in the way in that it consumed the airwaves in Los Angeles and nationally, disrupting regularly scheduled programming with continuous (and commercial-free) coverage of fires, looting, and violence. During the uprising, the most chaotic period of the catastrophe, John Caldwell argues that the television apparatus recklessly historicized and contextualized the events in real time. Between making immediate references to the

1965 Watts Rebellion and categorizing the Los Angeles Uprising as such framed the way in which viewers comprehended what they saw happening on their screens. Caldwell argues that modes of presentation, including the use of simultaneous and overlapping images, editorialized the crisis, while the coverage structured the events in terms of simplistic binaries (Black and white; good and evil). Live coverage of the uprising in real time turned it into something needing containment, which the news media did by emphasizing order and likening the unfolding events as something temporal (with a beginning, middle, and eventual end).[10] Even in the midst of live, catastrophic coverage, television cannot help but use familiar structures of time and the return to stasis as a means of resolving a crisis. These attempts to create order in the immediate moment of crisis became a mode of containment in the uprising's aftermath.

In that aftermath, VSEs occupied a smaller role within the larger catastrophic narrative and its conclusion as both ruptures and mechanisms of resolution. While catastrophes create prolonged anxiety and rupture televisual flow, both of which are useful for drawing television viewers, they must ultimately be resolved. Without resolution and the ability to re-create feelings of stasis via the normal flow of regularly scheduled television, catastrophic moments lose their power. In the aftermath of the uprising, after networks exhausted crisis coverage, Caldwell argues that the placement of "rebellion-specific entertainment programs" as the kickoff to the 1992–1993 television season represents what "appeared to be a more reasoned and planned strategy for reconciling the effects of the rebellion," a strategy crafted collectively by politicians and entertainment industry heavyweights.[11] Scripted television and sitcoms in particular are primed to do the work of containment because that is built into their narrative formulas. However, the work of containment is by no means a neutral endeavor. While the familiar rules that define genres help bring order to viewing experiences, Robin Means Coleman argues that "genre is generally delimited by cultural consensus" and that the normative cultural consensus defines Blackness as aberrant. Given this—and compounded by the fact that most shows, even ones featuring primarily Black casts, were written and directed by white people—Black sitcoms "revea[l] a 'cultural practice' (Fiske, 1987) that orders Blackness, organizes the meanings or shared expectations surrounding Black culture, and ultimately reifies dominant ideology about racial minorities."[12]

Fiske reminds us that in writing narratives of containment, there "is a discourse of racism that advances the interests of whites and that has an identifiable repertoire of words, images, and practices through which racial power is applied."[13] Fiske identifies this practice as occurring during the Los Angeles Uprising, noting that the dominant voices structuring the events for mainstream consumption were white and arguing that "the few Black voices that struggled to push Black meanings into public discussion were overwhelmed by white voices and marginalized by the media."[14] These tendencies bleed into scripted television, where most of the people behind the scenes, on-screen, and in the audience are presumed to be white. Shows featuring Black casts constitute a rupture as—by including nonwhite characters—they deviate from the racial hierarchies that privilege whiteness. In his analysis of *That's So Raven*, Hollis Griffin applies Doane's idea of the catastrophe to the way in which episodes that acknowledge racial difference are themselves ruptures within dominant television narratives. Although VSEs are not catastrophic in the way in which Doane conceptualized, Griffin argues that they are still narrative ruptures due to the way in which they temporally disrupt the ordinary flow of the run of episodes, calling attention to themselves on the schedule. VSEs that call attention to race as a site of difference further rupture regularly scheduled programming because of their "momentarily foregrounding the complex history of racial inequality in America."[15] "Will Gets Committed" exemplifies Griffin's application of Doane's concept as an instance "that problematizes social issues by emphasizing the social inequities rooted in racial difference."[16] However, this VSE serves a dual purpose: it both highlights race and is a timely response to a cultural crisis predicated on race. If VSEs with Black casts are a way to acknowledge race, audiences were especially primed to hear this story at this time because of the way in which race was so prevalent at this moment.

Populating Television with Shows Featuring Black Casts

By the early 1990s, shows featuring Black casts, especially sitcoms, had proliferated due to larger industrial changes. The 1970s saw a shift in programming to address younger, urban people's sensibilities as a result of changing population demographics. The concentration of people of color in urban areas contributed to the racialization of the term "urban," creating a shorthand that collapses racial, class, and geographic issues into one term. In attempting to reach these untapped audiences, television shows began to address contemporary issues such as race relations and gender more directly. In the 1980s, the proliferation of cable further segmented audiences and decreased overall viewership numbers, as there were more channels from which to choose. In these circumstances, minority-group audiences actually had more viewing power than they had previously. Minorities were among the few demographic groups whose television consumption increased in this period of overall declining viewership.[17] On top of this, the concentration of Black and Latino audiences in major media markets gave networks an extra competitive edge against cable. As Kristal Zook argues, because Black and Latino audiences' access to new television technologies was delayed, they became a larger concentration of the audiences still watching the free networks: "black audiences watched 44 percent more network television than non-blacks. What's more, they clearly preferred black shows."[18] These trends were clear enough to affect the programming strategy of the emerging Fox network, which, at least temporarily, recognized the viewing power of Black audiences.

Although offerings featuring Black casts were expanded, that did not mean that the shows actually engaged with specific issues related to Blackness. Representations of Blackness that ended up on-screen were the product of concentrated white-dominated power structures designed to maintain white privilege. All aspects of production, and ultimately network boardrooms, were (and still are) overwhelming controlled by whites, and there was (and is) an underlying concern about scaring away white audiences. Moreover, the underlying values of mainstream film and television are also filtered through whiteness. In describing hegemonic definitions of racial progress, Kristen Warner asserts that "if minorities are to have a chance at a successful life, whites must see past their ethnic or racial makeup and cultural specificity and find common traits that make the others like them."[19] Racial progress can be shown through the presence of Black bodies, but those bodies must attempt to succeed in the same way as their white counterparts do so as not to reduce white privilege. Thus, whatever the intentions of Black producers or actors, the ultimate goal for shows like *FPBA* at the time they were made was to package Blackness in ways that affirmed whiteness. This push toward colorblind integration "becomes a strategy to translate racism from a systems issue to an individual's prerogative"—a strategy that is tailor-made for episodic television.[20]

In terms of television in the late 1980s and early 1990s, Herman Gray suggests a helpful model to use in thinking about the larger context of the normal functioning of shows featuring Black casts like *FPBA*, which in turn informs that show's very special, and very unusual, treatment of the Los Angeles Uprising. Gray argues that there are essentially three discursive practices that construct and frame issues of race: "assimilationist (invisibility), pluralist (separate-but-equal), and multiculturalist (diversity)."[21] Within this schema, Gray categorizes *FPBA* as pluralist, arguing that "race and cultural difference and diversity can be represented, even celebrated, but in ways that confirm and authorize dominant social, political, cultural, and economic positions and relationships."[22] Using this lens illuminates the ways in which *FBPA* was ultimately ill equipped to engage the larger issues that caused the Los Angeles Uprising, because to do so would have upended the ways in which the show solved issues of race by distancing its characters via their upward class mobility.

Flipped-Turned Upside Down: *FPBA* Returns to "the Old Neighborhood"

From its opening, "Will Gets Committed" works to distance audiences from actual issues emerging from the King beating videotape and the aftermath of its release. In a throwaway cold open, Will Smith (Will Smith) sits on a couch in his uncle's home. Uncle Phil (James Avery), who frequently butts heads with Will, chastises him for eating and having his feet up on the couch. Will points a remote at Uncle Phil, who turns to static and disappears. Will then looks directly at the camera and asks the audience, "Don't you wish you lived on TV?" The opening credits then roll. Before viewers even have the chance to become involved in the narrative, Will calls attention to the medium to distance them, setting an uneasy tone for the rest of episode.

FPBA is a fish-out-of-water story based on Will, who is transplanted from his urban, gang-populated, lower-class roots in West Philadelphia to live with the Banks family—his Aunt Vivian, Uncle Phil, and their children—in safe, white, rich Bel-Air. "Will Gets Committed," however, flips this premise on its head. Instead, it repositions Will and the Banks family as outsiders because of their physical and socioeconomic distance from the site of the uprising (marked by the family's money, their children's lives of privilege, their proximity to whiteness, and the time and space it takes to travel the twenty-plus miles between Bel-Air and South Central Los Angeles). Gray argues that pluralist shows like *FPBA* situate black characters in domestically centered black worlds and circumstances that essentially parallel those of whites."[23] With this in mind, the Banks family cannot ever really engage with the uprising because the show is based upon the underlying assumption that the stakes are the same for white people and people of color.

As a pluralist show, *FPBA* does not address many of the various forms of racism that people of color experience. The way in which the episode frames the uprising reflects this separate-but-equal mentality that privileges white perspectives on racialized violence. "Will Gets Committed" does not engage with the events of the uprising or any of the particularities that caused it. Instead, the uprising acted, as Caldwell asserts, to give a new narrative history of the Banks family, as it is revealed that "the sitcom family now had its economic roots and origins in South Central."[24] However, South Central is never named in the episode. Instead, characters refer to going back to help "the old neighborhood." This ambiguity calls upon viewers to fill in the background context about everything regarding the uprising and the events leading up to it. When they return to the "old neighborhood," Uncle Phil and Aunt Vivian (Janet Hubert-Whitten) are now out of place in their old neighborhood because of their current affluence, and the family is out of place in its new neighborhood as the only Black family that audiences see in Bel-Air. The fact that sitcoms focus on domestic space and issues further distances the Banks from the moment in which they live—the sitcom format excludes the outside world.

At the beginning of the episode, Will's cousins, the preppy Carlton (Alfonso Ribeiro) and the young and impressionable Ashley (Tatiana Ali) prepare boxes of food in the kitchen because their parents have insisted that the family go help "rebuild the old neighborhood." However, the kids don't really understand why they are going or why their help is important to their parents. Although this is a natural opportunity for the show to explain and contextualize the uprising, instead it leaves the audience with the same limited understanding as Will and his cousins have. The opening scenes present Uncle Phil and Aunt

Vivian fighting with one another because she has been avoiding him. Rather than point to the severity of the uprising or her commitment to the neighborhood in which her family lived before Uncle Phil was hired by a premier Beverly Hills law firm, Aunt Vivian frets that she can't leave the house because she needs to get her hair done.

When the family members arrive in the old neighborhood, each feels a different level of connection to the "old neighborhood," feelings largely divided along generational lines. In accordance with middle-class narratives asserting that parents should provide better conditions for their children, the Banks children feel little connection with or responsibility to the "old neighborhood," since their everyday standard of living is so physically, culturally, and economically removed from that space. The kids, specifically eldest sister Hilary (Karyn Parsons) and Carlton, instantly look out of place. Hilary is dressed up from her date the previous evening, while Carlton wears a pastel yellow T-shirt neatly tucked into his blue khaki pants. Such costume choices are usually shorthand that shows how out of place Will is. However, in this case Will's dress and speech, referents aligning him with a lower-class and primarily urban area, are now in line with the larger surroundings of the episode, while his family's wealth feels out of place. Will, the only young person in the show who has spent a significant amount of time in a poor and rough urban area, is the only one who can connect with the destruction caused by racism as well as any of the people who were directly affected.

The positions of the characters in normal episodes of the show are further upended when Will and Carlton check in with Simone (Rosemarie Jackson), the attractive female volunteer coordinator, for instructions about what to do. Another way in which Carlton and Will are diametrically opposed is in their interactions with girls. Will is most often the one who charms all the ladies around him, while Carlton is positioned as the butt of jokes for his inability to do or say the cool thing. However, in this episode, things are flipped-turned upside down. It's Carlton who impresses the attractive female volunteer coordinator, after she rolls her eyes at Will's advances. After this initial interaction, Carlton spends essentially the rest of the episode wooing Simone, which emotionally separates him from the destruction in the neighborhood and thus the severity of the uprising and its aftermath.

As the family spends the day at the site, Uncle Phil and Aunt Viv continue fighting, Carlton continues courting Simone, and Hilary and Ashley staff a refreshment table. Will is the only one actually doing the clean-up work the family came to do. Will meets Noah (Shavar Ross), who is visibly annoyed at the Bankses both because they are not working and because he recognizes that their commitment to "the old neighborhood" is fleeting. Their presence on the scene is to momentarily assuage their guilt about having left, while those who are still there will be have to live with the trauma of what happened and why. Will and Noah start cleaning the inside of an apartment that has been burned, ransacked, and vandalized. Noah asks Will if he'll be on the site again the next day, and Will reluctantly admits that he can't because he has school, and that he can't return the following weekend because he has a basketball game and a date. At this point, Will is exposed. Noah chastises him: "You're just like the rest of 'em. You're coming around with the 'X' cap and them cool Doc Martens and your 'dope' and 'word to your mother,' and you think that makes you committed. Let me tell you something, this ain't no game. If you think that it is, then maybe you should go home 'cause you're not welcome here. Tell Dan Quayle I said 'what's up?'" With these lines, Noah actually crosses into territory not typically covered in pluralist shows like *FPBA*. While *FPBA* may acknowledge the Blackness of its cast, the show does so in ways that are largely superficial, leaning on visual signifiers like baggy clothing and/or cultural references like Malcolm X or hip hop to reflect difference while maintaining that those differences are only skin-deep. What these lines do is recognize race as the basis of larger social inequality and the fact that there are "oppositions, struggles, survival strategies, and distinctive lifeways that result from these experiences."[25] Noah breaks the monolithic approach to understanding Blackness on television by calling out the class-based diversity within the Black community. With the title of the episode guiding our understanding of what happened, this is the moment when "Will Gets Committed" to the plight of Black people in communities like the one from which he came. However, in line with the rest of the episode, that conclusion is left for audiences to draw. While this connection may be more visible to audiences whose position more closely aligns with Noah's, it is in line with the work that audiences must do to place the Bankses in South Central after the uprising.

Noah's part in the narrative reflects another familiar trope in the VSE: the guest star. Although Ross is not a well-known star and he does not play a large part in the episode, his function is to carry the controversy of the issue so that no member of the main cast is tainted by potential negative repercussions. In programs that have little narrative continuity between episodes—like sitcoms—the very special guest makes it possible to address an issue in the narrative structure of the episode. Even if the issue is not resolved (as is the case in this particular episode), it leaves the show together with the departing character when the credits roll, never to be seen or spoken of again. In this case, Noah's anger at what happened to his community (both his physical space as well as the Los Angeles Black community) can be intense. Although Will may agree with him, Noah's more extreme viewpoint protects Will (as well as Will Smith the actor and rapper as a crossover star who appeals to both white and Black audiences).

After Noah leaves the room, Will continues cleaning until he is confronted by a Hispanic man armed with a bat who believes Will is a looter. The show cuts to a commercial, forcing audiences to remain in the discomfort of Will's belonging nowhere. He's been rejected by Noah for his merely temporary interest in the community, but his appearance and dress cause a non-Black person to assume that he's a "thug" who caused the destruction. After the commercial, Carlton and

FIG. 7.1 Will and the Bankses pitch in to clean up their old neighborhood after the L.A. Uprising.

Uncle Phil enter, and Uncle Phil immediately recognizes the man with the bat as Hector (Gregory Sierra), the Banks' former neighbor. Uncle Phil calls the rest of the family, and a reunion ensues.

When Uncle Phil informs Ashley—who had not been born when the family lived in "the old neighborhood"—that they lived above Hector's grocery store, it dawns upon all of the Bankses and the audience that this reunion is taking place inside their old apartment. With this realization, the scene fades into a sepia flashback of the Banks family when they lived there. The flashback takes place moments before Uncle Phil gets the call hiring him for the job that will take them out of poverty and "the old neighborhood." This temporal device literally separates viewers from the present struggles of the Black community in South Central and repositions them within the confines of the family. Instead of serving the devastated community of South Central and the issues of oppression within the larger Black community, *FPBA* uses the apartment as a way to pivot the narrative and erase the larger issues by relocating the episode's larger conflict into the domestic sphere.

As the episode draws to a close, it remains focused on settling domestic tension over addressing larger social issues. The domestic tension confronted by a Black family in a burned-out apartment radiates outward to soothe lingering societal tension surrounding the racial inequities that culminated in the uprising. In the final moments of the flashback, Uncle Phil vows to never turn his back on this community. However, except for this very special visit, he has done and will continue to do just that. In the moments before each character exits the room (and thus the neighborhood and the episode), familiar and familial order is restored so that the Bankses (and by extension the audience) can feel good about themselves. Within the episode, the family reflects on how far they've come (or how far they've gone from their roots) in ways that reaffirm their characters. Aunt Vivian warmly reflects on the place where they started their family. Uncle Phil is remorseful about not fulfilling his commitment to the neighborhood. Will commits to canceling his plans so he can return the next weekend, and Ashley follows his example. Carlton schedules a date with Simone, and Hilary plans to celebrate their absence by throwing a party at the Bel-Air mansion. After the kids leave the room, Uncle Phil and Aunt Vivian have the confrontation that their fighting has been leading up to the entire episode. Positioning them in their old home to have this fight connects them with the idealistic people they were before upward mobility distracted them (especially Uncle Phil) from larger commitments to societal change. As Uncle Phil laments the road his life has taken, Aunt Vivian announces that she's pregnant. Uncle Phil faints and falls on the floor in shock, as the episode ends suddenly and cuts to the credits.

Will's promise to come back and continue cleaning up only moments earlier suggests a collaborative effort to rebuild both the physical neighborhood and the larger Black community in response to the uprising. However, the sudden announcement of the pregnancy is shocking enough to draw viewers away from racial problems in the present and refocus them on excitement for the family in future episodes. Ultimately, diffusing the tension between Uncle Phil and Aunt Vivians's interpersonal relationship also resolves the larger racially specific tensions in the episode. Although Aunt Vivian's pregnancy was going to become part of the season's plotlines due to Hubert-Whitten's real-life pregnancy, this is an interesting place to insert it. The announcement of her pregnancy at the end of the episode represents a further generational distancing from the "old neighborhood" because unlike Aunt Vivian's three older children, this baby will be brought up strictly within the confines of Bel-Air's wealthy and gated white community. The announcement is the impetus to leave the narrative and the neighborhood behind to return to the status quo.

This episode's allusions to the uprising suggests that race is the basis for inequality, which marks it as different from conventional episodes of *FPBA* as well as other pluralist shows like it. Because pluralist shows also "situate black characters in domestically centered black worlds and circumstances that essentially parallel those of whites," this ending does important ideological work in reestablishing the pretense of racial equality.[26] While the destruction of their original family home because of systemic racism resonates enough with the Bankses for them to temporarily leave the comfort of their recent privilege, the announcement of the pregnancy provides a compelling (and sympathetic) reason for them to return to it. This resolution signals the end of calling attention to racial inequality (however limited) as experienced by Black Angelenos by celebrating how this Black family has transcended social and economic barriers in relocating to Bel-Air. Realigning the concerns about racism and guilt over social mobility (that is, highlighting culturally specific Black problems) onto issues related to the family (the central unit in dominant American ideology) and the baby in the future diverts the concerns of this episode and reestablishes the show's normal state of affairs. The focus on celebrating (and protecting) their impending future gets to move the family forward in television time, and viewers' attention in actual time, while the problem of institutionalized racism and the promise of flip-turning white privilege upside down are left behind in "the old neighborhood."

Notes

1 Alex Altman, "Why the Killing of George Floyd Sparked an American Uprising," *Time*, June 4, 2020, https://time.com/5847967/george-floyd-protests-trump/.
2 John Fiske, *Media Matters: Race and Gender in U.S. Politics*, rev. ed. (Minneapolis: University of Minnesota Press, 1996), 14–15.
3 Ibid., 2.
4 Ibid., 3.
5 Mary Ann Doane, "Information, Crisis, Catastrophe," in *New Media, Old Media: A History and Theory Reader*, ed. Wendy Hui Kyong Chun and Thomas Keenan (New York: Routledge, 2006), 262.
6 Raymond Williams, *Television: Technology and Cultural Form* (New York: Routledge, 1974), 84; Nick Browne, "The Political Economy of the Television (Super) Text," in *Television: The Critical View*, ed. Horace Newcomb, 4th ed. (New York: Oxford University Press, 1987), 588–89.
7 Doane, "Information, Crisis, Catastrophe," 255.
8 Ibid., 251.
9 Robert Reinhold, "Violence and Racism Are Routine in Los Angeles Police, Study Says," *New York Times*, July 10, 1991.
10 John Thornton Caldwell, *Televisuality: Style, Crisis, and Authority in American Television* (New Brunswick, N.J.: Rutgers University Press, 1995), 313–14.
11 Ibid., 319–20.
12 Robin R. Means Coleman, *African American Viewers and the Black Situation Comedy: Situating Racial Humor* (New York: Garland, 1998), 75.
13 Fiske, *Media Matters*, 5.
14 Ibid., 187.
15 Hollis Griffin, "Never, Sometimes, Always: The Multiple Temporalities of 'Post-Race' Discourse in Convergence Television Narrative," *Popular Communication* 9, no. 4 (October 2011): 245.
16 Ibid., 244.
17 Herman Gray, "Television, Black Americans, and the American Dream," *Critical Studies in Mass Communication* 6, no. 4 (December 1989): 67.
18 Kristal Bryant Zook, *Color by Fox: The Fox Network and the Revolution in Black Television* (New York: Oxford University Press, 1999), 3.
19 Kristen J. Warner, *The Cultural Politics of Colorblind TV Casting* (New York: Routledge, 2015), 5.

20 Ibid.

21 Herman Gray, *Watching Race: Television and the Struggle for Blackness* (Minneapolis: University of Minnesota Press, 2004), 84.

22 Ibid., 87–88.

23 Ibid., 87.

24 Caldwell, *Televisuality*, 326.

25 Gray, *Watching Race*, 87.

26 Ibid.

8

The Night the Lights Went out at (Most of) NBC

Producing a Network with 1994's Must See TV Blackout Stunt

ERIN COPPLE SMITH

On November 3, 1994, New York City experienced a widespread blackout—not in reality but on television, as NBC staged an elaborate crossover night during what it called its Must See TV Thursday. At the time, all four of the network's sitcoms were set in New York, leaving an opportunity for an elaborate stunt event that could tie the series together. *Seinfeld* held out, but the network's other series—*Mad About You*, *Friends*, and the short-lived *Madman of the People*—all had episodes centered on the fictional blackout, a move that raised ratings for them and *Seinfeld*.

In hindsight, the outrageous success of NBC's "Must See TV" lineup seems inevitable. The series that aired as part of the lineup's run (most notably *Friends*, *Seinfeld*, *Frasier*, and *Will & Grace*) have become legendary. But in 1994, the executives at the network were primarily interested in developing a brand identity that would draw audiences to NBC not only on Thursdays but throughout the week. In a move that those involved refer to as "producing the network," cultivating a sense of cohesion among the shows' content was key, and they settled on comedies with a more adult tone rather than the family-oriented fare that had previously dominated television's 8:00–9:00 hour. Their efforts paid off when, in the fall of 1994, they realized not only that they had four series with a similar tone but also that all four were set in New York City, laying the groundwork for a potential sweeps stunt.

Investigating sweeps stunts offers a new way to understand the logics of television networks as they compete for the attention of audiences, and the 1994 NBC blackout stunt in particular provides key insights into the building of the Must See TV era at NBC. But more than that, examining the blackout stunt provides a new way of understanding what makes very special episodes (VSEs) special. Though most definitions of that specialness focus on narrative, in this case the institutional structures and strategies mark the event as special. Crossover sweeps stunts like this one constitute their own variety of VSE because they are deliberately set apart from the rest of the multiple series involved. Their distinctiveness—marked by combining multiple series into one televisual event—marks them as special. Indeed, the networks promote them as one-of-a-kind event in their efforts to entice audiences of one series to sample the others. And in taking place during a period of ratings sweeps, the NBC blackout of 1994 highlights a special crossover held during a special time of year. Little has been written about ratings stunts or the origin and purpose of the sweeps periods in the ratings calendar. As this chapter illuminates, sweeps have long played a role in determining the ad prices that are the engine of broadcast television. Planning and executing an elaborate stunt like the blackout had multiple advantages for the network: highlighting the cohesion among its Thursday night comedies, building the Thursday comedy block into a brand, introducing fans of longer-running series like *Mad About You* and *Seinfeld* to new ones like *Friends* and *Madman of the People*, and generating an uptick in ratings during a crucial period. The case of the very special NBC blackout highlights several key elements of the broadcast television industry in the 1990s—most notably, NBC's interest in building a successful Thursday night comedy block and broadcasters' efforts to stage sweeps-related stunts to inflate ratings during key periods.

NBC in the Must See TV Era

The fall of 1994, the backdrop for the subject of this chapter, was a watershed moment for NBC, a network looking to rebuild its once successful Thursday night comedy block. The first wave of NBC's success with its comedy block in the 1985–2000 era peaked during the 1987–1988 season, when, as Amanda Lotz explains, the Thursday prime-time schedule featured five series all ranked in the top fifteen: "*The Cosby Show* (1), *A Different World* (2), *Cheers* (3), *Night Court* (7), and *LA Law* (12)."[1] This dominance didn't last. By the 1991–1992 season, NBC had only one series in the top ten, and the rest of the original batch had lost their appeal. In 1993, *Time*'s Richard Zoglin said: "NBC, the onetime kingpin of prime time, has seen its fortunes turn sour almost overnight. Its biggest hit of the '80s, *The Cosby Show,* took early retirement last spring, while several other veterans—*The Golden Girls, Matlock* and *In the Heat of the Night*—were given their unconditional release. The network's last remaining Top 10 hit, *Cheers,* will call it quits at the end of this season."[2] After several years of dominance built on the strength of its comedies, NBC found itself right back where it had started.

It did not help that the network's struggle to replace its aging content occurred concurrently with other larger institutional forces. By 1992, there was increased competition for broadcasters coming from the addition of upstart Fox as well as cable channels. Lotz highlights the declining viewership during this era: "Only 19 percent of television households had access to thirty or more networks in 1985, whereas 76 percent of television homes could access more than thirty channels and 25 percent could access sixty channels or more by 1999. As a result, the Big Three networks saw their share of the prime-time audience decrease from 74 percent in the 1984–85 season to 54 percent in 1998–99."[3] Viewership declines are a problem for broadcasters because their revenue is based on advertising, and advertisers pay to reach audiences. As the head of NBC programming Warren Littlefield explained, "A strong advertising marketplace can cover up a lot of scheduling weaknesses, but when both the ad market is weak and your schedule is weak, that's the worst double whammy you can have."[4] Amid a massive downturn in viewership and thus advertising revenue, NBC found itself with a weak schedule full of series that were rapidly losing audiences' interest.

To make it through this difficult period, NBC worked to build up its comedy lineup yet again. That lineup had saved the network in the 1980s, and it hoped the same thing would happen in the new decade. Though the earliest years of the 1990s were choppy for NBC, its star rose again. By the season of the blackout, "the components of the second wave of success were in place, with *Seinfeld* ranking first, *Friends* eighth, and the new *ER* second."[5] With both *Friends* and *ER* debuting in the fall of 1994, NBC was on the precipice of a new era—one that would eventually become widely known as NBC's Must See TV. This breakout year was simply the beginning: in the 1996–1997 season, NBC surpassed its own record, with seven series in the top ten and sixteen in the top thirty.[6]

Littlefield and others at NBC refer to the process of turning the Thursday night schedule into a brand as "producing the network."[7] Rather than just think about shows as individual blocks, the executives at NBC conceptualized how the blocks would work together and could build a specific brand identity for the network—a brand identity that they could then leverage to attract audiences and thus advertisers. Individual series could last only so long (as the network saw with *Cosby* and *Cheers*), but a strong network identity could last long after specific series ended. To begin, the network had to successfully brand its content. John Miller, then czar of advertising and promotion at NBC, claims this somewhat inauspicious origin for Must See TV: "Don Ohlmeyer [then president of West

Coast operations] said he wanted to label our night of appointment television on Thursday. 'You guys figure out what you want to call it.' That first lineup was *Mad About You*, *Wings*, *Seinfeld*, and *Madman of the People*, *LA Law* at 10:00. That was the fall of 1993. We wanted to come up with a name for this night because we wanted to package it. There was a guy who worked for us then named Dan Holm. He suggested, 'How about Must See TV. It rhymes.' We said, 'Okay. Let's go with Must See TV.'"[8]

Once they had a catchy name, executives got to work on building support for the brand they were developing. Miller describes the process: "Producing the network was a year in the making, and then we had a year on the air by ourselves doing this . . . we had a unit make what we called promotainment. Not pure promos, but talking about our shows, the stars, where they'd come from. It was to keep people engaged."[9] This "promotainment" suffused the network, which helped NBC build and maintain a brand identity. Littlefield explains: "The quality of our Must See shows became our greatest sales tool to the creative community. Better still, we'd begun to promote our shows in a way no other network had attempted at the time. We produced the network rather than just the shows."[10]

The key for the Must See era was that all of the series that were part of the Thursday night lineup needed to be cohesive, as it's difficult to build a brand identity around series that are substantively different in content, style, or tone. In the 1990s, as viewing habits changed, NBC shifted its strategy from broad-based family content to series designed to appeal to narrower audiences. As Lotz explains, "its winning strategy was to schedule programs that featured characters reflecting, and themes targeted to, a narrower demographic, namely a younger and more affluent urban audience."[11]

But the brand of the Thursday NBC comedies was more than just adult: it was also focused on maintaining a particular tone and approach. With the success of *Seinfeld* and then *Mad About You*, NBC had already set the table for urban comedies with a smart, almost erudite, tone. Paul Reiser describes his series *Mad About You* as "adult, smart, introspective. Perhaps overly introspective. The show was simple. It was about simple things."[12] Littlefield explains that in his search for a "*Friends*-like show" in the early 1990s, "we wanted to reach that young, urban audience, those kids starting out on their own."[13] This was part of the NBC strategy—focusing on a specific audience that was attractive to advertisers and selecting programming designed to appeal to that audience. Christopher Anderson highlights the fact that during this era, "NBC executives dissected audience demographics and measured the advertising potential of each program developed for the network, carefully weighing program costs against advertising revenue for each portion of the schedule."[14] Lotz points to the various series that occupied the Thursday night comedy block, emphasizing their unity in terms of the audience they were clearly attempting to reach: "The network's demographic specificity is most apparent in the various series scheduled in the Thursday sitcom block during the second cycle [begun in 1994]. With varying success, the network repeatedly told stories about young, affluent, white urbanites who lived in worlds curiously devoid of people different from themselves."[15] Steve Levitan, writer and producer of *Frasier*, notes: "We talked about that NBC brand all the time. That brand represented smart, sophisticated, urban comedy. It stood for quality."[16]

Though appealing to young adults might seem like common sense now, it was fairly revolutionary in the 1990s. Describing the origins of *Friends*, Littlefield claims, "It may seem hard to believe today, but in 1994 we were playing in core conceptual territory that hadn't been explored that much on network TV—young adult relationships."[17] Karey Burke, then a programmer working in development for NBC, echoes Littlefield: "Some people thought [*Friends*] was too Gen X, way too narrow."[18] In the fall of 1994, all four comedy series on NBC featured childless young adults in New York City, engaging in romantic and often sexual entanglements. For example, of the episodes involved in the 1994 blackout, *Mad About You* featured Paul and Jamie finding a porn channel on cable, *Friends* included the gang discussing the most shocking places they'd had sex, and Kramer urged Jerry to have sex with a Romanian gymnast on *Seinfeld*. Without a doubt, both the content and the audiences were distinctively adult at NBC.

Though it seems surprising in hindsight, NBC got pushback from local affiliate stations concerned about airing adult-targeted programming in the 8:00–9:00 hour. Historically, that hour had been devoted to family-friendly series, and *Friends* and *Mad About You* were controversial. In desperation, Littlefield pushed back, using the growing availability of content to the network's advantage: "I argued that the world was changing. There were plenty of kid and family choices available on network and cable. . . . No one had ever tried the grown-up stuff this early before, but I was desperate, and Thursday night needed to work."[19] As we know with the benefit of hindsight, it did work. In 1994, NBC was looking to reestablish the dominance it had enjoyed in the late 1980s by building a strong schedule and network identity, and, as mentioned before, the network had four sitcoms that were similar in theme, tone, and target audience, with all four set in New York City. Because NBC programming during this era was so uniformly focused on appealing to a white, urban, and affluent segment of the audience, the sitcoms airing in November of 1994 were all more or less similar in their subject matter and audience composition, which made it more plausible that all four sitcoms took place in the *same* New York City. The blackout worked because the series not only shared a geographical setting but also had very similar characters. The fact that the series appealed to a similar audience meant that NBC had even more reason to believe that the crossover would work to its advantage, raising ratings for all four series—not just on that Thursday, but for the rest of the season.

Ratings, Sweeps, and Stunts

The stage was set for a successful crossover, but the question remains: why stage one? Crossovers are notoriously difficult to pull off. Dick Wolf, a producer on successful franchises such as *Law & Order* and *Chicago Fire*, once grumbled to critics: "Crossovers are a pain in the ass. Everybody hates doing them" due to the complexity and difficulty of writing and scheduling them. Nonetheless, he admitted, crossovers are "like ratings crack."[20] Ratings are the fundamental currency of broadcast television. Advertisers purchase time on broadcast television to air advertisements to audiences. The price of the time varies depending on a variety of things, including the time of day, the nature of the programming being aired, and the locations where the programming is available—but all of these boil down to two factors: the size and demographic characeristics of the audience. Advertisers' interests center on getting their ads in front of viewers who are likely to buy what they're selling—whether that's cars, makeup, fast food, or pharmaceuticals—and the more viewers, the better. What advertisers need to know from television networks and stations is how many people are watching and who is watching. In other words, they want to know both the size of the audience and the nature of the people in the audience—where they live, their income level, their gender, and so on. The problem is that audience measurement can only be done after the ad has aired. In short, advertisers must purchase ad time based on projections of the audience. Those projections are crucial to both advertisers (who want as much assurance as possible that their ads will reach large numbers of the right types of viewers) and the networks and stations (who want to get the most money possible for the time they're selling).

Those projections are made by companies specializing in audience analysis, of which Nielsen is the best known and most widely used. Audiences are measured at the local level. For example, Nielsen has broken down the national television marketplace into designated market areas (DMAs)—segments of the country that service audiences. As James Webster, Patricia Phalen, and Lawrence Lichty explain, "Each DMA is a collection of counties in which the preponderance of total viewing can be attributed to local or home-market stations. That is, counties are assigned to markets on the basis of which stations the people in those counties actually view."[21] As of 2020, Nielsen recognized 210 DMAs nationwide, and each is measured differently depending on how many audience members it contains. In the twenty-five biggest markets in the country, Nielsen uses local people meters (LPMs), electronic devices that are able to track audience members twenty-four hours per day and 365 days per year. As one might expect, these superpowered people meters are located in the twenty-five largest markets in the country (accounting for roughly half of the national TV audience), meaning that the most granular data is collected in the largest markets encompassing the largest portion of the national audience.[22] An additional thirty-one mid-level markets use a combination of methods, including electronic set meters and paper diaries. The meters measure daily viewing for overall household data, with demographic data available only a few times per year.[23] As of 2019, in the additional 154 markets, participants use only paper diaries to record their viewing habits. These diaries are issued, collected, and used to create ratings data during only four months of the year—February, May, July, and November. These periods are known as ratings sweeps.

Because sweeps periods are the only time during the year when half the national audience is measured on a demographic level, they are crucial to the industry in terms of determining advertising rates. Ratings are useful in this determination in two ways, both before and after an ad actually airs. As Webster, Phalen, and Lichty explain, "all ratings data are historical. They describe something that has already happened. . . . [R]emember that the buying and selling of audiences is always conducted in anticipation of future events. Although it is certainly useful to know which program had the largest audience last week, what really determines the allocation of advertising dollars is an expectation of who will have the largest audience next week or next season."[24] Sweeps data are considered to be a representative measurement of a station's audience for a specific segment of the year. The data from each of these periods are used by both national networks and local stations to project audience sizes and demographics for the purposes of setting prices for ad time. Additionally, the data are used to determine whether or not expectations for audiences were met. If an advertiser purchased time based on a particular projected audience, it will be interested in whether or not the projections held true. In the post-buy analysis, advertisers and stations or networks revisit the terms of the contract and the data to ensure that the expected audience was actually delivered. A 10 percent margin of error in projections is considered acceptable, but if an ad spot underdelivers (meaning the projection, and thus the price, was too high), stations or networks might have to offer additional advertising time for free or at reduced cost to make up the difference.

Because sweeps are so central to the process of determining ad prices, network and station programmers put a great deal of emphasis on building up audiences during sweeps periods. Local stations often include highly sensational stories (such as "Your garage may be trying to kill you!" and "What you need to know to keep your family safe!") as part of the local news programming to encourage audiences to tune to their station rather than a competitor. National networks typically air high-profile programming during these months, including anticipated miniseries (including *Roots*), ripped-from-the-headlines made-for-TV movies (*The Day After*), the television premiere of blockbuster movies, big events (the Super Bowl and the Oscars are both scheduled during the sweeps month of February), or—as this chapter explores—heavily promoted stunts designed to attract audiences. These stunts can include all manner of tactics: celebrity guest stars, a VSE dealing with a particularly hot social issue, a wedding or vacation, or a musical episode. Historically, sweeps months are the epicenter of content that's in some way outside the norm, designed to get audiences to tune in so as to inflate ratings.

The crossover is one popular type of ratings stunt. Crossover episodes, when characters from one series visit another series, are appealing stunts because they are likely to draw fans of both series and improve ratings. J. Richard Kjelstrup, writing about television crossovers, begins by noting, "Crossover is a strategy designed to attract (more) viewers so that the networks in turn can negotiate (higher) advertising rates."[25] In addition to the temporary ratings boost for any given episode, crossovers are appealing to networks because they can cross-promote series, encouraging audiences to move from the series they are familiar with to one that may be new to them but is housed on the same network. As Kjelstrup observes, "The intended spillover of viewers from one show to the other in a crossover is obvious as an industry strategy and should not be underplayed."[26] In short, crossovers appeal to networks due to their potential to increase viewership in the short and long terms.

"Thursday, the Lights Go out on NBC! It's Blackout Thursday!"[27]

The fall of 1994 proved fertile ground for a crossover: NBC was looking to produce the network by reestablishing its comedy dominance on Thursday nights, and sales of ad time were in decline as audiences were stretched thinner than ever before across multiple competitors—making sweeps periods particularly important for establishing high viewership and thus advertising rates. The way each series handled the blackout demonstrates how NBC worked to maintain some continuity across all three episodes. The blackout begins at the very end of *Mad About You*, which aired in the 8:00–8:30 slot. The series, in its third season in 1994, focused on a married couple, Jamie and Paul Buchman. In the episode, Jamie and Paul are arguing because the two are both working out of their apartment home and struggling for space and resources.[28] To get Paul out of the living room and watching TV (for his documentary project) in the bedroom, Jamie eventually steals cable via their building's rooftop box—and comedic chaos ensues. It's not until the very end of the episode that the blackout comes into play. About two minutes before the end of the twenty-two-minute episode, Jamie and Ira, Paul's cousin, pull a cable on the roof that causes lights across the entire city—on view behind them—wink out. In the final shot of the episode, Paul sets the stage for the rest of the evening on NBC, admonishing Jamie as the credits start to roll: "Do you realize what you've done? Do you realize now the entire city . . . the city! Stop smiling!" Behind the credits sits the longtime NBC meteorologist and newsman Al Roker, who intones: "It seems the city of New York has been thrown into a mysterious blackout. ConEd believes it was caused by either a power surge in a series of sensitive grid relays or some yutz trying to steal cable. Fortunately, New Yorkers can always be counted on in an emergency. Looters have asked for our patience, and they'll get to everyone just as soon as possible.

I'm Al Roker of NBC in New York, filling in for Tom Brokaw, who's stuck in an elevator." This interstitial material, though brief, sets the stage for the rest of the night by establishing that the blackout will extend beyond the borders of *Mad About You*. It also reinforces the "NBC-ness" of the stunt by invoking not only Roker but also Brokaw—it helps produce the network as a cohesive unit. And narratively, it sets up common themes that would carry across all of the blackout episodes.

In the other participating series, the blackout functions as a backdrop for the action. *Friends* begins with Phoebe taking the stage at Central Perk, a coffeehouse, explaining, "I want to start with a song that's about that moment when you suddenly realize what life is really all about." She strums her guitar once and the lights go out—thirty seconds into the episode.[29] Cut to Chandler, about to leave a bank's ATM vestibule when the power goes out, leaving him in the dark and locked in. The episode continues in typical *Friends* fashion, following a few different plots all set against the backdrop of the blackout. With one minute remaining in the episode, the lights of New York City come back on, revealing Rachel kissing Paolo, her neighbor, as Ross looks on in horror.[30] The 9:00–9:30 slot was *Seinfeld*'s, and (as noted above) the series elected not to participate in the stunt. Not only were the lights on in New York for that half-hour, but the episode also makes no mention of the blackout. The final blackout episode was in the short-lived *Madman of the People*, a series starring Dabney Coleman as an outspoken newspaper columnist.[31] The episode isn't available for viewing, but various episode guides describe the events: "A blackout in the city finds Jack [Coleman] enduring a miserable birthday, and Meg and Sasha stuck on an elevator with a hunk."[32]

Certainly, the three episodes all shared the narrative component of the blackout, but perhaps most interesting are the other ways the three managed to achieve further thematic unity, based largely on the Roker material aired after *Mad About You*. First, there is the theme of characters stuck in small spaces. In *Mad About You*, Paul spends the episode trying to cross paths with a neighbor who has gotten stuck in an elevator when the blackout hits. Roker tells us that Brokaw gets stuck in an elevator in the interstitial material. Chandler gets stuck in an ATM vestibule, and two characters on *Madman* are stuck in an elevator. Further, Roker's fake news brief indicates that there will be looting in New York City as the blackout continues, and looting is a key theme of the *Madman* episode later that night. It is clear that NBC worked hard to make the crossover episodes have more in common than just the blackout.

The blackout itself was a success. Dan Holm, then a senior director at NBC (and originator of the phrase "Must See TV," as noted above), claims, "It solidified the Thursday legacy that NBC had at the time. The chemistry was there. It was a tremendous success."[33] If the goal of the stunt was to get audiences of one series to watch the next one, it was indeed a success. As *Esquire*'s Rose Maura Lorre reports, "*Friends* gained about five million viewers from the week before, and even *Seinfeld*'s blackout-boycotting 'The Gymnast' saw

FIG. 8.1 *On Friends*, the city-wide blackout traps Chandler in an ATM vestibule with model Jill Goodacre.

a 2.5 million-viewer bump."[34] As Holm continued, "You're always looking for audience from one show to the next to fill the night, from early in the first sitcom to the end of the last drama. You're looking to escalate the night. In this case, [the blackout] gave them a great reason to stick around." Ultimately, the blackout accomplished several of NBC's goals simultaneously: by giving audiences a reason to stick around for the entire night, it elevated ratings (and thus future advertising revenue) during the crucial November sweeps. Though it started as a straightforward sweeps stunt, the event managed to accomplish a great deal more for NBC: at the start of Must See TV's dominance in the 1990s, the blackout helped establish the network's Thursday comedy block as a cohesive unit.

Conclusion

There is no doubt that the Must See TV era was a massive success for NBC, launching it into the new millennium. The phrase still lingers, even many years past the era's heyday. But just how profitable was it? Littlefield highlights the incredibly high ad rates for the block: "[The Must See era was] *really* profitable. Looking at ad sales figures, I could see in black and white the vast differential between what was charged for a spot on Thursday versus what we would get on a Saturday. At the height of Must-See madness, a thirty-second spot on *Seinfeld* sold for $800,000 while *ER* commanded $550,000 for thirty seconds."[35] He also notes: "At the height of the Must See era, NBC was generating over $1 billion in annual profit for GE. During my last three seasons, NBC sold an industry record $6.5 billion in prime-time advertising, $2 billion more than our closest competitor. On Thursday night in the 1997–98 season we beat our combined competition by margins of 60 percent."[36]

The blackout stunt of 1994 provides a useful example of a VSE that can be analyzed from an institutional perspective. As with other VSEs, stunts like these demonstrate an effort to rise above the clutter of the broadcast airwaves by marking themselves as distinctive. Sweeps stunts—televisual events meant to boost ratings during key periods of the year—reveal key strategies at NBC. The blackout offered the network an opportunity to accomplish several tasks at once: improve ratings during sweeps, highlight the cohesion of its Thursday comedy block, and establish a strong night with a very particular audience segment. The blackout was very special indeed.

Much has changed in the television industry since 1994. With the advent of streaming services and digital video recorders (DVRs), sweeps no longer have the power they once did. As Tim Kenneally of *The Wrap* explains, "With audiences watching content when and where they want it, it matters less and less what a sample audience is watching during specific times of the year."[37] And as audiences have continued to flee broadcast TV first for cable and then for streaming services, ratings have dropped precipitously. The highest-rated TV series of 2018, CBS's *Roseanne*, averaged 20.0 million viewers. In 1994 (its first season), *Friends* averaged 31.3 million and ranked only eighth for the year. *Seinfeld*, number one that year, averaged 36.6 million. As audiences continue to move away from broadcast TV, the profitability of a crossover stunt like the blackout becomes less and less likely. Moreover, the development of blocks like Must See TV doesn't mean as much today as it did in 1994. Must See TV didn't last long into the new century. In the early 2000s, NBC moved on from that brand after losing its biggest hit series, including *Friends*, *Seinfeld*, *Frasier*, and *Will & Grace*. In 2004, it put a noncomedy show (the reality series *The Apprentice*) on at 9:00–10:00, breaking with the tradition begun in the early 1980s and clearly signaling the end of the era. As Dan Harrison (then a strategic planner and scheduler at NBC) explains, "Today the average home has two hundred channels. You're never going to aggregate up an audience like there was in the Must See TV era. It was as much of a cultural milestone and touchstone in size and scope as Frank Sinatra or Elvis or the Beatles were in the music business."[38]

The 1994 blackout stunt highlights NBC's efforts to produce the network, using a high-profile sweeps stunt to reinforce its brand of adult-targeted comedy. The lights might have gone out at 8:20 P.M. in New York City that night, but by the time they came on again at 10:00, the Must See TV era was well and truly begun.

Notes

1 Amanda Lotz, "Must-See TV: NBC's Dominant Decades," in *NBC: America's Network*, ed. Michele Hilmes (Berkeley: University of California Press, 2007), 267.

2 Richard Zoglin, "Baltimore Bullets," *Time*, February 1, 1993.

3 Lotz, "Must-See TV," 262.
4 Warren Littlefield, *Top of the Rock: Inside the Rise and Fall of Must See* (New York: Anchor, 2012), 145.
5 Lotz, "Must-See TV," 269.
6 The seven series in the top ten were *ER* (1), *Seinfeld* (2), *Suddenly Susan* (3), *Friends* (4), *The Naked Truth* (5), *Fired Up* (6), and *The Single Guy* (8).
7 Quoted in Littlefield, *Top of the Rock*, 239.
8 Quoted in Littlefield, *Top of the Rock*, 235. Miller was mistaken about the original lineup, which included *Frasier* (seventh in the top ten series), not *Madman of the People*.
9 Quoted in Littlefield, *Top of the Rock*, 259.
10 Ibid.
11 Lotz, "Must-See TV," 262.
12 Quoted in Littlefield, *Top of the Rock*, 129.
13 Ibid., 153.
14 Christopher Anderson, "Creating the Twenty-First-Century Television Network: NBC in the Age of Media Conglomerates," in *NBC: America's Network*, ed. Michele Hilmes (Berkeley: University of California Press, 2007), 283.
15 Lotz, "Must-See TV," 270–271.
16 Quoted in Littlefield, *Top of the Rock*, 313.
17 Ibid., 170.
18 Quoted in Ibid., 175.
19 Ibid., 125.
20 Quoted in Kate Stanhope, "'Chicago Justice': Dick Wolf Talks 3-Show Crossover, 'Law & Order' Comparisons," *Hollywood Reporter*, January 18, 2017.
21 James G. Webster, Patricia F. Phalen, and Lawrence W. Lichty, *Ratings Analysis: The Theory and Practice of Audience Research*, 3rd ed. (Mahwah, NJ: Lawrence Erlbaum Associates, 2006), 148.
22 Markets using LPM technology in 2019 included Atlanta, Baltimore, Boston, Charlotte, Chicago, Cleveland-Akron, Dallas–Fort Worth, Denver, Detroit, Houston, Los Angeles, Miami–Fort Lauderdale, Minneapolis–St. Paul, New York, Orlando, Philadelphia, Phoenix, Pittsburgh, Portland (OR), Sacramento, San Francisco, Seattle-Tacoma, St. Louis, Tampa–St. Petersburg, and Washington (the D.C. area). See Nielsen, *Local Measurement: Methodology*, April 1, 2019, https://www.nielsen.com/wp-content/uploads/sites/3/2019/04/Local-Measurement-Methodology-Ex.pdf; Nielsen—Client Knowledge Service Team, *Local Measurement: Methodology, LPM, Set-Meter, Diary Only*, 2019. https://www.nielsen.com/wp-content/uploads/sites/3/2019/04/Local-Measurement-Methodology-Ex.pdf.
23 Information on the 2019 projected TV market breakdown is available at Nielsen, *Local Measurement Methodology*, April 1, 2019, https://www.nielsen.com/wp-content/uploads/sites/3/2019/04/Local-Measurement-Methodology-Ex.pdf.
24 Webster, Phalen, and Lichty, *Ratings Analysis*, 227.
25 J. Richard Kjelstrup, "Challenging Narratives: Crossovers in Prime Time," *Journal of Film and Video* 59, no. 1 (Spring 2007): 32.
26 Ibid., 43.
27 The quote is from the blackout promotion aired on NBC.
28 The episode is "Pandora's Box," episode 6 in season 3.
29 The episode is "The One with the Blackout," episode 7 in season 1.
30 The episode is "The Gymnast," episode 6 in season 6.
31 The episode is "Birthday in the Big House," episode 9 in season 1.

32 "*Madman of the People*: Episode Guide," *TV Guide*.
33 Quoted in Rose Maura Lorre, "Revisiting 'Blackout Thursday,' NBC's Epic 1994 Promo Stunt," *Esquire*, November 3, 2014.
34 Ibid.
35 Littlefield, *Top of the Rock*, 237.
36 Ibid., 309.
37 Tim Kenneally, "TV Sweeps' Dirty Little Secret: They're Not as Important as They Used to Be," *The Wrap*, November 18, 2014, www.thewrap.com/tv-sweeps-dirty-little-secret-theyre-not-nearly-as-important-as-they-used-to-be/.
38 Quoted in Littlefield, *Top of the Rock*, 311.

9

Ellen, "The Puppy Episode," and a Special TV Milestone?

RON BECKER

A full-page ad in the April 26, 1997, issue of *TV Guide* announced: "The Wait Is Over. Tonight the episode everyone is talking about. A special all-new one-hour *Ellen*." The buildup for this very special episode (VSE) of the ABC sitcom began the previous September, when rumors started that the series' title character, Ellen Morgan, might come out of the closet during the show's fourth season. *Ellen* had been a moderately successful sitcom in the vein of *Seinfeld* and *Friends* since its 1994 debut. It followed the daily lives of Ellen Morgan, a thirty-something Los Angeles bookstore owner, and her circle of friends. Although jokes had often centered on Ellen's aversion to dresses and her mother's continually thwarted desire to see her get married, the series had treated Ellen as straight. In March 1997, after months of coy jokes, the series finally announced that Ellen Morgan would come out in April. The story became a major news item, discussed everywhere from CNN's *Crossfire* to the editorial pages of local newspapers. Public attention grew still more when Ellen DeGeneres, the actor who played the title character, came out on the cover of *Time* and in televised interviews with Oprah Winfrey and Diane Sawyer. Gay activists heralded the episode as a cultural milestone and organized "Come Out with Ellen" viewing parties in cities nationwide. In contrast, the religious right denounced it; for example, the conservative Media Research Center took out a full-page ad in *Variety* imploring ABC and its parent company Disney to rethink "this slap in the face to America's families."[1] Some cynical industry observers saw the episode as a brazen, year-long ploy to improve ratings. According to the *Washington Post*, "In the long history of network competition, there's never been a stunt like this one."[2]

The wait ended when "The Puppy Episode"—a title based on the code name producers playfully used to maintain secrecy during the script's development—aired at 8:00 P.M. on Wednesday, April 30. Ellen Morgan's coming-out story begins when Ellen meets up with Richard, an old college friend who is in town for work. At dinner, she meets and instantly clicks with Susan, one of Richard's coworkers. When she learns that Susan is a lesbian and that Susan had assumed she was too, Ellen panics. After a comically bad sexual encounter with Richard and with the help of her therapist, Ellen realizes that she is gay and has feelings for Susan. When she thinks that Susan is flying home to Pittsburgh, Ellen rushes to the airport—where, in what became the episode's most iconic moment, she accidentally announces her sexual identity over the public address system. While things don't work out with Susan, Ellen comes out to her friends who, in the final scene, show their support by taking her to a lesbian coffeehouse.

In this chapter, I examine the relationship between the concept of the VSE and "The Puppy Episode" from various angles. First, I discuss the episode as an example of a certain kind of VSE—what we might call the TV-milestone VSE. Second, I discuss why "The Puppy Episode" could be considered the last VSE of its (and perhaps any) kind, linking the concept of VSEs to historically specific assumptions about TV's social role. Third, I help us gain a critical distance from the claims made about "The Puppy Episode" and about VSEs in general, approaching the concept of VSEs as a cultural discourse. And finally, I use the notion of the VSE to explore why the series struggled in its final season.

A Very Special TV Milestone

As a TV-milestone VSE, "The Puppy Episode" was special in two interconnected ways. All VSEs are special in relation to television's persistent predictability and assumed banality. The medium's rigid schedule and efficient formulas form the background against which all VSEs stand out. TV-milestone VSEs, however, depend on a second assumption about TV—namely, that the medium plays an important sociopolitical role through its power to establish what is considered normal, mainstream, or acceptable. From this perspective, the medium's predictability and formulas function as a normalizing tool, and in certain cases, an episode that disrupts those formulas can disrupt that normalizing influence.

In 1997, having the title character of an established prime-time network sitcom come out was a big disruption. Just the rumor that it might happen led *Newsweek* to ask: "Is America ready for a TV sitcom where the leading character is a lesbian?"[3] For several decades, homosexuality seemed somehow incompatible with a medium that seemed to have an ingrained conservative bent. As the chief home-media technology from the 1950s to the 1990s, TV was firmly entangled with the intense heteronormativity of suburban life after World War II.[4] Expected to deliver content that was appropriate for the public airwaves and safe for the whole family, TV was constrained by government oversight, skittish sponsors worried about their products being associated with controversial material, and network executives' interest in reaching a mass audience through the use of the least objectionable programming. While queer characters had appeared on TV since its beginning, and openly lesbian, gay, and bisexual characters had appeared sporadically since 1970, the medium's reputation for being unwelcoming to LGB characters persisted.

That reputation began to shift in the mid-1990s as more LGB characters appeared on prime-time network TV. Importantly, however, they had appeared only in supporting roles. Thus, while the existence of gay people was increasingly acknowledged, the televisual conventions still helped reinforce the idea that straight people were at the center of American life. For viewers raised on decades of such heterocentric TV, it was hard to imagine that there could be a lesbian Mary Tyler Moore or Roseanne Conner. Thus, "The Puppy Episode" seemed very special indeed. It wouldn't just be unusual or even unprecedented: it promised to be important. It wouldn't just disrupt TV's routine flow: it promised to change TV and—given TV's role as the culture's most pervasive storytelling medium—society itself. In that way, "The Puppy Episode" is a quintessential example of a TV-milestone VSE.

Considering what it was trying to do, it isn't surprising that "The Puppy Episode" would include several features common to VSEs. While the decision to expand it to sixty minutes was likely motivated (at least in part) by ABC's desire to squeeze more ad revenue out of the event, it also signaled that this wasn't a normal sitcom episode and might have led viewers to assume that Ellen Morgan's story line was too momentous, serious, controversial, or complicated for the series' typical format to handle. The decision to include A-list celebrity guest stars such as Oprah Winfrey, Laura Dern, Billy Bob Thornton, Demi Moore, k.d. lang, Gina Gershon, Melissa Etheridge, and Dwight Yoakam likely worked similarly, helping give the episode an expanded sense of cultural significance.

"The Puppy Episode" also has a wider range of emotional tones than a normal installment. The series' standard comic tone and timing were interrupted by several moments of heartfelt drama. The opening title sequence, for example, which had featured DeGeneres clowning around in different zany situations each week, was stripped down to just an empty chair and title card with no audio. This brief moment of silence sets a serious opening mood. That mood returns when Ellen comes out to her therapist (played by Winfrey). Laugh-track cues disappear, and the actors deliver the following dialogue with quiet gravitas:

FIG. 9.1 The mood gets serious when Ellen talks to her therapist (played by guest star Oprah Winfrey) about the challenges of coming out.

THERAPIST: You kept it to yourself and never acted on it. Why do you think that is?

ELLEN: I don't know. I guess I thought if I just ignored it, you know, it would just go away and I could just live a normal life.

THERAPIST: And what is a normal life, Ellen?

ELLEN: I don't know. Normal, I mean, just the same thing everybody wants. I want a house, with a picket fence, you know, a dog, a cat, Sunday barbeques. Someone to love, someone who loves me, someone I can build a life with. I just want to be happy.

THERAPIST: And you don't think you can have those things with a woman?

ELLEN: Well, society has a pretty big problem with it, you know. There are a lot of people out there who think people like me are sick.

During this forty-five-second exchange, jokes get sidelined by the emotional weight of Ellen's hopes and fears. Because Ellen Morgan's fictional life can be conflated so easily with DeGeneres's real life as well as with the experiences of millions of queer people, the scene takes on an earnest and educational quality, as if it wants to teach straight viewers that gay people simply want the same thing they do and help closeted gay people see that they can be gay and have a normal life.

Before the scene can get "too" serious, however, Ellen breaks the mood with a joke: "Oh God, why did I ever rent *Personal Best*?" The tonal shift, of course, reminds viewers that despite the seemingly historic weight of the moment, they are still watching a sitcom. In general, the episode obeys usual sitcom conventions, presenting Ellen's coming out through a steady stream of jokes and comic situations. It is funny in the way that well-written network TV sitcoms are funny. Many critics applauded this balance. *Daily Variety*'s Ray Richmond, for example, declared it "the funniest and most moving in the sitcom's four years on the air thanks to a script . . . that steers clear of the typical heavy-handed messages and speechifying."[5] Of course, Richmond's final dig about "speechifying" reflects a criticism many people have made about VSEs: that they can be overly wrought or overly political which are bad things (at least according to certain gendered and classed taste cultures). However, his praise of the episode for its ability to be both funny and moving points to a key feature of many VSEs: their pleasures are often rooted in the tensions that can arise when things that seem incompatible, like the comic and the dramatic, are intertwined. The jokey attitude people often have when talking about VSEs, for example, plays upon the seeming incongruity or even paradox of the idea that an episode of a bland series on a quotidian medium like TV could be special.

As a TV-milestone VSE, "The Puppy Episode" exploited such tensions in ways that depended on TV's reputation as both banal and culturally powerful. There can be unique pleasures and thrills in encountering the pathos of Ellen's coming-out story within the comic formulas of a sitcom; learning something new and profound about a prosaic character you had gotten to know well over the course of four seasons; watching a politically charged topic like gay rights play out in a genre considered trivial and on a medium considered banal; watching the climax of a heated public debate while sitting in the privacy of your living room; and seeing a social group long marginalized in both the media and society suddenly included at the center of that society's most ubiquitous cultural platform. Thus, the "The Puppy Episode" not only balanced humor and heartfelt drama but also intertwined the familiar and the unexpected, the mainstream and the marginal, the public and the private, the political and the personal, the mundane and the monumental, and the queer and the (hetero)normal. Network TV was a meaningful site for many gays and lesbians because it was uniquely suited to generating these very special experiences and feelings.

The Last TV-Milestone VSE?

While "The Puppy Episode" is as a clear example of a TV-milestone VSE, it could also be considered the last one. Why? The idea that an episode is special because of its social importance rests, as I have said, on assumptions about the medium's social power. Those assumptions were rooted in the way TV seemed to have functioned as a mechanism of social integration. Before cable, the internet, and smartphones, TV dominated a relatively sparse media landscape as the most pervasive form of mass media. On any given evening in the 1970s, for example,

90 percent of people watching TV were watching one of the three broadcast networks, and the most popular programs often had an enormous cultural footprint. These dynamics helped make broadcast TV feel like an important cultural forum, where society's values got negotiated and its sense of what was mainstream got established.[6]

Even before Ellen Morgan came out, however, TV had changed. By the 1990s, the three-network era had started to give way to a period marked by audience fragmentation and a shift to narrowcasting practices. Such developments had helped make prime time more welcoming to gay-themed programming and helped make "The Puppy Episode" possible. Faced with intense competition, ABC moved away from trying to reach a mass audience and more aggressively targeted well-educated, upscale 18–49-year-olds, whom they conceptualized as having cosmopolitan sensibilities and a taste for edgier programming. Having the title character of one of the network's prime-time series come out may have been controversial and may have turned off older, younger, or more conservative viewers, but it was seen as a way to attract the audience segment ABC was most interested in. Thus, "The Puppy Episode" was enabled by the fact that prime-time network shows were drawing significantly smaller audiences and sorting viewers into narrower demographic and psychographic bubbles. In other words, TV was moving away from the role it had played as America's unifying cultural storyteller.

Public perceptions about TV and its social role changed more slowly than industry practices, however. That lag helps explain the intense debate around and coverage of "The Puppy Episode." People on various sides of the issue clearly felt very strongly that having an openly lesbian title character on a network sitcom mattered because they believed that TV mattered—that it still said something about mainstream American values and that it still had the power to change people's opinions about gay rights. Those assumptions helped make the episode feel like a special milestone, even as some of the foundations underpinning those assumptions were eroding.

Since 1997, of course, TV has fragmented further. In the era of Netflix, YouTube, and microcasting, the idea of TV as a unifying social force and a site to advance or even just gauge political change has lost much of its sway in the popular imagination. As a result, it is harder for people to believe that a TV episode could be socially significant to the degree people may have in the 1970s. At the very least, the fragmentation of our engagement with the medium means that it is more difficult for the industry or its critics to focus enough attention on a single episode to fuel the kind of widespread public celebration, outcry, and debate that surrounded "The Puppy Episode." Because of such shifts, I argue, the TV-milestone VSE is disappearing.

To push this point further, one could argue that such shifts undermined not just the conditions that supported TV-milestone VSEs but also the broader notion of VSEs. Admittedly, some VSEs depend more than others on the perceived social significance of the medium. But in some ways and to some extent, all VSEs—even those that are special because they disrupt certain genre conventions or TV's predictability—depend on a general notion of TV's importance. In part, I argue, the disruption of a certain TV show's formula warranted being called a VSE because of the general aura of cultural significance associated with TV as the preeminent mass medium. Furthermore, the idea that disrupting TV's formulaic predictability could be special has also been undermined by the fact that TV has become less formulaic and predictable, as an era defined by content scarcity has given way to one marked by relative plenty. Of course, there are still formulas that can be disrupted and silences that can be ruptured, but such constraints don't define the medium in the way they once did. In other words, VSEs emerged during the network era, and much of their resonance depended on specific circumstances that marked U.S. television in the 1970s and 1980s.

TV-Milestone VSEs as Cultural Discourse

Linking VSEs to the historically specific conditions of the network era pushes us to recognize the concept of VSEs as a cultural discourse (in other words, the term enables and encourages a way of talking, promoting, and assessing television that emerged from a specific context and that are deployed to specific ends). To approach the concept as a discourse is to acknowledge that the term "VSE" doesn't help us accurately identify TV shows that are *objectively* special or *truly* TV milestones. Instead, to use the term is to make a claim in an effort to shape our understanding of certain shows and of TV as a medium. I raise this rather "meta" point to give us some critical distance from the VSE discourse that surrounded "The Puppy Episode."

For example, thinking of VSEs as a discourse encourages us to question the concept's founding assumptions and claims. I argued above that the TV-milestone VSE depends on and reinforces certain assumptions about TV's social function. TV's actual social impact and that impact as presented in discourse are not the same thing. For example, TV in the network era may or may not have played the kind of social role discourses attributed to it. Conversely, just because the TV-milestone VSE discourse seems to be losing its relevance doesn't mean that TV isn't as powerful today as it always was. I don't have the space here to debate the nature of TV's social function or whether "The Puppy Episode" should or shouldn't be considered a meaningful political milestone. Those are certainly worthwhile and complex questions to ponder. For example, we might find that an episode becomes politically meaningful only if it gets dubbed a TV-milestone VSE, in which case the discourse about the episode would be said to generate the thing it claimed to merely describe. Here, however, I sidestep the thorniest of those questions and simply aim to reframe claims made about the episode.

As the *TV Guide* ad mentioned above illustrates, discourses about TV-milestone VSEs are usually driven by the TV industry's promotional goals. ABC's marketing team deployed the VSE discourse strategically, leading cynical observers to dismiss "The Puppy Episode" as a brazen ratings stunt designed to attract key viewers and channel ad revenue to ABC's coffers. In the end, it did just that. Anticipating a huge audience, companies paid as much as $330,00 for a thirty-second spot on the episode—nearly twice what ABC had been charging for *Ellen*. When the Nielsen figures came in, the episode exceeded even the most optimistic projections, scoring a 23.4 rating and a 35 share (compared to *Ellen*'s year-to-date average of 9.6 rating/16 share).[7] Deploying the TV-milestone discourse seemed to pay off for ABC.

Of course, such a cynical economy-focused read fails to convey the complex dynamics at play in the VSE discourse surrounding "The Puppy Episode." Even if *Ellen*'s producers and writers, as well as DeGeneres, hoped the episode would be a ratings success, they were also no doubt motivated by a sincere desire to make *Ellen* a better TV show, to change the medium of TV, and perhaps to impact society. Furthermore, while ABC's marketing team initiated the VSE discourse, it was circulated and strengthened by activist organizations like the Gay and Lesbian Alliance Against Defamation and the Human Rights Campaign, which lauded the episode in their press releases; and by the millions of viewers who talked about it with each other, invited friends over to watch it, or went to one of the official viewing parties.

Having said that, it is still important to recognize that the TV industry and its huge promotional resources are usually responsible for defining an episode as a VSE. As a result, usually only certain moments and the experiences linked to them are publicly validated as meaningful. Take the decades-long history of LGB representations on TV. "The Puppy Episode" was just one of many episodes that disrupted TV's heterocentricism. When it served their interests, TV executives deployed the VSE discourse to help promote LGB-inclusive programs like *That Certain Summer* (aired in ABC's *Movie of the Week* show in 1972); "Killing All the Right People" (a 1987 episode of CBS's *Designing Women*) or "The One with the Lesbian Wedding" (a 1996 episode of NBC's *Friends*). Like many members of minority groups historically excluded from network-era TV, however, many LGB viewers have strong memories of many other TV episodes that included a queer character and was very special to them. Many of those TV moments were fleeting and passed by without the legitimating frame of the VSE discourse, yet they still offered those viewers something powerful—perhaps a sense of community, identification, or sexual desire. Reminding ourselves of this helps us better understand the work that VSE discourses do.

The Challenges of a Very Special Season

I now want to take a slight detour to consider the way the concept of the VSE might help us understand the challenges *Ellen* faced in its fifth (and what would prove to be its final) season. "The Puppy Episode" and the subsequent two episodes that closed out the fourth season were considered creative and ratings successes. When the fifth season began the following fall, there was intense curiosity about how the series and viewers would handle the unprecedented situation of a sitcom centered on a lesbian character. Over the course of the season, ratings started to drop, leading to an intense debate about why that was happening. Some critics argued that the show was "too" gay—that episodes focused too much on Ellen's coming-out experience, undermining the show's old charm and turning off straight viewers. DeGeneres and the show's producers argued that ABC had undermined the show's success by failing to promote it, scheduling it in an unpopular time slot, and placing a parental advisory warning on episodes. The public debate about the show's problems seemed to undermine the series even more. In April 1998, ABC announced *Ellen* would not be renewed for a sixth season.

In retrospect, there were clearly many factors that contributed to the series' problems. Here, however, I want to briefly discuss one that is especially relevant to this volume. In part, I argue, the series struggled in its fifth season because it was never able to move past the VSE discourse that surrounded the "The Puppy Episode." Heightened audience expectations, for example, proved to be a burden for *Ellen*'s producers. After viewers had been caught up in the excitement surrounding the VSE, it was always going to be difficult to get them to transition back to expecting and enjoying the standard formulas and banality of a weekly network sitcom. That challenge was only exacerbated by the unprecedented nature of what the producers were trying to do: make a network sitcom in which the title character, whom most viewers had assumed was straight for four seasons, was now openly gay.

That premise—or, more precisely, a sense of responsibility producers felt to honor Ellen DeGeneres's coming out and LGB viewers' investments in the show's story line—pushed them to put Ellen Morgan in situations that seemed to demand a certain seriousness and earnestly educational tone. For example, when Ellen tries to win the approval of Holly, the teenage daughter of her new girlfriend, Laurie, Ellen is forced to confront her own internal homophobia ("Public Displays of Affection," November 12, 1997). "Are you ashamed of being gay?" Holly asks, trying to understand why Ellen wouldn't hold Laurie's hand at the movie theater. During a heartfelt conversation, Ellen admits that it is difficult for her to be affectionate in public. "I'm trying to let go of a lot of old ideas," she says. Ellen and Holly have worked through the issue by the time Laurie comes home, and the three head out to dinner. As they get into a crowded elevator, Ellen takes Laurie's hand and smiles, at which point the studio audience erupts in applause. Although Ellen and Holly's conversation is peppered with typical sitcom jokes, its earnest tone is more akin to a VSE than a standard sitcom episode. Furthermore, the audience applause (which occurred in various episodes in the show's fifth season) signals that they think (and by extension the home viewer is supposed to think) something consequential just happened. The prevalence of such moments likely led viewers to expect the fifth season to be a string of VSEs. For viewers less invested in Ellen's gay life, it is easy to see how such moments could feel too political, serious, earnest, or gay. But even for viewers poised to applaud these special gay moments, maintaining the intensity needed to watch a VSE every week could be difficult and could position them to be disappointed if a given episode wasn't special enough.

I also argue that the producers made key decisions that made it even harder for the series and its viewers to move beyond the VSE discourse and return to normal. A defining feature of the production of TV series, especially sitcoms, is the cost-saving reliance on a minimal number of sets where scenes can play out every week. Those sets become a show's visual identity and help establish the familiarity and predictability that is so characteristic of episodic series television. For almost all of *Ellen*'s first four seasons, the show's defining locations were the living room and kitchen in Ellen's apartment and the bookstore where she worked. In the last episode of the fourth season, however, Ellen moves into a new house and quits her job at the bookstore. As a result, when viewers returned for the fifth season, ready to follow Ellen on her new journey as an out lesbian, two key elements that could have kept the series and viewers grounded in the familiar by harking back to the mundane and predictable experience they had watching *Ellen* during its first four seasons were gone. The new sets likely distanced viewers from Ellen and made the new gay-themed jokes and situations more jarring. With these changes, the fifth season of *Ellen* also failed to deliver some of the key pleasures and political impacts promised by "The Puppy Episode." If VSEs exploit the tension between the special and the normal, or the unusual and the familiar, *Ellen*'s writers reduced some of the tension by changing things too much.

Ellen's strikingly reinvented fifth season could also lead us to reconsider the fundamental argument of this chapter: that "The Puppy Episode" is a quintessential TV-milestone VSE. In fact, "The Puppy Episode" might exist in a category by itself. There are certainly other VSEs whose special status was rooted in assumptions about the importance of TV's social role (for example, *Star Trek* depicts an interracial kiss, the title character on *Maude* decides to have an abortion, and *All in the Family*'s Edith Bunker is sexually assaulted). These episodes went places both their series and TV had never gone before and raised awareness of important sociopolitical issues on a medium that seemed politically important but routinely cautious. In all of these examples, however, the disruption to the series and the medium were limited to the VSE. The dynamics of episodic TV made it relatively easy for writers and viewers to return the next week with no memory of what had happened the week before. The fact that many other TV-milestone moments have been made-for-TV movies or miniseries (for example, the 1977 slavery miniseries *Roots*, the 1984 domestic abuse drama *The Burning Bed*, and the 1984 family incest drama *Something About Amelia*) illustrates that broadcast TV often responded to forces pushing it to address politically sensitive topics (such as producers' creative aspirations and viewers' desire for socially relevant programming) through a one-off strategy that contained the disruption.

However, Ellen Morgan's coming out—affecting as it did the core identity of the title character—fundamentally shifted the series' premise in a way that couldn't be confined to the VSE. That feature distinguishes "The Puppy Episode" from any other VSE I can think of in TV history. In fact, it might push us to consider "The Puppy Episode" as having more in common with pilot episodes of groundbreaking series like *Mary Tyler Moore*, *One Day at a Time*, or *The Cosby Show*. Those series were touted for disrupting TV much as TV-milestone VSEs do. And by placing characters from groups long excluded from network lineups (that is, unmarried working women, a divorced mom, and an upscale Black family) into a very familiar and formulaic genre, they likely offered pleasures rooted in mixing the special and the banal, which VSEs often do. Unlike "The Puppy Episode," however, those pilot episodes get to start with a relatively clean slate. They disrupted TV's norms, but they did so by establishing the series' premise (that is, the foundation upon which the series' familiar predictability would be built). "The Puppy Episode" disrupted TV's norms as well as *Ellen*'s well-established premise—a disruption only exacerbated by Ellen Morgan's new home and employment status.

Just four months after *Ellen*'s finale, *Will & Grace*, an NBC sitcom with an openly gay title character, debuted. Given *Ellen*'s troubled fifth season, many observers wondered how the show would be received. When it became a critical and ratings hit, pundits tried to explain the two series' different fates. Some argued that *Ellen* had paved the way for *Will & Grace*. Although vague, there's likely some truth in that assessment. But part of the difference certainly lies in the fact that episodes of *Will & Grace* never carried the burden of having to live up to or move past the kind of expectations every episode in *Ellen*'s last season faced because of "The Puppy Episode" and its status as a milestone VSE.

Conclusion

In 2017, Ellen DeGeneres used the platform of her successful daytime talk show to celebrate the twentieth anniversary of "The Puppy Episode." Her monologue and an accompanying video reflected a common assumption about the episode: that it had ushered in a new era of gay media visibility and helped advance LGBT political equality. The video tells that story by tracing Ellen's personal journey: the coming-out episode, the whirlwind of controversy about the episode and the series' cancellation, her reputation as ratings poison, a career revived by *Finding Nemo*, her multiple Emmy award wins, a white wedding to Portia de Rossi, and a Medal of Freedom awarded by President Barack Obama. "It was the hardest thing I ever did in my life," DeGeneres says about the episode and its aftermath. "And I would not change one moment of it, because it led me to be exactly where I am today." A common narrative suggests that "The Puppy Episode" helped lead U.S. television and American society to where they are today in terms of gay inclusion. That claim undoubtedly inflates the episode's significance, yet the fact that it has gained a foothold in the popular imagination makes "The Puppy Episode" a very special episode indeed and reflects the power that discourses about VSEs can have.

Notes

1 Quoted in Tom Shales, "Closet Space and Selling 'Ellen,'" *Washington Post*, April 27, 1997.
2 Ibid. Also see Bettina Boxall, "Is 'Ellen' an Opportunity—Or Just Opportunist?," *Los Angeles Times*, April 30, 1997.
3 Jean Seligmann, "A Sitcom Coming Out?," *Newsweek*, September 23, 1996, 87.
4 Lynn Spigel, *Make Room for Television: Television and the Family Ideal in Postwar America* (Chicago: University of Chicago Press, 1992).
5 Ray Richmond, "Ellen: The Puppy Episode," *Daily Variety*, April 30, 1997. The episode would win an Emmy for best writing in a comedy series.
6 Horace Newcomb and Paul M. Hirsch, "Television as a Cultural Forum," in *Television: The Critical View*, 5th ed., ed. Horace Newcomb (New York: Oxford University Press, 1994): 503–515.
7 Joe Flint, "Out "Ellen" Gives ABC Rating Rout," *Daily Variety*, May 2, 1997.

10

"And Was There a Lesson in All This?"

Weaponizing—and Subverting—the Very Special Episode

ERIN GIANNINI

Following the discovery that popular prime-time game shows such as *Twenty-One* and *Dotto* were rigged, television networks used the situation to eliminate the sponsorship model of TV's early years and move to their preferred "magazine" style (that is, content interrupted by advertisements).[1] With multiple advertisers rather than a single sponsor, no one advertiser would be able to dictate content by any other means than buying (or not buying) time in series that were appropriate or advantageous for its products. A congressional investigation of the rigging was initiated, but neither sponsors nor networks were willing to implicate one another, and no charges were brought against either. The only result was a few mild provisions added to the Communications Act of 1934, barring game shows from rigging results.

Much scholarship has focused on how these scandals and their aftermath became a primary way in which the relationship between the government and television has evolved—that is, the two sides are allied when expedient, but each frequently views the other with distrust and derision.[2] Here I analyze the relationship between the public service announcement (PSA) and very special episode (VSE) to illustrate how they constitute a less discussed but arguably more important way in which the U.S. government continues to work in tandem with the television industry as a public service. The initial licenses for radio and the nascent television networks were granted based on the idea that they were public services and should be used for the public good,[3] similar to the U.K. and European public broadcasting models. However, U.S. telecommunications did not follow those models. Until the Public Broadcasting Service (PBS) debuted in 1969, U.S. television followed the commercial model: public service was relegated to the related but separate PSAs and VSEs. The PSAs, frequently developed by the nonprofit Ad Council through funding from both government agencies and private corporations, appear as either print or radio or television ads. Famous television examples include 1971's "Crying Indian" spot that highlighted the problem of littering.[4]

As Reba Wissner describes in chapter 1, the U.S. government has historically used not only the PSA but also the VSE as a way to both publicly and clandestinely shape television content to simultaneously spread important messages and shape what it means to be American. This propagandistic tactic was not only used in the distant past but continued at least into the late 1990s, when the Office of National Drug Control Policy (ONDCP; created by the Anti-Drug Abuse Act of 1988 and responsible for both managing an administration's policies on drug use and abuse and advising the president on drug control strategy) instituted a program offering additional advertising time to series willing to incorporate antidrug or antidrinking messages into their programs—similar to the product placement common in early television. By the time the program was terminated as a result of concerns about lack of transparency, regulatory sponsorship rules, and potential First Amendment violations, it was estimated that the ONDCP had given at least $25 million in advertising to the six broadcast networks in exchange for reviewing episodes or scripts that did (or could) incorporate an antidrug message.[5] While all broadcast networks participated, the WB network was particularly involved due to both its status as a struggling network and the teen demographic that comprised its primary viewers. Neither the head of the program, Alan Levitt, nor the networks revealed precisely which episodes had received these incentives, and the program and networks provided only a partial list of series that received them, including the WB's sitcoms *Smart Guy* and *The Wayan Brothers* and its dramas such as 7th *Heaven* and *ER*.

Indeed, only one series' episode was named in connection with the ONDCP's program, mentioned because it was rejected: "Beer Bad" (4.5), from the WB's *Buffy the Vampire Slayer.* Calling the episode "other-worldly nonsense," a spokesperson for the ONDCP claimed that "viewers wouldn't make the link to our message,"[6] a claim that is worded to suggest both the language of and purpose behind advertising (that is, persuasion), suggesting that the didacticism of VSEs was still a goal for both networks and the ONDCP, and serving as a particularly insidious form of propaganda that few, from episode writers to network executives, seemed comfortable objecting to. I first present a brief history of governmental advertising on television and then examine two episodes from the WB, "Beer Bad" (the rejected *Buffy* episode that, possibly unintentionally, would have subverted the goal of the program) and "Great Xpectations" (an episode from the arguably more mainstream *Dawson's Creek*, which was a likely candidate for ONDCP participation). Contrasting these episodes offers a window into governmental or social policy, embedded advertising, and the effects of this messaging on narrative and characters. While antidrug messaging is hardly the worst thing in the world, I argue that while "Beer Bad" displays addiction as fundamentally related to socioeconomic structures, what really makes "Great Xpectations" propagandistic is how it instead makes drug abuse into an individualized moral problem easily solved by eliminating the bad apples.

"You Can Learn a Lot from a Dummy": Government Advertising on Television[7]

To explain how the U.S. government now employs VSEs that resemble PSAs to spread its messaging in the name of the public good, I first describe the messaging's historical connections and roots at the beginning of the television industry. Television's paradoxical role as both a public good and a commercial enterprise has been debated throughout its near-century-long existence. Networks and advertisers argue that the programming they offer and goods they display are inherently part of the public good, introducing viewers to products and services they might find useful. Yet depending on the era in question, government agencies view programs and their advertising as either a "vast wasteland"[8] and a "toaster with pictures"[9] or as an entity that is ethical and capable enough to regulate itself without governmental interference.[10] The creation of PBS in 1969 provided an outlet for educational programming and thus met some of the need for it, and the idea that PBS's entertainment could be used to educate or enlighten the audience seems to be some of the impetus behind both PSAs and VSEs.

This combination of commercial and educational goals has continually spurred debates about the susceptibility of audiences to both programming and commercial messages.[11] The start of World War II brought such topics to the forefront. Uniting the country around the war effort and providing necessary information about rations, war bonds, and national security became a significant concern for the administration of President Franklin D. Roosevelt, but worries that airing such messages could be construed as propaganda made them reluctant to ask broadcasters for programming time to spread their messages. Instead, the administration partnered with the newly formed War Advertising Council[12] to publicize, via print and radio, issues such as the importance of war bonds and national security (one famous slogan used was "Loose Lips Sink Ships"), using time donated by both air and print media. In that respect, the administration (and those that followed) could theoretically avoid the charge that the government had a propaganda arm.[13]

However, the nature of the Ad Council's work was itself problematic. As Erik Barnouw argues, most of their campaigns have a "pervasive innocuousness that is apparently intentional."[14] That is, the causes they champion tend to be ones few people would object to: vehicle safety, preventing littering, forest management, and stopping drunk driving. Worse, Barnouw cites well-founded objections to these campaigns, including the United Auto Workers' statement that the Ad Council's PSAs tended to put the onus for solving issues like pollution on citizens, rather than taking on the corporate polluters;[15] and the fact that the abovementioned "Crying Indian" spot was both sponsored by Bethlehem Steel, U.S. Steel, and Allied Chemical, among others,[16] and suggested that littering was the problem, rather than the toxic chemicals that such corporations released into the air and water. Nor could the Ad Council's anticommunism campaigns of the 1950s be considered apolitical, given that their spokespeople included Dwight D. Eisenhower and Eleanor Roosevelt.[17] Indeed, Eisenhower frequently turned to the Ad Council for PSAs on anticommunism and economic issues, calling the organization "one of our great agencies for the preservation of freedom."[18] Finally, the effectiveness of the Ad Council or later programs such as Partnership for a Drug-Free America (founded in 1985) has never been fully examined. Perhaps worse from the programs' perspective, some of the campaigns (such as "This Is Your Brain on Drugs") stuck in the public consciousness as parody at best, and as showing a significant misunderstanding of both their audience and how various drugs affect individuals. (Various portrayals of the effects of alcohol or marijuana in television and film also include such misunderstandings.)

Currently, there are various outlets for targeting PSAs to youth, including the internet and Channel One (1989–2018), a content provider that provided news (with significant commercial content) to thousands of schools. Channel One itself was controversial, in that it mixed commercials and news content for what was considered a captive audience. A 2006 study by the American Academy of Pediatrics found not only that surveyed students recalled the ads more than the news items, but also that students said ads had influenced their purchasing.[19] However, one of the more egregious collusions between government, television, and the advertising industry was perpetrated by the ONDCP. During the administration of President Bill Clinton, the ONDCP responded to concerns about the effectiveness of its antidrug and antidrinking PSAs by launching an initiative that used the $1 billion the government had allocated for purchasing advertising as a trade—that is, the time allocated for PSA advertisements could be resold—to pay series to embed antidrug messages into their story lines.[20] While the series involved denied that they had changed their scripts,[21] at least one individual came forward to indicate that they had, in fact, changed a scene in an episode of the sitcom *Smart Guy* to make drinking teens look less "cool."[22] Rick Mater, who at the time was the WB's senior vice president for broadcast standards, admitted that "the White House did view scripts. . . . They did sign off on them."[23] While many of the series featuring episodes approved by the ONDCP were targeted at younger audiences (*Smart Guy*, *Beverly Hills, 90210*, and *7th Heaven*), the fact that programs offering more adult fare (such as *ER* and *Chicago Hope*) also participated indicated the wide range of demographic groups whose members would be watching. With a single exception (the *Buffy* episode "Beer Bad"), particular episodes that were part of the ONDCP's program were not named, but a review of series airing at the time (1998–2000) reveals some likely candidates. These include *ER*'s "Responsible Parties" (5.11), which featured the consequences of drunk driving, and *Chicago Hope*'s "The Heavens Can Wait" (5.23), an episode that combined alcohol abuse preventing a patient from becoming an astronaut and teens overdosing at a rave. It does not seem accidental that both episodes featured teenagers as the individuals engaging in targeted behaviors and paying significant prices, including near-fatal burns ("Responsible Parties") and a trifecta of death, sexual assault, and psychosis ("The Heavens Can Wait")—prices dating back to such propaganda films as *Reefer Madness* (1936).

During the congressional hearings on this initiative, Jeff Loeb, an advertising executive, drew a parallel between the embedded antidrug messages and product placement, referring to ONDCP's actions as "anti-product placement" (that is, drugs and drinking were "anti-brands").[24] The difference, as Loeb elucidates, is that unlike traditional product placement, which requires the tag "promotional consideration provided by" to appear in an episode's credits, the ONDCP's indirect sponsorship was not indicated. Given the importance that the ONDCP placed on influence, its staff members likely felt that revealing its sponsorship would alienate the very audience they wished to reach through this program: children and teens. However, this led to the precise charge that earlier administrations had sought to avoid through outsourcing their PSAs: that the government (in this case via the ONDCP) was producing propaganda.[25] Despite the assertions of advertisers, network executives, and some members of the congressional committee that the purpose of the initiative was laudable,[26] it was terminated in 2004.[27] Moreover, this problematic coordination between networks, advertisers, and the ONDCP was not useful. Neither its PSAs or the antidrug messaging inserted into programs made a difference in behavior,[28] except in some instances—in which researchers found that the campaigns had unintentionally encouraged the behavior they were meant to prevent.[29]

Due to the networks and the ONDCP's unwillingness to indicate which episodes were reviewed or changed (barring the exceptions mentioned above), assessing their effectiveness in transforming behavior becomes complicated, if not impossible. In that respect, the real issue becomes precisely what advertisers, networks, and the ONDCP sought to avoid: the apparent use of government resources to spread a particular message, also known as propaganda. As a *Washington Post* editorial asserted, there were few objections to these particular messages (don't abuse drugs or alcohol), but what about other messages? The example used in the editorial—a hypothetical episode of *ER* paid to weigh in on the health-care debate and parrot the administration's policy position—would at least alienate a portion of the audience (an effect that would be important to both networks and advertisers) and potentially violate propaganda rules.[30]

This is not to suggest that any series' message qualifies as propaganda because the show deals with contemporary issues. VSEs often include PSA-like messaging on everything from sexually transmitted diseases to symptoms of post-traumatic stress disorder. What sets the ONDCP's program apart is that by involving a government agency in the process, without transparency, it ran the risk of weaponizing these episodes in service of a particular biased and/or misleading agenda that was parallel to the episode's stated purpose of shedding light on social issues such as eating disorders or drug abuse but was unacknowledged—thus meeting the definition of propaganda. To examine the ways in which this operated during the ONDCP's program, I examine the two WB episodes mentioned above: "Great Xpectations" and "Beer Bad."

"One Big Fat Empty": Weaponizing the VSE for Millennial Youth[31]

In the final moments of *Dawson's Creek*'s "Great Xpectations," longtime friends Joey (Katie Holmes) and Dawson (James Van Der Beek) talk about the perils of growing up in the new millennium, where parties, which used to involve "bowling and birthday cakes," have become "high-risk adventures that could actually kill you." The episode revolves around the changing interpersonal dynamics and hopes for the future of the main characters—Dawson, Joey, Pacey (Joshua Jackson), Jen (Michelle Williams), Jack (Kerr Smith), and Andie (Meredith Monroe)—as they start their senior year of high school and prepare for the next stage in their lives. Andie, who was recently hospitalized with depression and anxiety, receives an early acceptance to Harvard University. However, due to her illness (and likely the medication used to treat it), she finds it difficult to celebrate, telling Jack (her brother) that she "feels nothing." Jack suggests that they attend a rave on the outskirts of town, where all of the main characters converge to dance (or not), chat about their love lives, wave glow sticks, and jump around in a bouncy castle. Hoping to get into the right mood, after a discussion with Jen about 3,4-Methyl enedioxy methamphetamine (MDMA) (in which Jen emphasizes its negative effects at great length), Andie sneaks a tab and proceeds to dance wildly and talk endlessly about various personal matters to her friends. Unfortunately, she has a bad reaction to the drug and ends up hospitalized with tachycardia and fever. She survives, and she and her family vow to better communicate.

The high drama and suggestion of a lesson learned are not limited to this episode. During its run, *Dawson's Creek* did not shy away from either serious issues (infidelity ["Pilot," 1.1], divorce ["The Election," 2.9], and suicide ["Abby Morgan, Rest in Peace," 2.19]) or melodramatic events or plots (secret half-siblings ["Indian Summer," 3.5], a teacher-student affair ["Baby," 1.6], parental death ["Capeside Revisited," 5.3], and killer storms ["The Two Gentlemen of Capeside," 4.3]). That said, the events of this episode are an anomaly within the series' overarching narrative and shade into propaganda, particularly Jen's lengthy speech regarding the dangers of MDMA. The use of alcohol and drugs by the main characters is relatively minimal and mostly has to do with alcohol ("Be Careful What You Wish For," 2.16; "Something Wilder," 5.13; and "100 Light Years From Home," 5.19). Even as the series transitions to college, there are no significant plots revolving around the use of marijuana, performance-enhancing drugs, or even prescription drugs such as Adderall. Aside from a second season plot point related to Joey's father selling (not using) drugs to improve his family's finances, drug use on the series is limited to the spoken (but not seen) stories about the past of Jen, a New York City transplant. Jen's sexual and substance-use history frequently positions her as a scapegoat for the other characters' misdeeds.[32] It is thus not surprising that Jen ends up being the accidental drug source in the episode, having a few tabs of MDMA left over from her clubbing days.

To the series' credit, Andie's adverse reaction to mixing Nardil, a monoamine oxidase inhibitor used to treat depression and anxiety, and MDMA is a realistic outcome. This sets "Great XPectations" apart from other likely ONDCP episodes, including one in which marijuana causes a character to act hyper and erratic, an outcome more in line with cocaine ingestion (*The Wayans Brothers*, "The High Life," 5.7). Yet despite that, "Great XPectations" still serves the ONDCP's propagandistic purposes. As suggested above, not only were the plot (the only story line in which illegal substances were used) and character elements (the choice of the driven and hyperefficient Andie as the one to take MDMA) anomalous, but so were the ways in which the episode's narrative essentially stopped at various points to provide ONDCP-mandated messaging. In a scene in line with the ONDCP's goals, the final moments of the episode feature both enlightening moments between Andie and her family about the dangers of drugs, and a lengthy conversation between Dawson and Joey (a bookend to Jen's early monologue regarding the dangers of MDMA) about how "real" the experience was and how it made them want to enjoy every moment (without resorting to substance use, of course). Andie's near-death experience thus enlightens them about what is important—an element that will carry into the next episode, in which Andie brings everyone together to forgive one another and themselves before she leaves the series, never to be heard from again ("You Had Me at Goodbye," 4.6).

While the series had several characters and plotlines that were dropped (and, in the latter case, never resolved)—an issue with any number of long-running series—none of these plotlines featured a main cast member who was so thoroughly excised as to barely warrant a mention in the remaining two seasons (even by her own family). In that respect, by situating Andie at the center of this VSE, the narrative ends up both objectifying and dismissing her in the service of a sponsored antidrug message. No wonder Andie claims she feels nothing: she becomes the antiproduct placement the ONDCP was striving for.

"The Id Wants": Subverting the VSE[33]

In contrast, *Buffy*'s "Beer Bad" offers an interesting example of what happens when television producers are less interested in bowing to governmental pressures. Given the didactic nature of the episode as a whole, it is not entirely surprising that this fairly forgettable episode from *Buffy*'s fourth season starts in a classroom with a lecture on Freud's theory of the ego, superego, and id. This was not the first time that *Buffy*—a series about a young woman chosen to fight vampires and other forces of evil—used a classroom lecture or discussion to either introduce or underscore an episode's theme: a class discussion of Othello in "Earshot" (3.18) suggested the episode's subtext about envy, and a postlecture conversation about Quasimodo's motivations in *The Hunchback of Notre Dame* offers a direct link to the characterization of Spike (James Marsters), a soulless vampire motivated to do good only because of his love for Buffy ("Crush," 5.14).

True to form, "Beer Bad" focuses on the conflict among the id, ego, and superego. Buffy (Sarah Michelle Gellar) is depressed about being rejected by a fellow college student, Parker Abrams (Adam Kaufman), after they slept together, and feels that this is the pattern of all her relationships ("The Harsh Light of Day," 4.3). Her friend Xander (Nicholas Brendan) secures a job (though he is underage) tending bar on campus, and Buffy goes to the bar to drown her sorrows. After seeing Parker with another woman, Buffy is approached by a group of young men, who invite her to join them for a pint.

The group spends that night and the next getting drunk, before they all turn into cavemen (or, in Buffy's case, a cavewoman): the beer had been cursed by the bar's owner as revenge for years of being looked down on by his college-age customers. The male patrons end up terrorizing the campus before dragging women into an underground coffee bar, which they proceed to accidentally set on fire. Buffy, while still in "cave" mode, manages to pull everyone to safety. The young men are locked in a convenient car where they can't do any more damage, and Buffy deals with her feelings for Parker by knocking him out with a tree branch.

"Beer Bad" was the only episode mentioned by name in stories about the ONDCP script-review program, explicitly because it was rejected as "other-worldly nonsense," and not "on-strategy . . . very abstract and not like real-life kids taking drugs."[34] This implies that episodes such as the above-mentioned *Wayan Brothers* episode, in which a character reacts to marijuana as if he had snorted cocaine were in line with "real-life" reactions to controlled substances. Both investigative articles and the congressional committee transcripts indicate that most of the writers and producers of participating series did not know that either scripts or completed episodes were being submitted. While certainty is impossible—as noted above, the networks were silent about which episodes were involved—it does seem unlikely that either the episode's writer, Tracey Forbes,[35] or executive producer, Joss Whedon, would have selected this episode for consideration. "Beer Bad" seems

FIG. 10.1 Buffy drowns her sorrows with evil beer.

to have been selected primarily for its title, which suggests that the episode was intended to warn viewers of the dangers of drinking—a reading that the text of "Beer Bad" does not support. (Indeed, when Xander asks Buffy: "What did we learn about beer?," Buffy's reply is simply "Foamy!")[36] Instead, "Beer Bad" focuses more on the abovementioned conflict among the ego, superego, and id. Buffy deals with the fallout from an impulsive hookup by fantasizing about an apologetic—and shirtless—Parker bearing ice cream and flowers, while the guys drinking with Buffy attempt to rationalize their alcohol consumption, and Parker to justify his promiscuity to Buffy's best friend, Willow (Alyson Hannigan). However, Willow sees through Parker's comments and calls him "id boy."

Yet the other narrative thread running through the episode is the issue of class and socioeconomic status, and it is one of the ways in which "Beer Bad" subverts the intent of the ONDCP-sponsored VSE. The bar owner, Jack (Steven M. Porter), deliberately taints the beer with a formula created by his warlock brother to reduce the well-off and pompous college students to Neanderthals. He explicitly paints beer as a social equalizer: "That's the great thing about beer. It makes all men the same." His contention is paralleled by the young men, who assert that: "Had the earliest morality developed under the influence of beer, there would be no good or evil. There would just be kinda nice and pretty cool." Furthermore, the owner offers Xander a potential glimpse of his own future: as the only one of his friends coded working class and unable to afford college, Xander struggles throughout the fourth season to find his place, both among his friends and in the wider community. Jack's bitterness over his bad treatment by his bar's patrons suggests one possible future for Xander, as the bar's customers mock and talk down to him as well.

This conflation of alcohol and class dynamics is a feature of the series in general. Not only are Xander's parents alcoholics ("Amends," 3.10, and "Hell's Bells," 6.16), implying that his poor academic performance and socioeconomic status are related to his parents' addictive behavior, but the other episode in which drinking is featured significantly ("Reptile Boy," 2.5) touched on issues of class and misogyny. The episode is set at a fraternity house, where Buffy and her frenemy Cordelia (Charisma Carpenter) are served spiked drinks and pass out. They wake up chained in the house's basement and designated to be sacrificed to a giant snake demon that is the source of the fraternity members' socioeconomic success. As in "Beer Bad," the Freudian implications are clear, and class issues are a significant subplot. Not only does the demon require a sacrifice of women to ensure its upper-class male followers' success, but Xander, who crashes the party in an ill-fated attempt to rescue his friends, is relentlessly mocked by the fraternity brothers: he is stripped naked, forced to wear women's undergarments and a blonde wig, and made to dance before being thrown out. As he storms off, he complains to himself that even if he were successful later in life, they would "still have more" than he would ("Reptile Boy"). Like the later "Beer Bad," however, any VSE moralizing is tempered with humor. For example, when Buffy says she had "one drink, told one lie," her mentor, Giles (Anthony Steward Head), replies: "And you were nearly devoured by a giant demon snake. The words 'let that be a lesson' are a tad redundant" ("Reptile Boy").

In both episodes, the focus is less on the toxic effects of drinking than it is on gender and class bias. The contemporaneous *Dawson's Creek* also featured a working-class character (Joey Potter) on whose family substance abuse had taken its toll, but Joey is presented as highly intelligent and is accepted to an Ivy League university, with fees paid for by a scholarship and her wealthier friends' generosity ("Admissions," 4.17). In contrast, Xander has a series of minimum-wage jobs as his friends start college, only eventually realizing he is skilled at carpentry and finding a degree of success in the trades ("The Replacement," 5.3). Studies have found that income does play a part in the "hazardous use" of alcohol[37]; that is, people of lower socioeconomic status tend to be prey to more of the negative consequences of alcohol use.[38] The *Buffy* twist is that Xander, despite not consuming alcohol himself in either "Reptile Boy" or "Beer Bad," does experience the consequences of drinking both through his general upbringing and the individual events of these episodes.

Thus, since the ONDCP linked substance abuse—and its consequences—to socioeconomic characteristics rather than the ostensibly individualized and private problems seen in other VSEs (such as driving under the influence, overdosing, death, and alienation from friends and/or family members), it is not surprising that the organization dismissed "Beer Bad" as not being on message. Despite the episode's simplistic moral—alcohol can have a detrimental effect on the drinkers' behavior and attitudes—neither Buffy nor her companions seem to suffer any long-term consequences: no one dies, drops out, or becomes addicted to alcohol. Indeed, Buffy's reversion to "Cave Slayer" ("Beer Bad") puts an end to her grief over Parker and allows her to move on. In both respects, "Beer Bad" subverts the ONDCP-sponsored intended use of VSEs and refuses to overtly moralize or propagandize about the use of alcohol.

Conclusion

Given both the secrecy surrounding participation in and the accusations of producing governmental propaganda, it is unsurprising that the ONDCP terminated its program of embedded messaging and antiproduct placement when it was discovered. Such messaging, at least in contemporary television, is supposed to be woven organically into programs. Unlike early, single-sponsor television, which frequently had hosts and actors pause to shill products, contemporary placements can range from the sight of an Apple iPod in use by a character (*Supernatural*'s "Lazarus Rising," 4.1) to the Fox network's building an entire episode around characters trying to score tickets to the premiere of the film *Avatar*, which shared a studio with the series in question (*Bones*' "The Gamer in the Grease," 5.9). While the latter example was more over-the-top than the former, the idea that those individuals would be excited by the film was not out of line with their established characters.[39]

Yet by definition, VSEs are supposed to stand out, to impart a message to the audience. It may not have been explicitly stated by the ONDCP or the advertisers and networks that participated, but it was inherent to the program that the sponsored episodes be "special" and impactful. Both the episodes examined here as well as others suspected of participating in the program aired near or during one of the three sweeps periods (November, February, and May), also suggesting these episodes constituted event programming. *Dawson's Creek*'s "Great XPectations" served as a de facto two-part episode that simultaneously operated as a swan song for a central character, underscoring its "event" status.

The danger of this type of initiative, however, is not only the lack of transparency and undeniable propagandizing but the near-uniform way neither the Congressional subcommittee nor commentators were comfortable expressing outright condemnation of the ONDCP's collusion with networks or the questionable use of taxpayer money. To do so, it seems, would suggest that either elected leaders or editorial staffs were not antidrug. The ONDCP, in essence, weaponized the VSE to forward an agenda few would feel comfortable objecting to.

Notes

Chapter title quotation taken from the *Buffy the Vampire Slayer* episode "Beer Bad" (4.5). Numbers following episode titles throughout chapter denote season number and episode number.

1 Michele Hilmes, *Only Connect: A Cultural History of Broadcasting in the United States*, 3rd ed. (Boston: Wadsworth Cengage Learning, 2011); William Boddy, *Fifties Television: The Industry and Its Critics* (Urbana: University of Illinois Press, 1993).
2 Hilmes, *Only Connect*; Boddy, *Fifties Television*; Erik Barnouw, *The Sponsor: Notes on a Modern Potentate* (New York: Oxford University Press, 1978); Robert W. McChesney, *Rich Media, Poor Democracy: Communication Politics in Dubious Times* (New York: New Press, 2000).
3 Hilmes, *Only Connect*, 43 and 180–181.
4 The actor featured in the spot, Iron Eyes Cody, was in fact an Italian-American actor who had played Native Americans in several films and television series from the 1930s to the 1960s. His actual ethnicity was not revealed until after his death in 1999.
5 Daniel Forbes, "Prime-Time Propaganda: How the White House Secretly Hooked Network TV on Its AntiDrug Message," *Salon*, January 13, 2000, https://www.salon.com/2000/01/13/drugs_6/.
6 Quoted in ibid.
7 This quote appears in a PSA on seatbelt usage and driver safety for the US Department of Transportation, which ran from 1985 to 1999.
8 Newton N. Minow, "Television and Public Interest," May 9, 1961, American Rhetoric Speech Online Speech Bank, http://www.americanrhetoric.com/speeches/newtonminow.htm..
9 Caroline E. Mayer, "FCC Chief's Fears Fowler Sees Threat in Regulation," *Washington Post*, February 6, 1983, https://www.washingtonpost.com/archive/business/1983/02/06/fcc-chiefs-fears-fowler-sees-threat-in-regulation/06611aaf-15b8-420d-97ec-e239ddffb93b/.
10 Val E. Limburg, "Ethics and Television," in *Encyclopedia of Television*, ed. Horace Newcomb (New York: Fitzroy Dearborn, 2004), 1:817–818.
11 Hilmes, *Only Connect*; Barnouw, *The Sponsor*.
12 The council was a joint effort of the Association of National Advertisers and the American Association of Advertising Agencies.
13 Hilmes, *Only Connect*, 154–155.
14 Barnouw, *The Sponsor*, 141.
15 Ibid., 141–142.
16 John Mcdonough, "Ad Council at 60—Facing a Crossroads," *Ad Age*, April 29, 2002, https://adage.com/article/special-report-innovations-in-print/ad-council-60-facing-a-crossroads/52328.
17 The choice of political spokespeople was not limited to the 1950s. For example, Nancy Reagan (then the first lady) appeared on "The Reporter," an episode in the fifth season of *Diff'rent Strokes*, to discuss her newly launched "Just Say No" antidrug program.
18 Quoted in Craig Allen, *Eisenhower and the Mass Media: Peace, Prosperity, and Prime-Time TV* (Chapel Hill: University of North Carolina Press, 1993), 38–39.
19 Erica Weintraub Austin, Yi-Chun Chen, Bruce E. Pinkleton, et al., "Benefits and Costs of *Channel One* in a Middle-School Setting and the Role of Media-Literacy Training," *Pediatrics* 117, no. 3 (March 2006): e423–e433.
20 Forbes, "Prime-Time Propaganda."
21 "The White House, the Networks and TV Censorship," Hearing before the Subcommittee on Telecommunications, Trade, and Consumer Protection, February 9, 2000, https://www.govinfo.gov/content/pkg/CHRG-106hhrg62969/html/CHRG-106hhrg62969.htm.

22 Quoted in Veronika Bondarenko, "The Anti-Drug Agency Trump Wants to Gut Was Once in Charge of a Scandal-Filled Media Campaign," *Business Insider*, May 9, 2017, https://www.businessinsider.in/the-anti-drug-agency-trump-wants-to-gut-was-once-in-charge-of-a-scandal-filled-media-campaign/articleshow/58602304.cms

23 Quoted in Forbes, "Prime-Time Propaganda."

24 Quoted in ibid.

25 "Drugs, TV and Propaganda" (editorial), *Washington Post*, January 15, 2000, https://www.washingtonpost.com/archive/opinions/2000/01/15/drugs-tv-and-propaganda/099b0494-7663-4f1e-9cf3-541c2cc4d08f/.

26 Forbes, "Prime-Time Propaganda."

27 The ONDCP and its partners were involved in other scandals, including the creation of an antidrug news story sent to local news stations in 2004 without disclosing it had been produced by the agency (which violated domestic propaganda rules). In a separate case, two of the advertising executives working with the ONDCP were sentenced to fourteen months each in federal prison for defrauding the agency. See Bondarenko, "The Anti-Drug Agency Trump Wants to Gut Was Once in Charge of a Scandal-Filled Media Campaign."

28 Ira Teinowitz, "Study Faults White House Drug Ads," *Ad Age*, January 19, 2004, http://www.mapinc.org/newscsdp/v04/n124/a01.html; Elias Allara, Marica Ferri, Allesandra Bo, et al., "Are Mass-Media Campaigns Effective in Preventing Drug Use? A Cochrane Systematic Review and Meta-Analysis," *BMJ Open* 5, no. 9 (2015): e007449; Drug Policy Alliance, "Congress to Decide Whether to Renew Controversial and Costly Anti-Drug Ads," May 7, 2003, http://www.drugpolicy.org/news/2003/05/congress-decide-whether-renew-controversial-and-costly-anti-drug-ads.

29 Robert Hornik, Lela Jacobsohn, Robert Orwin, et al., "Effects of the National Anti-Drug Media Campaign on Youths," *American Journal of Public Health* 98, no. 12 (December 2008): 2229–2236.

30 "Drugs, TV and Propaganda."

31 Quotation is from the episode "Great XPectations".

32 Completing the trope of the reformed bad girl, Jen dies of an unspecified heart ailment at the end of the series (". . . Must Come to an End," 6.24).

33 Quotation from *Buffy the Vampire Slayer*'s "Beer Bad" (4.8).

34 Quoted in Forbes, "Prime-Time Propaganda."

35 The *Buffy* writing staff was remarkably stable throughout the series' seven seasons, as was also the case with other Whedon properties such as *Angel*, *Firefly*, and *Dollhouse*. Forbes was something of an anomaly, however: she wrote only three episodes of *Buffy*—all in the fourth season—with two of them ("Beer Bad" and "Where the Wild Things Are," 4.18) frequently topping lists of the worst *Buffy* episodes.

36 The attempts by Giles, Buffy's mentor and father figure, to moralize about substance use is similarly undermined by Xander's reminder of Giles's partying past, referring to him as "Mr. 'I spent the sixties in an electric-kool-aid-funky-Satan groove.'"

37 Katherine M. Keyes and Deborah S. Hasin, "Socio-Economic Status and Problem Alcohol Use: The Positive Relationship between Income and the DSM-IV Alcohol Abuse Diagnosis," *Addiction* 103, no. 7 (July 2008): 1120.

38 Susan E. Collins, "Associations between Socioeconomic Factors and Alcohol Outcomes," *Alcohol Research Current Reviews* 38, no. 1 (2016): 83–94. Another study found that binge drinking in college—as in "Beer Bad"—was not necessarily predictive of developing alcoholism as an adult. See Wendy S. Slutske, "Alcohol Use

Disorders among US College Students and Their Non-College-Attending Peers," *Archives of General Psychiatry* 62, no. 3 (March 2005): 321–327.

39 Whether Apple was pleased with the placement in *Supernatural* is questionable: the presence of an iPod in the series' iconic 1967 Chevy Impala was dismissed by the character of Dean (Jensen Ackles) as "douch[ing] it up," as he tossed the player into the backseat.

11

Animating Entertainment, or Very Special Media Reflexivity

MIMI WHITE

The Simpsons (Fox, 1989–present) and *Animaniacs* (Amblin Productions-Warner Bros., 1993–1998, Hulu, 2020–present) are animated series that thrived in the 1990s. In some respects, they are quite different. *The Simpsons* is a prime-time sitcom that has achieved iconic status in global popular culture. It debuted on Fox in December 1989 and completed its thirtieth season in May 2019. At that point, it was television's longest-running sitcom, with 662 episodes. *Animaniacs* was produced and scheduled for children's television[1] and had a shorter network run. It premiered in May 1994 with a season of 65 episodes and continued with four years of sporadic production (34 new episodes were produced between 1994 and 1998). The series was revived in 2020 for the streaming platform Hulu.[2] Despite the differences, both programs are known for their irreverent, parodic sensibility and their wide range of intertextual citation, with references to historical, cultural, and media figures and events—centrally including television.[3] The referential scope of *Animaniacs* in particular often seems well beyond the ken of the ostensible target audience.[4]

Both shows aired special episodes that call attention to their artifice and assert their place in media history. Because these shows are normally intertextual and self-reflective, it is arguable that they do this on a routine basis, if only tacitly. The very special episodes (VSEs) announce their difference from the outset, often breaking the routine fiction to signal their difference, and the self-conscious reflexivity goes beyond that of regular episodes. In the process, the VSEs of *The Simpsons* and *Animaniacs* diverge from the stereotypical image of VSEs on network television, because they emphasize media forms and histories rather than social issues, cultural celebrations, or current events. Yet the episodes are instructive, demonstrating how VSEs are an amplification rather than a disruption of routine television, because the exceptional tenor and tone of VSEs always play out in the familiar context of a specific show.

The Simpsons and *Animaniacs* are routinely self-aware, self-reflexive, and parodic texts, so it makes sense that their VSEs intensify these tendencies. Indeed, the shows make fun of VSEs. In the process, they not only comment on themselves and their place in media history but also offer insights into television more generally—especially broadcast television. They draw on, and thwart, expectations about the VSE, live television, and television's engagement with history and nostalgia.

Consider the following episodes:

May 23, 1994. *Animaniacs*, season 1, episode 65: "The Warners 65th Anniversary Special" presented itself as the live broadcast of a tribute to the program's central characters, Yakko, Wakko, and Dot Warner. An opening production number celebrates the Warner siblings. The emcee traces the arc of their career, supported by film clips with studio personnel, celebrities, and classic cartoon characters who tell stories about working with the Warners and the disruptive hijinks on the studio lot that led to their being locked up in the water tower on the Warner Bros.' studio lot.[5]

December 3, 1995. *The Simpsons*, season 7, episode 10: "The 138th Episode Spectacular" was a special live broadcast from the Springfield Civic Center, celebrating America's "favorite non-prehistoric cartoon family" and hosted by Troy McClure, a recurring character on the show. The episode briefly recounts the program's history, mentioning the program's creators (Matt Groening, James Brooks, and Sam Simon) and features clips from the program's history—beginning with sketches from *The Tracy Ullman Show*, "outtakes" from later episodes, letters from viewers, and trivia questions.

The titles of both of these episodes—the "65th Anniversary Special" and the "138th Episode Spectacular"—make similar jokes, referring to the programs' cumulative episode count as the occasion for a VSE. In the process, the titles suggest that celebratory and anniversary programs, which are one type of VSE, are prone to make overblown claims about their own specialness. In the case of *Animaniacs*, the 65th episode was simply the last episode of the first season, and 138th episode of *The Simpsons* came in the middle of the seventh season. In the context of the television program schedule, these are unexceptional moments.

Both episodes also profess to be live, even though that is obviously not the case: the programs are animated, so the characters are not even alive, let alone live. The episodes lay claim to liveness to celebrate the characters at the center of their animated fictions and self-consciously mimic television's self-congratulatory practices that typically combine liveness with historical film and video clips. Furthermore, they explore their own status as television shows and confound relative levels of fiction. For example, although Troy McClure is a recurring fictional character on *The Simpsons*, he hosts the live special in the characters' honor that identifies *The Simpsons* as a television show, positioning him both inside and outside the fiction of *The Simpsons*.

In programs that are thick with references to other texts and that regularly flaunt their artifice, these special episodes amplify the parodic self-reflexivity. In the process, they highlight the self-referential tendencies of American television more generally, as well as the many ways that it self-consciously displays its own history, liveness, and artifice. They also cite Hollywood's cartoon history, animated texts that also demonstrate self-referential awareness, often through caricature and parody.[6] In this larger context of multiple media intertexts—including film, television, animation, and Warner Bros. cartoons (as the proximate reference for *Animaniacs* in particular)—it is hardly surprising that *The Simpsons* and *Animaniacs* flagrantly promote their own fictive status. They do this most aggressively and explicitly in their VSEs, where they position themselves in television and media history and at the same time explore their own representational contradictions and contortions. The live spectacular or anniversary episodes make clear that in many ways, liveness is an animating, performative discourse as much as or more than it is an inherent quality of television. As a result, *The Simpsons* and *Animaniacs* advance themselves as savvy television texts that know their own history, media culture, and American culture and society more generally.[7] In short, the VSEs of *The Simpsons* and *Animaniacs* are instructive about the programs themselves and offer ways of thinking about VSEs, television, and media history.

On *The Simpsons* and Their Histories

The final episode of the eleventh season of *The Simpsons* presented itself as an episode of a television documentary series *Behind the Laughter* featuring the Simpson family. "Behind the Laughter" (May 21, 2000) was a parody of the cable television VH1 music documentary series *Behind the Music* (1997–2014).[8] The Simpsons are depicted as a real family that started a scripted television series, with the family members playing themselves on TV. The episode traces the genesis of the show, the family's rising fame and wealth, subsequent scandals and squabbles that lead to the breakup of their creative partnership, and an eventual reunion. While parody of this sort is typical for *The Simpsons*,[9] this episode is often singled out because, in the language of fandom, it is "outside the canon," shifting the premise that otherwise prevails on the program, where the Simpsons are a fictional, animated sitcom family.

The episode self-consciously asserts the program's place in a broader mediascape. *Behind the Music* told stories of well-known bands and musicians and their successes and woes. "Behind the Laughter" does something similar for the Simpson family, serving as an exposé of sorts, but it does this in terms that call attention to the program's status as animation and to the Simpson family and *The Simpsons* as an integral part of American media culture. The episode pushes the boundaries of the program's routine intertextuality, especially by granting the family a celebrity status that propels them into a wholly new television format, the celebrity documentary. It places the Simpson family at one remove from themselves, as a real family that plays a sitcom family on *The Simpsons*. What looks from one perspective like a one-time clever joke accrues critical depth by doubling the fiction and calling attention to the ways in which *The Simpsons* comments on American television, including itself.

"Behind the Laughter" also hints at narrative situations that one might find on VSEs elsewhere on television. As the story is told, Homer and Marge started using television to control their three unruly children. This initiates the family's television addiction, which in turn leads to the creation of *The Simpsons* once Homer decides that he could make programs that represent ordinary families better than the idealized TV families they constantly watch. As Bart notes, "TV families were always hugging and tackling issues." The idea that watching too much television is the instigation for *The Simpsons* is a self-reflexive joke, because the program is deeply versed in television and media culture. Its knowledge of what might be considered "too much" television and media culture is one of the things that makes *The Simpsons* a smart television show. In "Behind the Laughter," excess television watching is a symptom of bad parenting, which implies an adverse moral judgment of Homer and Marge. The episode also addresses Homer's addiction to painkillers owing to his frequent physical exertions and accidents on the show. Drug abuse is also at stake when Lisa mentions that the children were given hormones to delay their physical development to keep the series going.[10]

As "Behind the Laughter" breaks canon, it complicates the reflexive and intertextual logic of the show. The episode may be a parody of *Behind the Music*, but it also comments on *The Simpsons* as an animated show. For example, as a cartoon character, Homer can't really get hurt or addicted to drugs. Lisa's remarks about growth-delaying hormones similarly call attention to the show as animation. The Simpson children have stayed the same size and age not because of growth-delaying hormones but because they are animated figures; they can be any age and size the producers want.

"Behind the Laughter" is not the only *Simpsons* episode that breaks the fiction and calls attention to the show as a television show. Season seven's "The 138th Episode Spectacular" and season eight's "The Simpson's Spin-Off Showcase" also treat *The Simpsons* reflexively, as a television show. Both episodes are presented as gala events hosted by the actor Troy McClure, a featured character from *The Simpsons*, who is nonetheless able to separate himself from the fictive world of *The Simpsons* to celebrate the show as a show. Moreover,

"The 138th Episode Spectacular" presents a history of the show that is very different from the one presented on "Behind the Laughter."

Troy McClure hosts "The Simpsons Spin-Off Showcase" from the Museum of TV and Television.[11] He addresses the audience and explains that the Fox network asked the creators of *The Simpsons* to come up with thirty-five new shows. The "Spin-Off Showcase" offers previews of the three new programs they ended up developing: *Chief Wiggum, PI*, a crime series set in New Orleans; *The Love-Matic Grandpa*, a sitcom where Grandpa Abe Simpson is reincarnated as a novelty love-tester machine in Moe's Bar; and a live show, *The Simpson Family Smile-Time Variety Hour*. Each of these refers to a familiar television program or genre: the detective series (more specifically, *Magnum, P.I.* [CBS, 1980–1988]), the fantasy sitcom *My Mother the Car* (NBC, 1965–1966), and the live variety show.[12]

The representational play with levels of reality and fiction in all of these episodes flaunts their critical self-awareness with patent silliness, as they call attention to the elastic distinctions between fiction and reality. This is especially pointed in "The 138th Episode Spectacular," which claims to be broadcasting live. In addition to being animated (decidedly not live), most of the content for the spectacular is supplied by film clips.[13] By touting its live episode, *The Simpsons* both celebrates its own importance within legacy television as part of television history, and panders to the presumptive cachet of live television programming.

Many other episodes expressly deal with American media culture within the ongoing fictive world of *The Simpsons*.[14] For example, "Itchy & Scratchy & Marge" (season 2, episode 9; December 20, 1990) raises questions about violence in children's television and censorship; "Krusty Gets Cancelled," (season 4, episode 22; May 13, 1993) looks at television competition and assembles a cast of celebrities featured in a come-back show for Krusty; "Homer's Barbershop Quartet" (season 5, episode 1; September 30, 1993) and "Bart Gets Famous" (season 5, episode 12; February 3, 1994) look at the fleeting nature of popular culture celebrity; and "The Day the Violence Died" (season 7, episode 18; March 17, 1998) deals with plagiarism in the creative media industries, emphasizing the copying, imitation, and citation that are common in popular media culture and qualities of postmodern art. These episodes (and others) develop these issues in narrative forms. They also have a reflexive edge, because *The Simpsons* itself participates in these aesthetic practices.

In this context, it is also worth considering "Homer^3," one of the segments from the 1995 annual Halloween special ("Treehouse of Horror VI," season 7, episode 6; October 29, 1995). These annual specials offered parodies of a wide range of horror and science-fiction stories from literature, film, and television, and in the process they expanded the genre boundaries of *The Simpsons*. "Homer^3" goes further, literally transforming the form of the program's routine animation when Homer goes through a wall and ends up as a 3-D animated figure in an abstract space. While bemoaning his disorientation, he also comments on his thick form and makes a joke about the high cost of 3-D animation at the time: "This place feels expensive. It's like I'm wasting a fortune just standing here."

The VSEs of *The Simpsons* augment the program's routine media reflexivity and intertextuality, breaking the continuity of the fictive world. They emphasize the program's constructed artifice and its connections to American television history, despite the patent artifice of the animated series itself. They place the show and its characters in American media culture by telling its history, however variable that proves to be across episodes. This includes previewing the program's derivative spin-offs at the Museum of TV and Television, which explicitly positions *The Simpsons* itself as a reference text in lineages of television programming. With their distinctive self-awareness, the VSEs support the program's claims to cultural legitimacy, clinching the media legacy of *The Simpsons* even as the show ran for decades after these self-anointing, VSEs first aired on television.

On *Animaniacs* and Irreverent Citation

Animaniacs is even more intertextual and media-reflexive than *The Simpsons*, given its literal and fictive roots at Warner Bros. The Animaniacs live on the Warner Bros. lot, and the premise of the show places them squarely in Hollywood history. The Animaniacs are Yakko, Wakko, and Dot Warner, creatures of the Warner Bros. animation studio in its early days. In their escapades, they regularly interact with such studio personnel as Thaddeus Plotz, the producer; Ralph, the security guard; and Dr. Otto von Scratchansniff, the studio psychiatrist. They also encounter a wide array of historical and cultural figures in and beyond the studio.[15]

Animaniacs is sometimes labeled a variety show (for example, on IMDb and Wikipedia) because it offers a mix of sketches with recurring characters instead of a single, cohesive diegetic world. The recurring characters include the Goodfeathers, a trio of Italian-American pigeons modeled on a combination of Martin Scorsese's *Goodfellas* and Francis Ford Coppola's *The Godfather* (there is a Godpigeon); Mindy, a toddler who is often left in the care of Buttons, her dog, and who barely avoids calamitous accidents; Slappy Squirrel, a cartoon veteran, and her nephew, Skippy; Rita and Runt, a stray cat and dog; and Flavio and Marita, a wealthy, hip hippo couple. The lab mice Pinky and the Brain also originated on *Animaniacs* and were later featured on their own spin-off show.

Across the varied sketches, the program refers to a wide range of cultural intertexts, citing everything from Gilbert and Sullivan and *La Bohème* to mid-twentieth-century Swedish art cinema—specifically, Ingmar Bergman's *The Seventh Seal*. The Warners interact with Beethoven, Picasso, Einstein, and Michelangelo, among other figures, sowing disorder that variously fosters or stymies their work. The Goodfeathers sing about wanting to stand on the head of the Scorsese statue in the park to a melody borrowed from *West Side Story*.

Animaniacs also includes some references to children's culture, such as the classic children's book *Good Night Moon* and PBS's popular purple singing dinosaur, Barney (who is named Baloney on the *Animaniacs*). However, children's culture is not the dominant source of the program's references. Animated characters from classic Warner Bros. cartoons also make regular brief appearances. For example, a number of them are included in the clips for the anniversary special, and in "Turkey Jerky" (season 1, episode 46) Miles Standish, hunting turkeys for the first Thanksgiving, crosses paths with Elmer Fudd, who unsurprisingly is hunting rabbits.[16]

In this context of rampant and diverse intertextual references, "The Warners 65th Anniversary Special" was perhaps just another *Animaniacs* episode. Yet it expressly signals its special status, opening with a group of animated characters, including a giant fish, gathered around a couch. One of them addresses the camera and announces that *My Father the Tuna* won't be seen tonight because of a special presentation.[17] This is followed by a distinctive opening sequence, as the screen fills with the word "ANIMANIACS" in receding neon colors, which rotates and flies toward the viewer, followed by a second title card that says "An Animaniacs Special Presentation." A voice-over announces, "Live from the Dorothy Chandelier Pavilion, it's the *Animaniacs* 65th Anniversary Special." An opening production number featuring Liza Minnelli ends with the introduction of the host, Bob Hope (or an animated figure that looks and speaks like him), who tells some jokes before launching into the Warners' life story. Throughout the festive opening, the honorees (Yakko, Wakko, and Dot) complain about the dull production and bad jokes and wonder when they can leave, to the consternation of their tablemate, Dr. Scratchansniff.

Their story begins at the Warner Bros. animation studio, Termite Terrace, in 1930, when the Warner siblings were created to liven up cartoons featuring the good-natured but bland Buddy. From the start, they are a force of disorder, and the animator who created them immediately goes crazy. In his filmed recollections, their director describes working with them as the worst time of his life. Only Buddy reports fond memories of the Animaniacs. In a series of clips from the early films, Buddy goes about his business until the Warners show up with giant mallets and pummel him. Soon, Buddy is fired and replaced by Yakko, Wakko, and Dot, who terrorize directors and wreak havoc on the studio lot. Thus they end up—as the program's title sequence song recounts—locked in the studio water tower, from which they periodically break loose. For the anniversary special, a host of familiar characters appear in screened clips to help tell the Warners' story: Bugs Bunny, Porky Pig, and Yosemite Sam, among other cartoon characters alongside an array of actual and fictive studio figures and iconic fictional film characters such as Spartacus, George Bailey, Baby Jane, and the Gipper.

During transitions to commercial breaks, *Animaniacs* cuts to a brooding figure who is watching the live program and muttering about how the Warners

FIG. 11.1 History without nostalgia. Buddy joins the Animaniacs just before the bomb goes off.

wrecked his life. As the show reaches its climax, the figure is revealed to be Buddy, who plants a bomb in the podium, timed to go off when the Warners take the stage. However, when they finally get to the podium, they make special mention of Buddy and thank him graciously. He is so touched by their remarks that he joins them on stage for an unplanned reunion and, predictably, ends up the victim of the podium explosion. To cap things off, a giant mallet suspended above the stage as part of the decor falls and crushes him.

This VSE is playfully self-aware of its status as animation, and it is full of references to other texts and figures that situate *Animaniacs* and its characters in a longer history of American film and television. Buddy was a Warner Bros. cartoon character in the mid-1930s, created after a core group of animators led by Leon Schlesinger left Warner Bros. for MGM, taking the characters they had created with them. The episode tweaks history by dating the Warner siblings' creation to 1930—a few years before Buddy was originally created. But invoking this lesser-known animated character indicates the range of media knowledge and animation history that the program mobilized, albeit with a deeply irreverent sensibility.

With Buddy's appearance, the program also calls attention to its own storytelling. While the episode is initially presented as a live spectacular, the scenes of the shrouded figure watching the show on television shift the framework of the fiction. Buddy is not part of the live show, except in film clips. When the two strands of narrative—the live anniversary show and Buddy brooding about the Warners—come together in the final scene, events effectively play out as they did in the cartoon clips. In the process, the difference between live television and old film is collapsed, at least temporarily, as the punch line derives its force as much from what happened decades earlier as from the live celebration in the episode's present—though it also demonstrates the risks (and thrill) of television liveness, where the unexpected may erupt at any time.

Animaniacs routinely refers to film, animation, and entertainment history and focuses attention on the telling of that history in ways that disperse the textual strategies of VSEs across the series. "Testimonials" (season 1, episode 26) intersperses interviews about the Warners with aged actors and vaudevillians between three narrative sketches—including one with Rudolph Valentino, and animation resembling 1930s cartoons. The interviewees who provide the testimonials are evidently fictive characters, but they refer to prominent figures from the world of entertainment such as Jack Benny, George Burns, and Milton Berle (with multiple comments about his animosity toward the Warner kids, who regularly dropped anvils on him). These oral histories confirm what we see in the animated sketches: the Animaniacs are unruly, anti-authoritarian creatures who sow chaos in their wake.

"Animators Alley" (season 1, episode 42) frames a series of sketches with the Warner siblings interviewing the animation pioneer Cappy "Cap" Barnhouse. Cappy drones on, loses his focus, and bores the Animaniacs so much that they resort to a variety of tactics to avoid having to sit and listen to him. With the show's typical mix of historical self-awareness and irreverent silliness, Cappy claims that the Warner Bros. studio was originally established to make pies until Leon Schlesinger proposed that they make cartoons instead. He also mentions that Rudolf Ising and Hugh Harman created Bosko the Talk-Ink Kid—anticipating the "65th Anniversary Special," since Buddy was widely seen as a replacement for Bosko at Warner Bros., after Harman and Ising moved to MGM.

A number of episodes proclaim special status by using the same opening titles as the "65th Anniversary Special." "Very Special Opening" (season 1, episode 35) starts with the special titles, followed by the Warners addressing the camera and inviting all the members of the household to gather around the TV set and join them for a VSE. Dot asks, "And what's special about it?" In response, Wakko pulls up his long blue turtleneck and replies, "I'm not wearing any pants." As the episode transitions to the regular titles sequence, it seems that the "very special" status is a passing joke, especially since Wakko always wears the same long turtleneck, presumably without any pants. But it proves to be somewhat apt, since the episode scrambles the usual array of characters: Mindy the toddler is paired with Brain the lab mouse; Rita the stray cat appears with Pinky, and the cat ends up eating the mouse; Runt the stray dog is teamed up with Pesto from the Goodfeathers; and so on. Another episode that opens with the special titles sequence turns out to be a Christmas episode that includes a parody version of *A Christmas Carol* (season 1, episode 49). But its special status is questionable because it isn't the only Christmas episode of the season. In other words, the *Animaniacs* special opening titles may signal an exceptional VSE, but not necessarily. It is just as likely a way of making fun of network television's VSEs, or perhaps a way to add twenty or thirty seconds to an episode that would otherwise run just a bit short.

With every episode replete with references to media and culture, including an exceptional knowledge of animation history, it can be hard to clearly differentiate routine and special episodes. This is exacerbated by the show's ongoing play with the artifice of animation as the lines between fiction and reality and between fiction and history are redrawn.[18] In the "65th Anniversary Special" and other episodes, cartoon characters have a specific history as creations of studio animators. But once they are created, they don't stay in their cels. Instead, they assume full subjecthood in the world of the studio, as actors who perform in cartoons. Thus, the Warner siblings can drive directors crazy, and when Buddy gets fired, he isn't left on the drawing board but retires to Ojai and becomes a nut farmer.

More generally, animated creatures and fiction film characters have the same status as "human" characters; and the "human" characters include a mix of historical and fictional figures, including known actors and the prominent fictional characters they portrayed in films from the studio era. All of these characters readily move through the animated world of *Animaniacs* with equivalent status, whether they are walking around the studio in episodic sketches or appearing as celebrities in filmed clips as part of live specials. *Animaniacs* both calls attention to and existentially challenges the nature of television and film mediation by exploiting and calling attention to its own artificial, mediating status as an animated series.

The Animated VSE and Media History

While only a few episodes of *The Simpsons* and *Animaniacs* are singled out as very special, the textual dynamics at work in "The Warners 65th Anniversary Special" and "The 138th Episode Spectacular" are also evident in many other episodes. On this basis, one might wonder just how special these episodes (or others that similarly break the fiction or call attention to themselves as special) are. This uncertainty is a result of the way the episodes explicitly present themselves as special and thereby encourage reflection on what makes something exceptional in the context of network television's routines of production and the regularity of the schedule, including the occasional VSE.

The VSEs of *The Simpsons* and *Animaniacs* amplify the textual play in ways that highlight and transform their routine reflexivity. Both programs use their self-aware status as animated programs to explore and expose ideas about being special, live, on television, and part of media history. This includes an awareness of their fundamental artifice and the pleasure they take in flaunting that artifice by calling attention to the medium, its history, and the place of these shows in that history. At the same time, the self-conscious intertextuality of these programs with their roots in broadcast television is abetted by new media. There are many different ways to watch these programs repeatedly (broadcast and cable reruns, DVDs, DVRs, on-demand services, and media streaming), which makes it easier to see and savor the intertextuality and self-referentiality. Online resources such as Wikipedia, blogs, and fan wikis offer substantiating material by documenting many of the references.[19]

As they amplify the programs' routine parodic, intertextual, and reflexive dynamics, the VSEs also explore (or expose) aspects of television beyond the bounds of these specific shows, especially when it comes to liveness, history, and nostalgia. For example, some of the VSEs highlight the interdependence of history and liveness on television and emphasize the contingent and constructed nature of liveness. After all, if an animated show can deploy specific discourses, modes of address, and performative tropes to maintain that a particular episode is live (even as something of a joke), one might reasonably wonder about the liveness elsewhere on television that uses similar discourses, modes of address, and performative tropes. By undoing the naturalness of liveness while displaying historical self-consciousness, the animated specials also suggest television's role in preserving history. This challenges the idea that television is an amnesiac apparatus that keeps us in a perpetual present, minimizing any sense of history. *The Simpsons* and *Animaniacs* are examples of television shows that patently display a sense of history.[20] After all, *Animaniacs*—an exuberantly anarchic, often nonsensical, and irreverent text—is the show that brings Buddy, a relatively unknown animated figure from the 1930s, into the 1990s.

The combination of intertextual citation, parody, and play across categories is one of the crucial ways that *Animaniacs* comments on television and media with implications for thinking about history and nostalgia. The rich array of historical references in *Animaniacs* has sometimes been seen as nostalgic, and the show's references to classic cartoons and old Hollywood certainly could function nostalgically for some viewers. But invoking the past is not always or necessarily nostalgic.[21] After all, the intended target audience for the show was children, whose familiarity with the classic Warner Bros. cartoons would pretty much coincide with their viewing of *Animaniacs* (allowing no time lag for nostalgia), even though it also attracted an older audience segment (including people who constructed a guide to the cultural references in the show). Furthermore, Buddy (who appeared in the "65th Anniversary Special") is an example of a historical figure unlikely to function nostalgically for many viewers, owing to his short-lived career in 1930s cartoons. In other words, there are many issues that complicate the ways of understanding the program's wide-ranging references to media and culture, past and present.

At the same time, the irreverence of the show and its main characters challenge nostalgia as a prevailing sensibility. For example, in the "65th Anniversary Special," Yakko, Wakko, and Dot are utterly uninterested in the nostalgically figured spectacular being held in their honor. They are also bored by the old stories and the studio veteran storyteller in "Animators Alley," even though Termite Terrace was the site of their conception. The past has no distinctive allure for them. Moreover, the program's general tenor of silly irreverence, antiauthoritarianism, and its knowing (rather than feeling) use of figures from the past substantially mitigates the nostalgic possibilities. Media history is a resource for the show and contributes to its cultural cachet, in terms that might include nostalgia. But it uses history and intertextual references as sites of play, even mockery, more than as sources of affective attachment.

The Simpsons seems similarly wary of nostalgia, even as it evokes classic television as part of its intertextual repertoire. In the "Spin-Off Showcase," the featured programs, based on television shows from prior decades, are patently derivative. This is part of the self-legitimating joke, because when it first aired, *The Simpsons* was considered smart, innovative television with a critical edge. The showcase concludes with *The Simpson Family Smile-Time Variety Hour*, which parodied variety shows from the 1960s and 1970s—playing up the kitsch, not the fond memories. Moreover, as host Troy McClure explains, one member of the Simpson family refused to participate in the variety show, "but thanks to some creative casting you won't even notice." Specifically, Lisa appears as a tall, slender female with long blond hair, evincing no hint of nostalgia for the other Lisa. Indeed, the new Lisa introduces herself as a long-standing member of the Simpson family: "I'm Lisa, peppy, blonde, and stunning. Sophomore prom queen five years running." The *Smile-Time Variety Hour* doesn't simply use a stand-in for Lisa but implies a substantive revision of the show itself, one that is decidedly antinostalgic. This might seem to confirm the medium's disregard of history while introducing another version of Simpson family history and of *The Simpsons* program history that *The Simpsons* advances in VSEs. However, this occurs in an episode that places *The Simpsons* in the Museum of TV and Television, suggesting that self-conscious reflexive intertextuality is a strategy used to secure the program's cultural status. In other words, this complicated play with the nature of the representation of an animated family—including confounding its history—serves as a way of placing *The Simpsons* in media history.

VSEs of *The Simpsons* and *Animaniacs* engage with media irreverently to emphasize their legitimate place in American media culture. More generally, the insistent placement of these shows and their characters in history through these live VSEs, along with their persistent intertextual references to media, demonstrates the importance of media history and media knowledge as very special core values in American television and media culture.

Notes

1 The program initially aired on Fox Kids, the afternoon programming block on the Fox network. In 1995 it moved to the WB network, where it ran as part of the Kids WB afternoon programming and the number of new episodes produced was substantially reduced. The show also had a fan base of older viewers.

2 Counting the program's seasons and episodes is complicated by the release of the complete series on DVD in 2018. I follow the version given on Wikipedia and the *Animaniacs* Wiki, based on the original production and airing of the episodes in the 1990s. The 2018 DVD set divides the series into four seasons, with equal numbers of episodes, but this is not how they were originally produced and aired.

3 The programs have been analyzed in these terms from a range of perspectives. See Jonathan Gray, *Watching with The Simpsons: Television, Parody, and Intertextuality* (New York: Routledge, 2006); John Alberti, ed., *Leaving Springfield: The Simpsons and the Possibility of Oppositional Culture* (Detroit: Wayne State University Press, 2004); Tiffany L. Knoell, "The Usable Past and the Usable Present in Steven Spielberg Presents Animaniacs," in *The Dynamics of Interconnections in Popular Culture(s)*, ed. Ray B. Browne and Ben Urish (Newcastle upon Tyne, UK: Cambridge Scholars, 2014), 25–35; Lisa Scoggin, *The Music of Animaniacs: Postmodern Nostalgia in a Cartoon World* (Sheffield, MA: Pendragon Press, 2016); Bill Mikulak, "Fans versus Time Warner: Who Owns Looney Tunes?," in *Reading The Rabbit: Explorations in Warner Bros. Animation*, ed. Kevin S. Sandler (Piscataway, NJ: Rutgers University Press, 1998), 193–208.; Jason Mittell, *Genre and Television: From Cop Shows to Cartoons in American Culture* (New York: Routledge, 2004).

4 For one account of the program's range of references, see Knoell, "The Usable Past and the Usable Present." *Animaniacs* attracted an avid following of older viewers who could follow its dense and playful intertextual references. Fans compiled an online guide to cultural references on the program by episode, which is still being maintained and updated. There are multiple versions of this (including a Tumblr version with images), but for one that closely resembles the original, with additions, see Ron O'Dell, "Cultural References Guide for Animaniacs (CRGA) plus Other Random Ramblings from Alt.TV.Animaniacs," December 27, 2018, http://www.keeper1st.com/toons/crga2.txt.

5 The *Animaniacs* title sequence song also explains how the characters get locked up in the studio's water tower, from which they routinely escape.

6 Donald Crafton, "The View from Termite Terrace: Caricature and Parody in Warner Bros. Animation," in *Reading the Rabbit: Explorations in Warner Bros. Animation*, ed. Kevin S. Sandler (Piscataway, NJ: Rutgers University Press, 1998), 101–120.

7 Vincent Brook, "Myth or Consequences: Ideological Fault Lines in *The Simpsons*," in *Leaving Springfield: The Simpsons and the Possibility of Oppositional Culture*, ed. John Alberti (Detroit, MI: Wayne State University Press, 2004), 172–196; Kevin J. H. Dettmar, "Countercultural Literacy: Learning Irony with *The Simpsons*," in *Leaving Springfield*, 85–106; Knoell, "The Usable Past and the Usable Present"; Mikulak, "Fans versus Time Warner."

8 This episode is discussed in relation to the idea of *The Simpsons*' metareferentiality by Henry Keazor ("'The Stuff You May Have Missed': Art, Film and Metareference in *The Simpsons*," in *The Metareferential Turn in Contemporary Arts and Media: Forms, Functions, Attempts at Explanation*, ed. Werner Wolf [Amsterdam: Rodopi, 2011], 463–490) and as a mockumentary by Craig Hight (*Television Mockumentary:*

Reflexivity, Satire, and a Call to Play [Manchester, UK: Manchester University Press, 2010], 190–192) and Cristina Formenti ("When Imaginary Cartoon Worlds Get the 'Documentary Look': Understanding Mockumentary through Its Animated Variant," *Alphaville* 8 [Winter 2014], http://www.alphavillejournal.com/Issue8/HTML/ArticleFormenti.html).

9 Gray, *Watching with The Simpsons*; Alberti, *Leaving Springfield*.

10 Of course, this follows the parodied referent, because drug and alcohol abuse would be one possible fate for members of the bands featured on *Behind the Music*.

11 This episode is expressly discussed as a self-critical episode by Robert Sloane ("Who Wants Candy? Disenchantment in *The Simpsons*," in *Leaving Springfield: The Simpsons and the Possibility of Oppositional Culture*, ed. John Alberti [Detroit: Wayne State University Press, 2004], 137–171.

12 *My Mother the Car* was about a man whose deceased mother's spirit lived on in his car and spoke to him through the radio. As much as anything, its use ridicules the absurd plots of network television in the 1960s and 1970s—though it is worth considering the surreal and camp creative extremes of such programs.

13 Of course, liveness itself is a confounding aspect of television, and its meanings have changed over time. See Mimi White, "Television Liveness: History, Banality, Attractions," *Spectator* 20, no. 1 (1999): 38–56, and "The Attractions of Television: Reconsidering Liveness," in *Mediaspace: Place, Scale and Culture in a Media Age*, ed. by Nick Couldry and Anna McCarthy (New York: Routledge, 2004), 75–91; Karin Van Es, *The Future of Live* (Malden, MA: Polity, 2017).

14 Jonathan Gray in particular explores how the show "talks back" to television sitcoms, ads, and news (*Watching with The Simpsons*).

15 On *Animaniacs,* knowing references to studio history and a sophisticated sense of narrative reflexivity coexist with a comedic sensibility that is silly, often anarchistic, and also puerile, with sexual politics that often seem stuck in the Hollywood studio era. It was frequently cringe-inducing, even in the 1990s. In one courtroom sketch, for example, there are accusations of badgering the witness when a badger is literally held up in front of the person giving testimony (silly humor), and the judge repeatedly raises the need to "su-peenie" the witness (puerile humor). Yakko and Wakko routinely greet Dr. Scratchansniff's nurse, a buxom blonde, with an emphatic, leering "Hello Nurse" (which is also the name by which the character is known). Dot's girly affection for male stars is the gender-normative counterpart of her brothers' behavior.

16 These examples barely scratch the surface. It's worth consulting an episode guide or one of the cultural references guides to the *Animaniacs* (mentioned above in the notes) to appreciate the depth and breadth of references, especially since *Animaniacs* mixed fictive and actual historical figures with gleeful abandon.

17 The title "My Father the Tuna" evokes *My Mother the Car*, suggesting the importance of American television history—especially its patently absurd shows—to the comedic heritage of both *Animaniacs* and *The Simpsons*.

18 This is also common in classic cartoons. *Slick Hare* (1947), *The Scarlet Pumpernickel* (1950), and *Duck Amuck* (1953) are three exemplary Warner Bros. cartoons (among many others) in this category.

19 For example, there's a guide to all of the art that is cited on *The Simpsons* and another that describes all of the Itchy & Scratchy cartoons that appear on the show. In the case of *Animaniacs*, the persistence of an avid fan community provided support for the release of a complete DVD set of the 1990s series in 2018, and to the program's return on Hulu in 2020.

20 Fredric Jameson is one of the prominent cultural theorists who proffered the amnesia argument, identifying the presentism and historical amnesia of postmodern culture with television news, which was then generalized to television liveness and the medium as a whole ("Postmodernism and Consumer Society," in *The Anti-Aesthetic: Essays on Postmodern Culture*, ed. Hal Foster [New York: New Press, 1988], 127–144). For alternative views, see White, "Television Liveness" and "The Attractions of Television."

21 This is important, especially for programs that are as self-conscious and intertextual as *Animaniacs* and *The Simpsons*. "Nostalgia" can describe complex and productive affective engagements with culture, between past and present. But too often the term is used as a shorthand and ends up collapsing the complicated dynamics of culture (both past and present). This is especially the case when the term is applied to any representation of older popular media texts.

12

Liveness and the Live Episode in Television Comedy

BRETT MILLS

On October 28, 2018, the BBC broadcast "Dead Line," an episode of the comedy-horror anthology series *Inside No. 9* (BBC Two, 2014–present). Written by and starring Steve Pemberton and Reece Shearsmith, the program's blending of the comic and the ghastly aligns with previous series the two have collaborated on, such as *The League of Gentlemen* (BBC Two, 1999–2002 and 2017) and *Psychoville* (BBC Two, 2009–2011). Since it began, *Inside No. 9* has received considerable critical acclaim, with "A Quiet Night In" (February 12, 2014) being called "miraculously funny" and "The 12 Days of Christine" (April 2, 2015) being dubbed a "masterpiece."[1] The series continually experiments with form and content, including a dialogue-free episode ("A Quiet Night In") and one written in iambic pentameter ("Zanzibar," January 2, 2018). "Dead Line" continues in this vein, for it is an episode that was broadcast live.

Publicity material stated that the story would focus on a man who finds an abandoned mobile phone in a graveyard and the nightmare that follows as he seeks to find the device's owner.[2] But the audience watching the episode would have been disappointed, for a few minutes in the sound disappeared, and a BBC continuity announcer apologized for the technical mistake. When the problem was fixed, the episode continued, but not long after the sound disappeared a second time. Again, the announcer apologized, stating that the broadcaster had decided to abandon the episode and instead repeat a previous one, "A Quiet Night In." At this point, many viewers might have changed channels or turned off their televisions, but those who did would have missed "the biggest live TV surprise of the year."[3] The episode was instead about the haunted television studio that was being used for the broadcast, featuring CCTV footage of the cast backstage lamenting the technical failures and, as the story progressed, being killed one by one by the demons taking over their minds. Within the narrative, the actors no longer knew they were on television; at one point, they tweeted their followers to ask if they could see the backstage activities. It is a "perplexing" half-hour, whose pleasures lie in showing that television still has the "capacity to surprise, disconcert and delight."[4]

Live broadcasting such as this is an example of very special episodes (VSEs) of television. Live episodes are first and foremost special because the vast majority of comedy programming is not broadcast live, and thus they are marked as not typical or everyday in terms of the production processes of that particular program. This liveness is central to the marketing of such episodes as special; indeed, the promotional material for "Dead Line" refers to it as "a *special* live edition" (emphasis added).[5] This discourse constructs liveness as enabling narrative and production possibilities (as well as imposing limitations) that inform creative decisions. For example, Shearsmith noted that "Dead Line" was a result of "always striving to do storytelling in a different way," while Pemberton saw it as a "challenge" that was "impossible to ignore."[6] Many series have seen value in rising to such a challenge, for a number of comedy programs have broadcast live episodes—including *Will & Grace* (NBC, 1998–2006 and 2017–) in 2005; *30 Rock* (NBC, 2006–2013) in 2010 and 2012; *Two Pints of Lager and a Packet of Crisps* (BBC Two, BBC Choice, BBC Three, 2001–2011) in 2008; *Not Going Out* (BBC One, 2006–present) in 2018; and *The Drew Carey Show* (ABC, 1995–2004) in 1999, 2000, and 2001. Given that the vast majority of these series' episodes are not live, those that are function as special and are marketed and reviewed as such.

To outline how such broadcasting functions as special, therefore, this chapter examines a number of television comedy programs that have broadcast live episodes, and in doing so, focuses on television's relationships to liveness as a medium and technology. Given that such programming is, as noted above, a challenge, it is reasonable to ask why program makers should set themselves such obstacles—especially in an industry commonly critiqued for being conservative and risk-averse. In focusing on sitcoms, the chapter also attends to the particularities of live television comedy, given that comedy has a different relationship to liveness than do other, primarily serious forms of programming. To address these topics, I look at the history of television comedy to argue that while liveness may once have been a central component of the genre, over time it has developed into a way of making broadcasting special. The specialness of these VSEs, then, arises from contemporary audiences' understanding that television can be live but usually is not. This is in contrast to the experience of earlier audiences, for whom live television was much more common. Thus, a hitherto central component of broadcasting has been made into a marker of specialness.

Liveness and Comedy

The possibility of live broadcasting has been fundamental to television since its inception. Indeed, given that television has, for much of its history, been denigrated as a low form of culture, its potential to broadcast live has often been used as a marker of distinction.[7] Certainly many of what are seen as television's key moments—such as its coverage of the moon landings or sports events—are predicated on the medium's liveness. Liveness not only allows audiences to witness events as they happen but also encourages large numbers of people to watch simultaneously. Therefore, television offers the possibility of mass, communal belonging, suggesting a presence with others beyond physical proximity. This collective aspect has been core to television's promise from its inception, especially in countries with public service broadcasting—where the medium was understood as enabling togetherness and a sense of commonality. Thus, liveness's specialness may be predicated less on the ability to see things as they happen and more on the assumption that any individual audience member is seeing something at the same time as millions of other people, making it a "public phenomenon."[8]

This is why the analysis of liveness has typically been predicated less on its status as a technological possibility and more on it as a category.[9] Such a category is akin to a genre—that is, liveness's meanings and specialness are predicated on the rhetoric that deems it to have them, rather than anything inevitable arising out of the technology.[10] The question raised by this approach is why is television so seemingly obsessed with liveness, and so eager to let its audiences know when it uses liveness? This ideology of liveness is one that "must surely act to suppress contradictions," where one of those contradictions is the pretense of closeness offered to geographically dispersed viewers.[11] This sense of dispersed community means that television tells audiences that "nothing is lost, and much is gained, by staying home."[12] According to this argument, it is possible to critique television's display of liveness as it replaces genuine community and copresence with a mediatized substitute that has significantly less social power.

Newer media technologies continue to situate liveness as a special category with particular meanings. Indeed, social media make it easier for the moment of consumption of media to be communal, with viewers using multiple screens to simultaneously consume a text and communicate with others about it. This means that liveness "can no longer be seen solely in terms of the temporal immediacy between the transmitted event and the receivers" and should instead be understood as part of the "entire multiplatform and media landscape that it is part of."[13] It was such congruence that "Dead Line" exploited in its use of Twitter, in which audiences could respond immediately to a tweet they had just seen an actor on television post. The pleasures available here work from the temporal alignment of the narrative unfolding on television and the accompanying social media material, with their simultaneity inviting viewers to understand as live what they are consuming. This is precisely a special kind of pleasure, not commonly available in many media and, by definition, not what media normally do.

The sitcom has a distinct relationship to liveness that complicates this sense of community and the pleasures associated with it. Of course, the vast majority of sitcoms are not broadcast live, but the genre often incorporates some of the textual signifiers of liveness. These are most evident in the "traditions of sitcom,"[14] in which programs "are shot as if the performance was taking place in a proscenium theatre, with the audience positioned as the fourth wall."[15] Many such programs are filmed in front of studio audiences, whose reactions are recorded, constitute part of the aural makeup of the program, and function as an "electronic substitute for collective experience."[16] This mode of sitcom approximates liveness, with actors' pauses and performances responding to audience reactions. Sometimes sitcoms make this manner of recording explicit, with many American series stating in a voice-over at the beginning of each episode "filmed in front of a live studio audience" or, for example, including shots of the studio audience in the opening sequence, as in *Mrs. Brown's Boys* (RTÉ1, BBC One, 2011–present). The fact that sitcoms often function as "video approximations of theatre" is understood as a consequence of comedy's roots in music hall and vaudeville, with early television innovations a response to the problem of translating that theatrical, live, communal experience onto the broadcast screen.[17] The "three-headed monster" shooting style developed for *I Love Lucy* (CBS, 1951–1957)[18]—which remains prevalent in sitcoms to this day—was formulated with the goal of capturing "the spontaneity of Lucille Ball's comic performances, particularly her rapport with audiences."[19] Thus the sitcom's aesthetics were developed with the goal of somehow indicating a notion of recorded rather than real liveness as the source of their pleasure.

So how can we understand liveness in terms of the modern sitcom, given the genre's particular relationship to liveness? Perhaps most pertinent here is the question, why make a live episode at all? That is, if the pleasures of comedy are understood to be communicable via a recorded approximation of liveness, what extra pleasures are to be added by actual liveness? Furthermore, how can a genre that has markers of liveness built into its aesthetic signal real temporal liveness to its audience? The two case studies that follow outline how the answers to these questions also depend in part on national specificities of sitcoms, given that they explore a British and an American program. Thus, they show that there is no single unfailing way to do liveness, and liveness's status as a "category"[20] or "rhetoric"[21] requires program-specific solutions to the problem of how to indicate that something is live.

"When Johnny Met Sharky"

Two Pints of Lager and a Packet of Crisps (hereafter, *Two Pints*) is a sitcom about a group of five twenty-somethings in the North of England who are struggling with relationships, money, and their places in the world. For its first six episodes, it focused on two couples—Janet (Sheridan Smith) and Johnny (Ralf Little), and Donna (Natalie Casey) and Gaz (Will Mellor)—and their friend Louise (Kathryn Dynsdale). Broadcast for much of its run on the youth channels BBC Choice and its successor, BBC Three, the program aimed to reach a young adult audience, with its humor often centering on sexual matters and alcohol. Its aesthetic was aligned with that of many other sitcoms mentioned above, for it was filmed in front of a live studio audience, and it included an audience laugh track. It thus attempted to capture the theatrical nature of its recording process within its broadcast, offering as one of its pleasures the nuances of live performer–studio audience interaction.

In January 2008, though, an actually live episode was broadcast, titled "When Johnny Met Sharky" (hereafter, "Sharky"). The episode's title comes from one of its narratives, in which the central character, Johnny, is absent because he has won a competition to go to the United States and jump over a shark. At the end of the episode, the audience learns that he died during the event, and the tone quickly becomes more somber. While throughout its run *Two Pints* depicted noncomic moments, the death of a main character adds to the special nature of the episode. It is telling that the series employs liveness for an episode that fundamentally reshapes the program's format, with the specialness of the liveness congruent with the specialness of the narrative content.

Given that *Two Pints* is a program that adopts the sitcom aesthetic of recorded liveness, in this case it is required to indicate clearly to its viewers that this episode is actually live. It does so by beginning with an extradiegetic moment: the episode's first shot is of the television studio's main gallery, with the production team counting down to the program's "real" start. This cuts to a crane shot inside the television studio over the backs of the heads of the studio audience to a theater curtain. The camera swoops forward over the audience to the curtain, which opens to reveal the sets on which the narrative will be acted out. Here the particularities of sitcom liveness are made explicit by bringing together icons of theatricality (the curtain and audience) and the backstage matters of broadcast production (the gallery). By making the audience and production process visible, the episode shows how liveness is indicated less by the narrative, characters, or diegesis and more by making explicit the technical matters that are typically hidden in conventional fictional media forms. This revelatory process of liveness is common. For example, the live episode of *Will & Grace* ("Live and Schticking") begins with an almost identical sequence of shots from the production gallery, to a crane shot across the studio audience to a theater curtain. Significantly, these moments in both programs take place before the episode's narrative starts, cueing an audience to read the episode in terms of its liveness. Thus, these episodes' liveness is not incidental to their specialness but is instead intrinsic to the pleasures they offer. After all, it would be possible to broadcast a live episode of a sitcom without anyone knowing. The fact that "Sharky" instead indicates its liveness from its outset shows how central this aspect is to its meaning and pleasures.

Another pleasure central to the live episode is the possibility that something might go wrong. Whereas most broadcast television goes through editing and production processes with the aim of removing from the final version anything that is not categorized by the production team as intended, this is largely impossible with a live episode. Of course, the vast majority of live television is not actually simultaneously live: the limitations of the technology of broadcasting mean that there's always a delay between an event's happening in the studio and its being seen by audiences at home. But it is also the case that broadcasting guidance sometimes recommends delays for live programming to allow for the bleeping out of bad language or the erasure of accidents.[22] This means that even for supposedly live programming, the requirements of broadcasting intervene in the putative simultaneity that is ostensibly available. Despite all this, the potential for error remains a pleasure in live programming, with audiences likely to be closely attuned to the possibility of fluffed lines, poorly framed shots, and malfunctions of props, costumes, or sets.

"Sharky" foregrounds this pleasure by giving its cast members many narratively legitimized moments that produce a particular frisson because they must be achieved live, in a single take. One story line in the episode concerns Louise's diction, as other characters note how grating her voice is. To show her linguistic capabilities, Louise twice then recounts tongue twisters—such as "red lorry, yellow lorry"—at high speed, multiple times in succession, to rapturous applause from the studio audience. Such moments align with Steve Seidman's conceptualization of "comedian comedy," in which performative segments of a comedy's narratives do little more than offer the pleasure of seeing the performer's skills.[23] This disrupts the typical conventions of fictional representation, in which a performer's skill depends on their ability to disappear into the character they're playing. When the audience claps after the tongue twisters in "Sharky," it is not the character Louise who is being applauded. Rather, the actor, Kathryn Dynsdale, is being congratulated on her successful completion of a virtuosic act. Applause would likely be apparent in a recorded episode of the program as well, but it would be impossible for the viewing audience at home to know whether what they are seeing is the first take or a much later one. With a live episode there is only one take, and the successful completion of the tongue twisters is special because it is a moment that obviously could have gone wrong.

By the end of its narrative, "Sharky" is little more than a sequence of comparable acts, intended to show the abilities of the performers and make the possibility of error more likely. So Gaz rides around on a small motorbike, interacts with live snakes, and at the end does a fire-eating routine. Janet downs a pint of beer in one gulp and performs a cabaret-style song. Donna also sings a song and later does the splits. Not content with doing tongue twisters, Louise also completes some contortionism. Audience pleasure is available here, arising from wondering whether the actor already had the skills on display or had to learn them for this particular episode. While *Two Pints*—like much comedy—often draws on the skills and talents of its performers for its comedy, it is not normally the case that a single episode would contain quite so many moments that require the cast to pull things off in one take. Thus, "Sharky" begins to resemble a cabaret-style piece of music hall or vaudeville, re-creating the pleasures that underpinned the development of the sitcom in the first place.

It is easy to imagine the production team gleefully thinking about the array of challenges they could throw at their performers for a live episode and wondering if the actors could successfully meet them. The fact that a live episode is seen to be hard—for both the production crew and the performers—renders it special, and audiences are invited to find pleasure in the sheer effort expended to entertain them. It is for this reason that, at the end of the episode, the studio audience is invited to show its appreciation. The camera pulls back, revealing the episode's camera crew, and then sweeps across the studio audience as a voice-over announces, "Ladies and gentlemen, the cast of *Two Pints*!" The performers are then individually introduced, and they enter the stage to wild applause. This is not how a recorded episode of *Two Pints* typically ends, so this final moment, like the rest of "Sharky," is special. The cast members join hands and bow after Will Mellor has triumphantly punched the air, clearly relishing their success in completing the episode. In making clear the behind-the-scenes effort required for the episode, it thus returns to its beginnings, where the studio gallery similarly indicated the necessary production processes. Thus, the specialness of liveness is shown to be related to the production team's labor in achieving such a task, framing liveness as a "category" of television in which the medium congratulates itself on its diligence, skill, and effort.[24]

30 Rock

The live episodes of *30 Rock*, however, have a different congratulatory purpose. This sitcom focuses on the backstage production shenanigans of a satirical sketch comedy television program, centering on the conflicts of the lead writer Liz Lemon (Tina Fey) with a network executive, Jack Doneghy (Alec Baldwin), and series stars Jenna Maroney (Jane Krakowski) and Tracy Jordan (Tracy Morgan). While narratively structured like a traditional sitcom, with stories taking place within discrete episodes and a recurring set of characters and locations, the program does not employ the genre's traditional visual aesthetic as outlined above. It has no laugh track and is not filmed in front of a live studio audience. It aims for a naturalistic style that abandons the "three-headed monster" and instead uses a single camera, though that is often supplemented with a second, and hand-held shooting is more common than is the case in traditional sitcoms.[25] It is significant that the program does not adopt the theatrical visual style seen in *Two Pints*, given the aesthetic it employs in its live episodes.

30 Rock has broadcast two live episodes: "Live Show" in 2010 and "Live from Studio 6H" (hereafter, "Studio 6H") in 2012. Both episodes function as special precisely because they look unlike typical episodes of the series. They do have live studio audiences, whose laughter at the events in the episodes can be heard by audiences watching the broadcast at home. The episodes look like video, as opposed to the program's usual glossier aesthetic. Indeed, "Live Show" makes a joke about this, with Jack complaining that things look like "a Mexican soap opera." Where *Two Pints* re-creates the norms of that series in its live episodes, *30 Rock* instead abandons many of its norms and instead re-creates a form of television that it is usually understood to be in opposition to. And it is worth noting that this is a deliberate creative decision. After all, it would be possible to do a live episode of *30 Rock* that looked like its prerecorded norm, not in front of a studio audience and without a laugh track. But as noted above, live episodes' specialness depends on audiences' recognizing them as such, and in *30 Rock* that recognition is invited via the program looking and sounding quite different to what audiences would otherwise expect. The pleasures available here are ones of difference, and how these live episodes present and understand that difference is significant in terms of contemporary understandings of television.

Both live episodes of *30 Rock* structure narrative moments precisely around an assumed history of television in which the traditional sitcom aesthetic is rendered as historically obsolete. This is most evident in "Studio 6H," whose entire plot both celebrates the history of live television and renders that history as problematic and best moved on from. At the beginning of the episode, Jack announces that the network will no longer broadcast live television because it is too expensive, and this leads the intern, Kenneth Parnell (Jack McBrayer), to lock the majority of the other characters in a room so that he can persuade this captive audience of the value of live television. Throughout the series Kenneth is depicted as a fan of television both as an institution and for its programming, and this is often related to his conceptualization of the medium as a tool for nostalgia. Indeed, Kenneth's comic characteristics are his simplistic, homespun view of the world, coupled with a naïve optimism. Thus, while his defense of live television is depicted as heartfelt, the fact that *30 Rock* chooses such a character to encapsulate this view situates his argument as one that, while commendable in theory, can be understood as impractical in practice.

Kenneth's argument is played out via several sketches in which the *30 Rock* cast parody significant programs from television's history. Thus, Baldwin plays a crooner in "The Joey Monero Show," which is a parody of *The Dean Martin Show* (NBC, 1965–1974), and *The Honeymooners* (CBS, 1955–1956) is recreated as "The Lovebirds." These homages work from the assumption that contemporary audiences have an understanding of the referenced programs and thus allude to a presumed shared national consciousness related to the history of television. In this way such programming can be seen to be a kind of media event, which is live programming that, according to Daniel Dayan and Elihu Katz, "*integrate*[s] societies in a collective heartbeat" often centering on "a nation."[26] While Dayan and Katz's analysis focuses on supposedly more austere and rarefied television moments such as coronations or the Olympic Games, the discourses upon which such media events rely can be drawn upon for other forms of broadcasting, such as the sitcom. While adopting a comic mode in its presentation, "Studio 6H" clearly aims to appeal to a supposed "collective heartbeat" enacted via an assumed shared understanding of television history. If a viewer does not recognize the parodied program, this is not understood as a failure on the production team. Instead, it is a call to viewers to improve their knowledge of the collective national past. And it is unsurprising that all of this takes place in a live episode that looks different from usual episodes of *30 Rock*, because such "media events" function as "*interruptions* of routine."[27]

But "Studio 6H" also depicts a problematic relationship to that past, which serves to authorize the present in comparison. The key joke offered to audiences in "The Lovebirds" is that 1950s audiences were invited to see as funny physical threats made by men to their wives. The sketch ends with both performers dying of heart attacks, and this is followed by a mock 1950s advertisement in which a doctor encourages pregnant mothers to smoke cigarettes. Later in "Studio 6H," "Alfie 'n' Abner" parodies *Amos 'n' Andy* (CBS, 1951–1953), but the sketch is cut short as Jordan refuses to continue with the scene once Jon Hamm appears in blackface. Both this sequence and "The Lovebirds" end with a cut to a black-and-white 1950s-style "technical difficulties" test card, which aims to re-create broadcasters' responses to live television going wrong. But both of these sketches also serve to place ideologically problematic comedy in the past, where it can be mocked by contemporary—and therefore supposedly more culturally aware—series such as *30 Rock*. The shared national history presented here is one of progress, acknowledging the racism and sexism of earlier broadcasting and finding humor in the incongruity between such representations and contemporary, supposedly more civilized, social politics. In this way broadcasting aims to congratulate itself on its steady march toward inclusion and diversity, as if these debates are no longer ongoing and the necessary battles have already been fought and won.

30 Rock thus uses liveness for quite different purposes than *Two Pints*, and these differences indicate distinct national socio-historical understandings of the self for the countries that produced the shows. While *30 Rock*'s narrative celebrates live television, its comic matter critiques the kinds of humor that were historical characteristics of live television. The fact that *30 Rock*'s live episodes have a different visual aesthetic than its recorded episodes makes explicit that they are "*interruptions* of routine," normalizing the nonlive episodes. *Two Pints*'s live episode, in contrast, looks largely like its recorded ones, and it makes no attempt to situate live television as a historical anomaly.[28] Its specialness is grounded in what can be achieved by live broadcasting and the production team's ability to pull off technically complex moments. This points toward different national conceptualizations of both broadcasting and social history, as well as the purposes to which live television can and should be put. Thus, this indicates that despite the growth in international coproduction and the transnational circulation of television, programs such as *30 Rock* and *Two Pints* still arise from, and respond to, specific understandings of the nation as a meaningful concept that has informed television since its inception.

The "Was Live"

As the examples from *Two Pints*, *30 Rock*, and *Inside No. 9* show, liveness remains potent in broadcasting. While less common now than previously, liveness continues to be used as a tool to indicate a particular characteristic of broadcasting that marks it as different from many other cultural forms. Furthermore, it may be the case that liveness will increasingly become of significance to traditional forms of broadcasting, given that newer platforms such as Netflix have made clear they are not interested in streaming live programming.[29] Whereas television's liveness was once a way for it to distinguish itself from media such as cinema, liveness may now be mutating into a tool for distinguishing between different kinds of broadcast delivery. And where catch-up services function to disaggregate the television audience and dismantle the collective experience, the live episode serves to reestablish the communal nature of television, for its pleasures are most acute if it is watched when live. That said, how can we make sense of live episodes after the fact, when they are watched as broadcast repeats or at any time online? In these instances, the simultaneity is absent, as is the anticipation of mistakes. Instead, the live episode quickly becomes the recorded episode, and thus could be understood as being of a kind with all programming that is recorded and then broadcast.

Yet this is not the case. There remains a particular pleasure in watching an episode that was live, even when its liveness is no longer a constituent part of its consumption. The knowledge that such episodes were transmitted live—and therefore are a result of a particular logistical feat—enables continued appreciation of the means of their specialness, even if it is now a different kind. The live immediately becomes the "was live," even for those episodes in the United States that had to be performed twice for different time zones. Indeed, it is likely that the predominant consumption of live episodes of sitcoms is actually by people watching it as "was live," or after the fact, as these programs circulate in syndication and as repeats. The fact that something "was live" remains indicated through textual elements, such as *30 Rock*'s use of a laugh track and *Two Pints*'s cavalcade of performer trickery. This shows that liveness is a category of television rather than a technological fact, able to be signaled even when actual temporal liveness is entirely absent.[30] Even when the aspect that supposedly signaled their specialness—their liveness—becomes a matter of history, specialness remains because, at one point, this was live. To think about television's special episodes, then, is to be attentive to times when television was live, even when watching programming that is now—like the majority of television—simply recorded matter.

Notes

1 Rachel Aroesti, "Inside No. 9: The 10 Best Episodes So Far," *Guardian*, October 24, 2018; Andrew Billen, "TV Review: Inside No 9," *Times*, April 3, 2015, https://www.thetimes.co.uk/article/tv-review-inside-no-9-8rq2vtbxwox.
2 BBC, "Inside No. 9 Live—Dead Line," BBC Media Centre, October 17, 2018, https://www.bbc.co.uk/mediacentre/mediapacks/insideno9-halloweenlive.
3 Phil Harrison, "How Did Inside No 9 Spring the Biggest Live TV Surprise of the Year?," *Guardian*, October 30, 2018, https://www.theguardian.com/tv-and-radio/2018/oct/30/how-did-inside-no-9-spring-the-biggest-live-tv-surprise-of-the-year.
4 Ibid.
5 BBC, "Inside No. 9 Live—Dead Line."
6 Quoted in ibid.
7 Elana Levine, "Distinguishing Television: The Changing Meanings of Television Liveness," *Media, Culture and Society* 30, no. 3 (2008): 394.
8 Jérôme Bourdon, "Live Television Is Still Alive: On Television as an Unfulfilled Promise," *Media, Culture and Society* 22, no. 5 (2000): 534.
9 Nick Couldry, "Liveness, 'Reality,' and the Mediated Habitus from Television to the Mobile Phone," *Communication Review* 7, no. 4 (2004): 360.
10 Karen van Es, "Liveness Redux: On Media and Their Claim to Be Live," *Media, Culture and Society* 39, no. 8 (2017): 1247.
11 Jane Feuer, "The Concept of Live Television: Ontology as Ideology," in *Regarding Television: Critical Approaches—An Anthology*, ed. E. Ann Kaplan (Los Angeles: American Film Institute, 1983), 20.
12 Philip Auslander, *Liveness: Performance in a Mediatized Culture*, 2nd ed. (Abingdon, UK: Routledge, 2008), 23.
13 Inge Ejbye Sørenson, "The Revival of Live TV: Liveness in a Multiplatform Context," *Media, Culture and Society* 38, no. 3 (2016): 396.
14 Craig Hight, *Television Mockumentary: Reflexivity, Satire and a Call to Play* (Manchester, UK: Manchester University Press, 2010), 177.
15 Brett Mills, *Television Sitcom* (London: British Film Institute, 2005), 31.
16 Andy Medhurst and Lucy Tuck, "The Gender Game," in *BFI Dossier 17: Television Sitcom*, ed. Jim Cook (London: British Film Institute, 1982), 45.
17 David Marc, *Demographic Vistas: Television in American Culture*, rev. ed. (Philadelphia: University of Pennsylvania Press, 1996), 11.
18 Patricia Mellencamp, *High Anxiety: Catastrophe, Scandal, Age, and Comedy* (Bloomington: Indiana University Press, 1992), 322.
19 Christopher Anderson, *Hollywood TV: The Studio System in the Fifties* (Austin: University of Texas Press, 1994), 68.
20 Couldry, "Liveness, 'Reality,' and the Mediated Habitus from Television to the Mobile Phone," 360.
21 Van Es, "Liveness Redux," 1247.
22 For example, see BBC, "Guidance: Live Output," BBC Editorial Guidelines, 2021, https://www.bbc.com/editorialguidelines/guidance/live-output#guidanceinfull.

23 Steve Seidman, *Comedian Comedy: A Tradition in Hollywood Film* (Ann Arbor, MI: UMI Research Press, 1981).

24 Couldry, "Liveness, 'Reality,' and the Mediated Habitus from Television to the Mobile Phone," 360.

25 Jon Silberg, "Laugh Factory," *American Cinematographer* 89 no. 7 (2008): 64 and 67.

26 Daniel Dayan and Elihu Katz, *Media Events: The Live Broadcasting of History* (Cambridge, MA: Harvard University Press, 1992), 8–9.

27 Ibid., 5.

28 Ibid.

29 Edgar Alvarez, "Netflix Isn't Chasing the Competition into Sports or Live TV," Engadget, March 7, 2018, https://www.engadget.com/2018/03/07/netflix-ceo-reed-hastings-live-tv-disney-marvel/.

30 Couldry, "Liveness, 'Reality,' and the Mediated Habitus from Television to the Mobile Phone," 360.

13

Too *black-ish*?

Banned Very Special Episodes

APRYL ALEXANDER AND
JENNIFER PORST

Very special episodes (VSEs) of television shows often deal with notably heavy, topical, and controversial subject matter. They do so with the intent to positively influence the audience's behavior, educate the public on important topics, or even attract viewers by dealing with provocative themes. Often, VSEs encourage public discussion about controversial topics, but what happens when the topic and discussion are deemed too controversial? In those cases, we end up with VSEs that never air on television. Some of these episodes eventually air or leak on online platforms, while others never see the light of day. In most cases, they contained content that was deemed too salacious, taboo, or controversial for their time. Since these episodes were unaired, audiences can only speculate as to their content unless the writers and producers communicate with the press or audiences about them. One example of an unaired VSE is an episode of *Married with Children* (Fox, 1987–1997) titled "I'll See You in Court," which featured a motel that made unauthorized recordings of their guests, including Peggy and Al Bundy and their neighbors, Steve Rhoades and Marcy Rhoades D'Arcy. The episode contained frequent discussion of what were referred to as "sex tapes," and after audience and advertiser boycotts, Fox declined to air the episode in its initial run. In 1990, a year after it was originally scheduled to be broadcast, the episode aired internationally, and in 2002, it aired on FX.

Today, when cable networks and streaming platforms incorporate more adult content, it is rare for full episodes to be banned. Given the great expense of shooting an episode of a television show, an episode must be considered extremely controversial to warrant putting it in the vault. However, that happened in February 2018, when a VSE of *black-ish* (ABC, 2014-present) titled "Please, Baby, Please" did not make it to air. At the time the network and Kenya Barris, the show's creator, declined to provide specific information about the content of the episode, but it was rumored to deal, at least in part, with athletes' right to kneel during the national anthem. Official accounts given to the press stated that the network and Barris had agreed not to air the episode, but the decision still sparked controversy. Although both Barris and ABC swore that "Please, Baby, Please" would never see the light of day, in August 2020, ABC made it available on the streaming platform Hulu. By analyzing the unaired episode as well as other episodes of *black-ish* that were broadcast, this chapter highlights the way that VSEs reveal important cultural, industrial, and political issues of the day and the limits on what television is willing or able to handle. Ultimately, these examples show how corporate media hegemony functions to limit certain voices, as well as the potential for digital media and streaming services to provide new spaces for those voices to thrive.

black-ish

black-ish, a sitcom, was the first series since 2006 to feature a predominantly Black cast on one of the four major U.S. networks (ABC, NBC, CBS, and Fox). It has been nominated for fifteen Emmy awards and has won one. It has also been nominated for five Golden Globe awards, and Tracee Ellis Ross, who plays Rainbow "Bow" Johnson, took home the award for best actress in a television comedy or musical in 2017 (the first Black woman to win that award since 1983, when Debbie Allen won for her role in *Fame*). In 2016 and 2017, *black-ish* and *Modern Family* (ABC, 2009–present) were the only shows from one of the major broadcast networks to receive an Emmy nomination for outstanding comedy series. Averaging four million viewers an episode in its first couple of seasons, *black-ish*'s popularity spawned two spin-off series: *grown-ish* (Freeform, 2018–present) and *mixed-ish* (ABC, 2019–present). *black-ish* has been a commercial and critical hit for ABC, and throughout its existence, the series has successfully navigated real-world, ripped from the headlines topics from a Black perspective.

Since its beginning, the series has not shied away from controversial issues affecting Black Americans in particular, and many of the episodes can be considered VSEs because they incorporate some of the most pressing current events into their story arcs. For instance, the first episode from season two,

"THE Word," deals with when, how, and if it is appropriate to use the N-word. "Lemons" (season 3, episode 12), which aired January 11, 2017 (only days before the inauguration of President Donald Trump), featured the Johnson family and their friends and colleagues dealing with the outcome of the 2016 election. The timely episode reflected the issues of the day, depicting the characters grappling with challenges that many viewers likely experienced after the election—dealing with school and work cancellations the day after the election, becoming more involved in advocacy efforts, hearing about threats toward undocumented individuals and immigrants, experiencing fear of uncertainty, and questioning who colleagues had voted for. But as an article in the *Atlantic* pointed out, Barris "has generally resisted, he has said, the soapboxery of the Very Special Episode vein," and "Lemons" presented a nuanced discussion of the complexity of the time.[1]

In another topical episode, "Juneteenth," which opened the series' fourth season, Barris and his writers continued to push the envelope on controversial political and historical topics by centering their episode on the Juneteenth holiday. Juneteenth is the oldest celebration commemorating the abolition of slavery in the United States. On June 19, 1865, over two years after President Abraham Lincoln issued the Emancipation Proclamation, Union soldiers informed people enslaved in Galveston, Texas, that they were free. Today, many argue that this was the day that American slavery truly ended, and the Juneteenth celebrations around the United States recognize that liberation. The *black-ish* episode opens with twins Jack and Diane (played by Miles Brown and Marsai Martin) performing in a school play portraying historical inaccuracies such as Columbus discovering America. The episode then transitions into a *Schoolhouse Rock*–type cartoon, which features the twins' father, Andre "Dre" (played by Anthony Anderson), educating a colleague about Juneteenth via a musical. Of "Juneteenth," Barris stated: "The testing kept saying white viewers were uncomfortable. And I was like, *Wow, you mean the episode about how talking about slavery makes white people uncomfortable is actually making white people uncomfortable?* Shock! There were a lot of people from the network, to the writers and actors. This season was the season of trust. It took a lot of trust for people to get on board and trust what we were doing and hope that it worked out. And I really feel like, in my opinion, it did."[2] Episodes like these demonstrate some of the many ways that *black-ish* was able to feature boundary-pushing subject matter, particularly related to race, in its VSEs. However, that raises the question of what it was about the unaired VSE, "Please, Baby, Please," that was so controversial that ABC initially declined to run it.

The Black Lives Matter Movement

From the images, characters, and stories we see on screen to the logics of industrial and content regulation, the political and social climate influences the media. From the time *black-ish* debuted to the controversy over "Please, Baby, Please," there had been significant changes in the political and social climate, particularly as it related to race. *black-ish* hit the airwaves around the same time as the Black Lives Matter (BLM) movement began. BLM was founded in 2013 by the queer Black women Alicia Garza, Patrisse Cullors, and Opal Tometi in response to the acquittal of George Zimmerman, the murderer of seventeen-year-old Trayvon Martin. The movement is a sociopolitical force that has influenced the media, including news, television, movies, and social media. BLM is "an ideological and political intervention in a world where Black lives are systematically and intentionally targeted for demise. It is an affirmation of Black folks' humanity, our contributions to this society, and our resilience in the face of deadly oppression."[3]

Soon, the BLM movement extended beyond regional protests related to police-involved shootings, and athletes began engaging in public displays of support of the movement. One of the most high-profile examples occurred during a 2016 preseason game for the National Football League (NFL), when the San Francisco 49ers' quarterback Colin Kaepernick quietly sat during the singing of the national anthem rather than standing, as is the custom. His actions went unnoticed until the third preseason game, at which point he made media headlines by choosing to sit and then kneel during the anthem. Kaepernick explained: "I am not going to stand up to show pride in a flag for a country that oppresses black people and people of color. To me, this is bigger than football and it would be selfish on my part to look the other way. There are bodies in the street and people getting paid leave and getting away with murder."[4] While on the one hand, Kaepernick's became the best-selling jersey in the NFL, on the other hand, videos circulated of people burning his jersey in protest. Journalists debated his actions, scholars deconstructed the civil protest and action, the public was divided, and Trump weighed in during a press conference and called the protesting players "sons of bitches."[5] Ultimately, Kaepernick was dropped from his team, and allegations arose that he was being blackballed by the league. Athletes from around the world started emulating his protest, from the soccer star Megan Rapinoe to high-school athletes across the United States. Kaepernick's actions led to larger cultural and societal discussions, and he became a household name, even among those who may not have traditionally watched sports.

A Very Special Unaired Episode

Given the public attention to the Black Lives Matter movement and Kaepernick's NFL protests, some television writers decided to tackle the issue of police brutality in their work. Barris continued to push the envelope in *black-ish* by incorporating controversial content and felt a need to, as he explained, "talk about things that people might not want to talk about openly. But we have to dig in deeper and stay later and have more real conversations and argue amongst ourselves more and really bring our emotions to the surface and really say things that

FIG. 13.1 Dre uses a bedtime story to explain the state of the country to crying baby Devante.

people want to hear - have said. We have to do that more. We have a responsibility. It's not just TV for us anymore."[6] In 2018, during the series' fourth season, the episode "Please, Baby, Please" was produced. According to an official synopsis released before the episode was to air, in it "Dre is on baby duty for the night during a storm, and the household is wide awake. He decides to read a crying Devante a bedtime story, but when that doesn't do the trick, Dre tosses it aside and begins to tell a story of his own about the current state of the country in a way that Devante will understand, on a special episode."[7]

The usual production budget for an episode was raised to approximately $3 million to cover costs for things like using the Sam Cooke ballad "A Change Is Gonna Come," which Barris secured by meeting with Cooke's goddaughter. Part of the episode was animated, and a high-profile illustrator was hired to create those sequences. Spike Lee contributed the voice-over for the episode, which mixed animated political allegory with news footage of Trump and the attacks on protesters in Charlottesville, Virginia.[8] According to additional information that leaked about the episode, one scene depicted the father, Dre, and his oldest son, Junior (played by Marcus Scribner), arguing about the right of athletes to kneel during the national anthem at football games. The episode was scheduled to air on February 27, but on February 22, ABC announced that Barris and executives at ABC had agreed not to air the episode due to "creative differences." Barris stated, "Given our creative differences, neither ABC nor I were happy with the direction of the episode and mutually agreed not to air it." He continued: "We just had a difference of opinion. I don't think it's the first time an episode hasn't aired. You know what I'm saying? It probably won't be the last."[9] Channing Dungey, who was then the president of ABC Entertainment Group and the first Black executive to run the entertainment division at a major network, echoed Barris's sentiments when she explained:

> We have long been supportive of Kenya and team tackling challenging and controversial issues in the show and we have always traditionally been able to come to a place creatively where we felt good about the story he was telling, even if we felt it was pushing some hot buttons, and he felt he was getting to share the story in the way it should be shared. I think with this particular episode, there were a number of different elements to the episode that we had a hard time coming to terms on. Much has been made of the kneeling part of it, which was not even really the issue. But I don't want to get into that too much. At the end of the day, it was a mutual decision between Kenya and the network to not put the episode out and I think we all feel that was the best decision overall.[10]

After ABC announced that the episode would be shelved indefinitely, Anderson stated, "I don't think it's as controversial as people think it is. But hopefully, one day it will be aired. The lost episode of '*black-ish*' will see the light of day. I'd be interested to see and hear the comments once it does air. But everything we do is pretty good, and I think that was one of our better ones, so hopefully, it does see the light."[11] The cancellation of the episode made enough news that personalities unrelated to the show or ABC felt compelled to weigh in. The Black writer, producer, and director Issa Rae, known for the hit show *Insecure* (HBO, 2016–present), told *GQ* magazine: "That would *infuriate* me. You know? Like, I'm out here telling the truth, and I'm telling my authentic experience, and you pride yourself on having this show that exposes the plight of a black family in the United States, and then you're censoring: *No, not that. We don't want to see that part. The world isn't ready for that. America's not ready.* That's crazy to me. . . . Kenya tries to couch so much in a family show, and get so much across, in a way that I really respect and admire. But a lot of the time it is just mired in the Disney, ABC of it all."[12]

Content Regulation in Television

When Rae mentioned the "Disney, ABC of it all," she was referring in part to the different forces that work to regulate content for a broadcast network like ABC, which is a subsidiary of Disney, a larger media conglomerate. Those forces include network Standards and Practices (S&P) departments, corporate relationships and interests, Federal Communications Commission (FCC) oversight, and the economics of network television.

Often, when an episode of a television show does not make it to air, a group of people in an S&P department is involved. Most television networks and channels have such a department, which monitors the moral, ethical, and legal implications of aired programming. The department reviews scripts, occasionally sends staff members to visit sets, and reviews rough and final cuts of programming to ensure that only content deemed appropriate for audiences and corporate sponsors makes it to air. The department also runs test screenings of episodes to gauge audiences' reactions. For example, in the case of the *black-ish* episode "Juneteenth," ABC's S&P department ran test screenings and determined that the episode was "making the series' sizable white audience uncomfortable."[13] The episode was ultimately well received, and ABC ended up re-airing it along with "Hope" (season 2, episode 16) as a VSE in June 2020, in the wake of the murder of George Floyd and the Black Lives Matter protests. But if there is an unresolvable conflict between talent and the S&P department, or if there is a significant corporate interest at stake (for example, if a main character dies when a GE oven catches on fire, and GE is the network's parent company), network executives may get involved.

Broadcast networks also have an indirect responsibility to broadcast content in the public interest. That is monitored by the FCC, which has the power to license (or revoke the license of) local television stations and levy fines against those stations if they broadcast content that is indecent or obscene or deemed to not be in the public interest. Over the years, the interpretation of "public interest" has evolved, and the FCC has refused to provide clear guidelines as to what content rises to the level of indecent or obscene and is therefore finable. Although ABC, a network, is not subject to the exact same FCC regulation as other stations, ABC owns and operates or is affiliated with hundreds of stations across the nation, so the denial of a station license renewal or the levying of fines against stations for their broadcast content directly affect the network. Although a story line about NFL players kneeling during the national anthem would certainly not rise to the level of obscene or indecent, if the FCC receives enough audience complaints about a show, it is required to take those into consideration and determine whether or not a station is broadcasting in the public interest, and the complaints then could affect the station's license renewal.

In this case, the situation was further complicated by the fact that ABC is one of the subsidiary corporations in the Disney empire, as is ESPN—one of the largest sports broadcasters in the world. In the case of "Please, Baby, Please," Disney's CEO, Bob Iger, called Barris and "had a reasoned conversation with [him] about the political sensitivities of being a broadcast network in 2018."[14] Both ABC and ESPN have had close and lucrative relationships with the NFL for decades (for example, their deal for *Monday Night Football* alone is worth $1.9 billion), but in March 2018, stories were circulating that the relationship between ESPN and the NFL was the worst it had ever been. The NFL was reportedly upset about what it considered to be negative coverage aired by some ESPN shows and commentators, the controversies surrounding the anti-Trump tweets by Jemele Hill, coanchor of *SportsCenter*, and the broadcast of the football player Michael Sam kissing his boyfriend after being drafted by the NFL.[15] Other stories covered by ESPN that did not portray the NFL in the best light included things like the concussion crisis, infighting between the league's commissioner and team owners, and player protests like those by Kaepernick. In early 2018, James Pitaro became ESPN's new president, and he reportedly aimed to improve the relationship between the network and the NFL.[16] Since Pitaro took over, "ESPN has consciously steered away from programming and commentary that touches on Donald Trump, race relations, or anything else that might upset a theoretical viewer who wants the network to 'stick to sports.'"[17] Pitaro's stated goal of making the NFL his top priority had paid off when, by the time the 2019 season began, Brian Rolapp, the NFL's chief media and business officer, explained that the once troubled relationship between the league and ESPN was "on much more solid ground" because of "Pitaro's personal involvement as well as Disney's comprehensive coverage of the 2019 NFL Draft on ESPN and sister ABC Network."[18]

One of the things that might have made the NFL—and therefore ESPN and Disney—unhappy was airing an episode of one of ABC's most popular and critically acclaimed shows that either explicitly or implicitly criticized the NFL and supported a player who by that point had caused the league serious headaches. Another significant issue was the fact that in 2018, Disney was seeking approval from the U.S. Department of Justice for its proposed acquisition of the vast majority of 21st Century Fox, and that approval depended to no small extent on Trump's personal feelings about the company. At one point, Barris had agreed to have his editor test some of ABC's suggested cuts in "Please, Baby, Please," but "the sheer-tonnage of anti-Trump material rippling through the episode ultimately made the exercise futile."[19] Whether or not the NFL, ESPN, or Disney corporate leaders involved themselves in the postproduction discussions about the episode, those kinds of corporate pressures function as one more method of content regulation in the contemporary media industries and demonstrate the extent to which capitalist economic forces assert their power over the media.

Finally, all networks aim to avoid controversial content that might drive audiences and advertisers away. Broadcast networks, unlike premium cable channels or streaming platforms, rely on the income from advertisers that purchase air time in the networks' programming for their commercials. Even though the old adage holds that all publicity is good publicity, advertisers and the companies whose products they promote are notoriously averse to controversy. Historically, broadcast networks programmed what was known as "least objectionable programming" to ensure that audiences and advertisers would find no reason for offense that might cause viewers to change the channel and ratings to decline. In the age of premium cable and streaming services, which are not subject to the concerns of advertisers and which aim to provide content that appeals not to the broadest possible audience but to niche audiences, broadcast networks have struggled to keep up. Networks like ABC want relevant programming that attracts as many eyes as possible, but that is difficult to do if the networks want to avoid anything that might be controversial. In the case of *black-ish*, the high ratings throughout the series' first few seasons and its lucrative ad sales demonstrated that the show clearly had advertisers and audiences interested in the stories it was telling about contemporary cultural issues, including race and racism.

Indeed, *black-ish* had previously aired an episode dedicated to police-involved shootings. "Hope" originally aired on February 24, 2016, and directly tackled police brutality and BLM. The episode featured the Johnson family watching a news broadcast covering protests taking place about a decision not to indict a police officer who had shot and killed an unarmed Black man. Dre and his wife, Bow, struggle to answer their children's questions concerning police brutality and justice. The episode discusses the cases and displays pictures of Trayvon Martin, Freddie Grey, and Sandra Bland, as well as citing the work of the scholar Ta-Nehisi Coates and the writer James Baldwin. Additionally, the episode discusses the statistics concerning police shootings of unarmed Black people and how civil lawsuits following these cases result in millions of dollars in settlements each year. "Hope" aired to much critical acclaim, including reviews like the one in the *New York Times* that called the episode "remarkable" and gushed that it "proved how sitcoms can still matter; even in a time of fragmented audiences, they can connect."[20]

So what is the difference between "Hope" and "Please, Baby, Please," which went unaired only a year later? Timing was certainly one element. "Hope" aired before Kaepernick's preseason protests, which resulted in great controversy and intense debate in American culture about the nature of protests, race, sports, and BLM. In the post-Kaepernick and post-Charlottesville America, ABC may have felt a greater need to soften a potentially controversial episode that dealt directly with BLM and NFL players' protests and make it as unobjectionable as possible. In a time when there were shake-ups in the executive ranks at ABC and ESPN and Disney was pursuing an acquisition worth approximately $71 billion, it is highly likely that the desire to preserve those organizations' important relationship with the NFL and stay in the good graces of people in government who had the power to approve or deny their business plan was more valuable than the airing of one episode of a sitcom. These suspicions were largely confirmed when, in August 2020, "Please, Baby, Please" suddenly appeared on Hulu, which is another Disney subsidiary. Barris tweeted: "Following the re-airing of 'Juneteenth' and 'Hope,' I asked Walt Disney Television to revisit making the episode available. Recognizing the importance of the moment, they listened and agreed."[21] Again, timing likely played an important role in the eventual airing of the episode. Following the death of George Floyd, BLM protests were pervasive throughout the country. The *New York Times* observed that the BLM movement and the current protests might constitute the largest social justice movement in U.S. history.[22] While the episode dealt with a range of important social and cultural issues of the time, including BLM and Kaepernick's kneeling in protest during the national anthem, many critics noted that, at least from the perspective of 2020, the episode seemed less boldly combative than other episodes in the series.[23] However, many also recognized the extent to which it was anti-Trump. The episode even went so far as to include an extended allegorical animated sequence that outlined many of Trump's failings via a character Dre calls the "Shady King," and it likened Trump to superhero villains by highlighting footage of Trump seemingly parroting lines spoken by Bane in *The Dark Knight Rises* (2012). One thing is certain: the fact that this episode was too controversial to air in 2018 but it was then released and received as bland in 2020 highlights the power of VSEs to pinpoint the cultural, political, and industrial trouble spots at certain points in time and the ways that the episodes illuminate the extent to which those trouble spots evolve. In this case, "Please, Baby, Please" functions as a sort of bookend for the state of the United States and the media industry in 2018 versus 2020.

But the unaired *black-ish* episode was not the first instance that has caused concern about the hurdles faced by Black and women writers in getting their stories told on ABC. Over the years, the incredibly successful writer and producer Shonda Rhimes, a Black woman, had to advocate for certain controversial story arcs to air on her ABC shows. *Scandal*, a series featuring Olivia Pope (a Washington, D.C., political fixer played by Kerry Washington), became an incredibly popular staple for ABC in its Thursday night lineup, which was so dominated by Rhimes that it was dubbed "Shondaland."[24] In an episode of *Scandal* titled "Baby, It's Cold Outside" (November 19, 2015), characters advocate for government funding for Planned Parenthood. The episode culminates with Pope's having an abortion while Aretha Franklin's gospel rendition of "Silent Night" plays in the background. The episode aired as Congress was considering cuts to funding for reproductive justice advocacy groups like Planned Parenthood. Planned Parenthood praised the episode, but it angered conservative media watchdog groups such as the Media Research Center. ABC's S&P department had wanted the abortion scene removed to avoid such controversy, but Rhimes was able to use her clout to ensure that the episode aired in its original format.

Scandal had another episode that could be considered a VSE, "The Lawn Chair" (March 5, 2015), which centered on the BLM movement and aired shortly after the deaths of Michael Brown and Eric Garner. In the episode, seventeen-year-old Brandon Parker was shot and killed by a Washington, D.C., police officer after being suspected of shoplifting from a local convenience store. Brandon's father, Clarence, arrived at the scene with a shotgun, sat in a lawn chair over his son's body, and demanded answers. The episode concluded with the discovery that when Brandon had reached for his pocket, he was actually reaching for his store receipt, and the officer had planted the knife on Brandon after his murder. Reactions to this episode were divided: some critics and reviews remarked on its ability to highlight the current injustices of police-involved shootings, while others thought it was exploitative. In the cases of both of these episodes, Rhimes's powerful status at the network, which she earned as a result of her shows' high ratings and social media attention, allowed her to successfully integrate controversial topics in her show despite pushback from executives.

The Future of Black Television

Since Netflix introduced its streaming services in 2010, it has been a leader in pushing the media industry into the digital, over-the-top, streaming future. Just like premium cable channels such as HBO before them, streaming platforms are subscription based, and since they are not restrained by the content demands of the FCC or advertisers, their content often pushes boundaries by including graphic language, sex, violence, depictions of nudity, and other material that is more controversial than what might be aired on broadcast television.

In an effort to gain an edge in the streaming wars, many streaming platforms have offered talent more creative freedom and huge financial resources, and Netflix has succeeded in luring Barris, Rhimes, and even Dungey away from network television, giving them multiyear and multimillion-dollar deals. Rhimes was the first to make the move, when in July 2018, she signed a $150 million deal with Netflix, and although her existing Shondaland series remained on ABC, she was developing eight projects for Netflix that included comedies, dramas, and documentaries. During the announcement of the deal, Rhimes stated, "I wanted the new Shondaland to be a place where we expand the types of stories we tell, where my fellow talented creatives could thrive and make their best work and where we as a team come to the office each day filled with excitement."[25] The next month, Barris announced his eight-figure deal and the fact that Netflix would give him the space he needs to be "loud, bold, and unapologetic." Regarding Rhimes' influence, he stated: "I'm doing what I'm doing because of her. She's a black writer but she wrote shows and that opened up the door for the types of things I wanted to do, and for someone who was that successful at network TV for that long to make that move [to Netflix] made me understand the atrophy that can happen."[26] Barris considered staying with network television but was reluctant to do so, stating: "I worried that at the end of the day I was still gonna have to do pilots and I was still gonna have to do network television."[27] Then, in December, Dungey followed Rhimes and Barris and was hired as Netflix's vice president of original content. She explained her move by saying, "I'm drawn to the forward-thinking, risk-taking and creative culture at Netflix, and the deeply talented people there."[28] Dungey is responsible for overseeing Netflix's work with Barack and Michelle Obama and their Higher Ground Productions, Rhimes, and Barris, among others.

The perception of Netflix as a space where Black artists have the freedom to tell their stories without restriction is highlighted by a scene from the first trailer for Barris's first Netflix series, *#blackAF*. The trailer opens with Barris (who plays a version of himself) on a video conference call with Issa Rae, Ava DuVernay,

Tim Story, Will Packer, and Lena Waithe. Barris begins by saying: "I think we have to be able to talk honestly if we want our art to progress. What do you think about my show *black-ish*?" Everyone pauses and looks away from the camera to avoid Barris's gaze, and Rae finally responds, "Uh, it's fine." Story next says, "*black-ish* taps into the hearts and minds of fifty-five-year-old white women." Then everyone on the call laughs. Netflix captioned the trailer on YouTube with the phrase "Unapologetically Black," and the trailer promised a series that follows Barris's on-screen family members as they navigate life and success as a Black family. In this case, as in the cases of other storytellers like Rhimes and Dungey, writers and producers hoped that their move to streaming services had freed them from the limitations of traditional networks and allowed them to be more creative in telling stories featuring diverse points of view. Once *#blackAF* debuted on Netflix in April 2020, however, the reviews from critics and audiences were mixed. Critics noted that the series repeats many of the themes and tropes from *black-ish* without adding any complexity or depth,[29] and some observed that the primary way that Barris took advantage of his freedom from the broadcast networks' restrictions was by inserting "an abundance of expletives."[30] The critic Soraya Nadia McDonald very aptly noted: "It strikes me as strange and maybe even lazy to get an overall deal with a network that is worth $100 million dollars, and the first thing you come out with is of something you've already done? The candy store is open to you! You could do anything! That frustrates me."[31]

Conclusion

Providing a voice for the marginalized or voiceless requires shining a light on subjects that some segments of society find challenging, and one of the key things the unaired VSE "Please, Baby, Please" reveals is the fact that to tell relevant, controversial, and important stories, the people telling those stories must have enough power and status to influence the decision-making process. On this front, in the television industry there is still much work to be done. The Writers Guild of America West released its first Inclusion Report Card for the 2017–2018 television season, which highlighted systemic discrimination against television writers from underrepresented groups (that is, women, people of color, individuals with disabilities, LGBTQ+ people, and writers over the age of fifty).[32] The report revealed that only 27 percent of television writers are people of color, although that group accounts for 39 percent of the U.S. population. Moreover, only 12 percent of people who work as television showrunners are people of color. With the absence of diverse voices, stories on network television about people of color and other underrepresented populations will continue to be limited, and if writers and producers of color move toward streaming platforms, inclusive representation in the programming on traditional networks may continue to be scarce. The promise of media in the digital and streaming age is that it opens up new spaces in which a wider range of voices can emerge. Will that promise be fulfilled, or will the larger and even more powerful economic forces that arise with the concentration of ownership in the media industry eventually control the stories that are told in the digital space as well? Ultimately, unaired VSEs can shine a light on not only those important topics of the day, but also those topics that were at the time so controversial that their networks decided it was best to leave them unaired. The comparison between the unaired VSE of *black-ish* and other episodes in the series that were broadcast shows us the boundaries between acceptable controversy and controversy that pushes too far. Those boundaries reveal corporate media hegemony at work, and the fact that in times of media disruption when challengers like Netflix enter the scene, ruptures emerge that have the potential to challenge that corporate dominance and broaden the horizons of what is possible on screen.

Notes

1 Megan Garber, "*Black-ish*'s 'Lemons' Is Art for the Age of Trump," *Atlantic*, January 13, 2017, https://www.theatlantic.com/entertainment/archive/2017/01/black-ishs-lemons-is-art-for-the-age-of-trump/512978/.

2 Quoted in Maria Elena Fernandez, "ABC on the Unaired *Black-ish* Episode: The Kneeling Was 'Not Really the Issue,'" *Vulture*, May 15, 2018. https://www.vulture.com/2018/05/abc-unaired-blackish-episode-kneeling-was-not-the-issue.html.

3 "Herstory," Black Lives Matter, December 18, 2018, https://blacklivesmatter.com/herstory/.

4 Quoted in Steve Wyche, "Colin Kaepernick Explains Why He Sat during National Anthem," August 27, 2016, NFL.com, https://www.nfl.com/news/colin-kaepernick-explains-why-he-sat-during-national-anthem-0ap3000000691077.

5 Quoted in Bryan Armen Graham, "Donald Trump Blasts NFL Anthem Protesters: 'Get The Son of a Bitch Off the Field,'" *Guardian*, September 23, 2017.

6 Quoted in "'Black-ish' Creator Kenya Barris Says Show Will Take New Direction Post-Election," *Weekend Edition Sunday*, NPR, November 13, 2016, https://www.npr.org/2016/11/13/501904251/black-ish-creator-kenya-barris-says-show-will-take-new-direction-post-election.

7 Quoted in Greg Evans, "Topical 'Black-ish' Episode Pulled Over 'Creative Differences,'" *Deadline Hollywood*, March 10, 2018, https://deadline.com/2018/03/black-ish-episode-pulled-over-creative-differences-1202331217/.

8 Lacey Rose, "'Black-ish' Creator Kenya Barris Breaks Silence on That Shelved Anti-Trump Episode, His ABC Exit and 'Unapologetic' Netflix Plans," *Hollywood Reporter*, September 12, 2018, https://www.hollywoodreporter.com/features/black-ish-creator-kenya-barris-abc-exit-netflix-plans-interview-1141981.

9 Quoted in Maria Elena Fernandez, "Kenya Barris on Bow and Dre's Troubled Marriage and That Unaired Episode of *Black-ish*," *Vulture*, May 15, 2018, https://www.vulture.com/2018/05/kenya-barris-on-the-black-ish-finale.html.

10 Quoted in Fernandez, "ABC on the Unaired *Black-ish* Episode."

11 Quoted in Michael Schneider, "ABC Boss: 'Roseanne' Joke about Diverse Sitcoms Like 'Black-ish' Wasn't Meant to Offend," *Indiewire*, May 15, 2018, https://www.indiewire.com/2018/05/roseanne-blackish-fresh-off-the-boat-joke-abc-president-channing-dungey-1201964840/.

12 Quoted in Zach Baron, "Issa Rae's Uncompromising Comedy," *GQ*, May 22, 2018, https://www.gq.com/story/issa-rae-insecure-profile.

13 Rose, "'Black-ish' Creator Kenya Barris Breaks Silence."

14 Ibid.

15 James Andrew Miller, "Jemele Hill Waves Goodbye to ESPN and Hello to 'Places Where Discomfort Is OK,'" *Hollywood Reporter*, October 1, 2018, https://www.hollywoodreporter.com/news/jemele-hill-interview-leaving-espn-joining-atlantic-1148171.

16 Scott Davis, "ESPN's Relationship with the NFL Looks Like It's Never Been Worse, and It Boils Down to a Simple Problem," *Business Insider*, March 13, 2018, https://www.businessinsider.in/The-NFL-and-ESPNs-relationship-looks-like-its-never-been-worse-and-it-all-boils-down-to-a-simple-problem/articleshow/63289113.cms.

17 Peter Kafka, "Jimmy Pitaro Moved ESPN Away from Politics, Controversy, and Anything Else That Isn't Sports," *Recode*, May 30, 2019, https://www.vox.com/2019/5/30/18644638/espn-jimmy-pitaro-podcast-recode-media-peter-kafka-disney-streaming-sports-bob-iger.

18 Quoted in Michael McCarthy, "Mission Accomplished: ESPN's Jimmy Pitaro Healing Fractured NFL Relationship," *Front Office Sports*, September 5, 2019, https://frontofficesports.com/espn-nfl-relationship/.

19 Rose, "'Black-ish' Creator Kenya Barris Breaks Silence."

20 James Poniewozik, "With Police Brutality Episode, 'black-ish' Shows How Sitcoms Can Still Matter," *New York Times*, February 25, 2016.

21 Kenya Barris, @funnyblackdude, August 10, 2020, Twitter, https://twitter.com/funnyblackdude/status/1292910638608658434?s=20.

22 Larry Buchanan, Quoctrung Bui, and Jugal K. Patel, "Black Lives Matter May Be the Largest Movement in U.S. History," *New York Times*, July 3, 2020.

23 Daniel Fienberg, "Critic's Notebook: The Baffling Blandness of the Shelved 'Black-ish' Episode," *Hollywood Reporter*, August 10, 2020, https://www.hollywoodreporter.com/fien-print/critics-notebook-baffling-blandness-shelved-black-ish-episode-1306740.

24 Maryann Erigha, "Shonda Rhimes, *Scandal*, and the Politics of Crossing Over," *Black Scholar* 45, no. 1 (2015): 10–15.

25 Quoted in Nellie Andreeva and Denise Petski, "Shondaland Unveils Netflix Series Slate: 'The Warmth of Other Suns,' White House Drama 'The Residence,' Ellen Pao Project, More," *Deadline*, July 20, 2018, https://deadline.com/2018/07/shondaland-netflix-series-slate-1202430614/.

26 Quoted in Lacey Rose, "ABC Entertainment Chief on Pulled 'Black-ish' Episode and the 'Roseanne' Effect," *Hollywood Reporter*, May 15, 2018, https://www.hollywoodreporter.com/live-feed/abc-entertainment-chief-pulled-black-ish-episode-roseanne-effect-1111971.

27 Quoted in Rose, "'Black-ish' Creator Kenya Barris Breaks Silence."

28 Quoted in Joe Otterson, "Channing Dungey Joins Netflix as VP of Original Content," *Variety*, December 17, 2018, https://variety.com/2018/tv/news/channing-dungey-netflix-1203080928/.

29 Shamira Ibrahim, "What Kenya Barris Doesn't Understand About *#BlackAF*," *Atlantic*, April 26, 2020, https://www.theatlantic.com/culture/archive/2020/04/blackaf-fails-to-break-new-ground/610678/; Soraya Nadia McDonald, "'*BlackAF*' Is Painfully Devoid of New Ideas," *The Undefeated*, April 17, 2020, https://theundefeated.com/features/blackaf-is-painfully-devoid-of-new-ideas/.

30 Tambay Obenson, "IndieWire Critics Roundtable: '#blackAF' and the Dilemmas of Black Criticism," *IndieWire*, June 4, 2020, https://www.indiewire.com/2020/06/indiewire-critics-roundtable-blackaf-1202227144/.
31 Quoted in ibid.
32 "WGAW Inclusion Report Card: 2017–2018 TV Staffing Season," Writers Guild of America West, accessed January 29, 2021, https://www.wga.org/uploadedfiles/the-guild/inclusion-and-equity/wgaw_inclusion_report.pdf.

14

Knife Crime and Passion

A Very Special Episode of *EastEnders*

CHRISTINE BECKER

One could readily assume that the BBC's soap opera *EastEnders* is made up of nothing but special episodes, given its weighty context: the license fee–funded public broadcaster, BBC, operates under a public service mandate; British soap operas have traditionally tackled social issues; and *EastEnders*, in particular, has been distinguished by its commitment to social realism. But this volume makes a commitment to delineating the sometimes fine lines between standard television episodes, special episodes, and very special episodes (VSEs), and the soap opera genre in particular poses unique challenges to making these distinctions. Thus, a deep dive into a single *EastEnders* episode that focuses on how we can define the VSE in scripted television will help further establish the parameters under consideration in this collection.

With this larger aim in mind, I focus here on the *EastEnders* episode that aired on July 6, 2018, and explain why it deserves VSE status for reasons that go well beyond the above descriptions. In terms of its subject matter, this episode represented the apex of a story line intended to bring attention to the crisis of knife crimes in England overall and London in particular. With strict gun laws limiting the presence of firearms on the country's streets, violence is frequently perpetrated with knives instead of guns, and especially among youth groups in urban areas, knife-related crimes have skyrocketed. Between the first of January and early August 2018, shortly after the episode under consideration aired, fifty-one people in London—many of them young people—were fatally stabbed.[1]

EastEnders created a fictional showcase for this epidemic beginning on May 21, 2018, when two teenage male residents of the show's fictional London borough, both regular characters on the series, were stabbed in the wake of a dispute among local youths. One, Shakil Kazemi, died from his wounds three episodes later. Following weeks of legal fallout and community mourning over his death, Shakil was laid to rest in an early July episode that was indeed very special—not just in content but more importantly in form, with the show's executive producer referring to it as "format busting."[2] Specifically, the episode inserted direct-address testimonials from family members of real-life London knife-crime victims between scenes of the fictional characters attending Shakil's funeral. While some viewers and critics found this juxtaposition awkward, a creative flourish at the end of the episode convinced many that the episode had succeeded in being overwhelmingly affecting.

Such formal experimentation also seems key to defining a soap opera episode, or even more broadly a television drama episode, as very special, given that serious or socially relevant content is likely to be more prevalent in every episode than is the norm for their comedy counterparts. In this case, *EastEnders*'s producers seemed driven to elevate the weightiness of the subject matter by breaking from a typical episode's formal conventions, as if the stylistic norms were not sufficient to match what the content demanded. In interviews publicizing the episode, the actress who portrays Shakil's mother, Bonnie Langford, insisted that the episode's structural intermixture offered an ideal format through which to confront the knife-crime issue, because it combined the ability of the soap opera to illustrate long-term emotional impact on everyday lives with a documentary effect that underscored the real-life consequences of the crisis.[3] This coalition of representational codes is at the heart of the episode's status as very special, as this chapter explicates more thoroughly through an analysis of the series, story line, episode, and its closing scene. But the coalition raises additional questions about the dramatic effectiveness and societal benefit of this approach in a soap opera. How can genres with contrasting representational hierarchies, especially relative to realism, come together in broaching powerful subject matter? How can, or even should, VSEs function in relation to immediate and ongoing national traumas? And what can scripted genre television lend to both art and reality in times of tragedy?

The Specialness of *EastEnders*

The BBC launched the half-hour soap opera *EastEnders* on February 19, 1985, and the series had social relevance in its DNA from the start. Drawing upon the legacy of social realism in British film and television while still trying to distinguish itself from ITV's long-running northern England soap opera *Coronation Street*, *EastEnders* was set in London's working-class East End in the fictional borough of Walford, whose town center was Albert Square. The creators pledged to focus on everyday life in the inner city, albeit with heightened levels of personal and social drama. The original producer, Julia Smith, said in 1985 that they were aiming for "a realistic, fairly outspoken type of drama which could encompass stories about homosexuals, rape, unemployment, racial prejudice, etc. in a believable context. Above all, we wanted realism. . . . [W]e didn't want to fudge any issue except politics and swearing."[4] Those original goals are still a key part of *EastEnders* today. Some characters work multiple jobs to afford the rent on their small flats, others contend with restrictive community standards, and nearly all grapple with the consequences of larger social problems that seep into their lives at some point. The series' insistence on tackling socially relevant issues in ways intended to resonate in real lives is evidenced by the program's website, which offers links to information about and support for people dealing with concerns brought to the fore by recent story lines, such as sexual violence, post-traumatic stress disorder, suicide, and cyberbullying.[5]

These attributes may seem surprising to viewers more familiar with American versions of the daytime soap opera format. Both British and American soaps share the genre's defining characteristics of multiple serialized plotlines that focus on interpersonal relationships unfolding across a continuous timeline commensurate with that of everyday life and with resolutions that are continuously deferred. But American soaps tend to focus on upper-class aspirational worlds, compared to the grounding in working-class or everyday social realism characteristic of British soap operas (or continuing dramas, as they are labeled within the U.K. TV industry). Sonia Livingstone observes: "In general, British programmes seem both more down-to-earth, mundane . . . and yet also more ambitious, attempting to portray working-class communities coping with contemporary social problems. The genre is often thought of as being responsible, realistic and educative."[6] Lesley Henderson similarly discusses *EastEnders*'s focus on "social messages intertwined with entertainment," an orientation in alignment with the BBC's mission that goes back to the early days of its existence and the guidance of its most influential director general, John Reith. to inform, educate, and entertain.[7]

Given this background information about *EastEnders*'s social justice spirit, one might ask if the program's knife-crime story line of 2018 is just another story line and the July funeral episode just another episode among many, and thus not special, let alone very special. Given that many *EastEnders* episodes contain at least one story line that broaches a serious social issue, does that make all of the episodes special? Or would this mean that none is special, if each is on an equal plane of relevance and affect? These questions are additionally complicated by the fact that soap operas and continuing dramas are defined most broadly by ongoing story lines rather than individual episodes and are structurally conceived of more in terms of weekly installments than isolated daily portions. How can an individual episode be defined as very special in a storytelling format not geared toward individually distinguished episodes?

Very Special Content and Form

If many British soap opera episodes contain at least some socially relevant content and interweave it into the genre's archetypal serialized structure, we must consider how specialness beyond what is typical could be achieved. Dorothy Hobson coins the phrase "the Big Issue soap" to refer to story lines and episodes that take on social problems of even bigger import than is typical for a series. Notably, in presenting a standard by which one could assign "Big Issue" status, Hobson cites "the exploration of issues that might only be handled in other programme genres, such as documentaries" as a factor. She also frames her definition in terms of what the audience is typically exposed to in everyday life, television news, and scripted television drama: "for the majority of the audience, these same stories are never going to be part of their direct life experience; but they are part of the life about which they read and see reports on television.... [A]nd they can share in understanding it in greater depth by experiencing the representation in televisual form."[8]

Here the "Big Issue" intention, which I see as comparable to a VSE intention, is to help viewers who have not been personally exposed to a particular major social problem better understand its nature and consequences through dramatizing it via characters they have long been emotionally attached to, unlike the ephemeral and impersonal stories covered in news reports and one-off documentaries. Thus, achieving very special status for a British soap opera episode in terms of content would seem to require addressing not just average social issues that can regularly affect everyday lives, such as unemployment or discrimination, but ones that rise to the level of dictating special news and documentary coverage at key flash points in time. One could counter that this is too fine a distinction to rely on solely to designate a VSE in a soap opera: where is the line between what average viewers typically experience in their everyday lives and what they do not?

Thus, to add more rigor to this definition, we should also consider formal properties and the extent to which these diverge dramatically from the series norm in a particular episode, especially because soap opera storytelling is relentlessly formulaic across episodes, weeks, and years. In fact, much of everyday soap opera's viewing pleasure is based on the satisfaction of reliable formal patterns and story rhythms, and veteran viewers become amateur narratologists who are able to recognize any deviation, whether it's an episode that focuses on only one story line rather than the usual interweaving of multiple plots or a huge cliffhanger that comes at the end of an episode on any weekday other than Friday. In the case of British continuing dramas, particularly *EastEnders*, there is also dependence on formal codes of representational realism, such as verisimilitudinous elements of setting and costuming, the minimal use of stylistic flourishes, and strictly objective narration. A soap opera episode thus might have to formally diverge from the norm, significantly breaking with how an episode typically looks or sounds, to earn the VSE label.

Both of these content and form markers of specialness are evident in the *EastEnders* episode under consideration, with the formal divergences even standing out as historically unprecedented. In terms of subject matter, the knife-crime epidemic is not just another evergreen social issue like prejudice or poverty, and the vast majority of *EastEnders*'s viewers will never have their own lives directly touched by the problem presented. The issue at hand instead is a national trauma being traced out daily in broadsheets, tabloids, and, yes, numerous documentaries and current affairs programs. According to statements by the show's creators and actors, the aim in tackling the story line was not simply to draw attention to a controversy or to inform people who were ignorant of the issue, as is the case with many of the series' other socially minded plots. Instead, the goal was to spur people to take action, whether that would be to initiate conversations with young family members and friends that might result in knives being put down or to prompt viewers to participate in activist efforts to curb youth violence.[9] This is certainly well above and beyond the content goal for any standard episode of the series.

Additionally, the creators made the decision with the funeral episode to have it stand out as unusual formally, to be nothing short of "format busting." While every other episode featuring a strand of the knife-crime plotline unfolds structurally and aesthetically like any other episode of *EastEnders*, the funeral episode diverges significantly, and in fact, it is different from virtually any other soap opera episode in British or American television history. If the very special designation for a soap opera episode is indeed rooted most firmly in formal divergence, might such formal experimentation better serve the intended goal of spurring action in the audience, not just entertaining them—compared to a stylistically conventional episode?

A Very Special Formal Structure

In an institutional sign of the specialness of the episode that aired on July 6, 2018, the heads of BBC One and the BBC's Editorial Policy Department, neither of whom normally track the development of an individual episode of the series, were heavily involved throughout the creative process. Peter McKenna, who wrote the episode, explains that these BBC executives "had a big say in what we were doing in this episode," and this was "because if handled badly it had the potential to cause upset and offense—which is the last thing we wanted."[10] The creative evolution of the episode across multiple stages illustrates how seriously everyone took their responsibility for representing the episode's themes respectfully.

The plan to feature real family members of youths killed in knife crimes in the episode was on the table from the early stages. When John Yorke, *EastEnders*'s executive producer, first contacted McKenna about writing the script, he indicated that the episode would include the family members in attendance at Shakil's funeral. But this was just a vague starting point that posed logistical challenges, such as how to have viewers understand that these were real people, not extras. McKenna proposed having the family members tell their stories directly to the camera earlier in the episode, and subsequently revealing that they were at a group meeting also attended by Shakil's mother, Carmel.[11] According to John Greening, director of the episode, producers liked the testimonial idea but decided to remove Carmel from that space to more sharply distinguish the fictional from the real. Greening explained: "When I joined, the decision had been made to include real stories. The challenge was how to fit those into an episode of a soap. Visually it was important to separate fact from fiction. Initially, Carmel was to be present at a meeting for knife crime victims and would give her story straight to camera like they did, but this was soon dropped."[12] Evidently, there was an urge to lend legitimacy to the fiction via connections to reality but not to potentially dilute or depreciate the real by treating it as equal to the fictional. The episode in its script and shooting stages also contained two other separate character story lines, as is the norm for a typical soap opera episode, but the producers ultimately decided to have the episode's singular focus be on the knife-crime plot, and the extraneous scenes were dropped in the editing room.[13]

The storytelling structure presented in the twenty-eight-minute episode featured alternating segments that showcased the narrative events of Shakil's family preparing for and attending his funeral, intercut with stand-alone direct-address and seemingly extemporaneous testimonial interludes from real-life family members seated in Walford's community center. There are five interludes of parent testimonials inserted across the episode, with each interlude lasting anywhere from 25 seconds to 105 seconds.[14] For example, one scene two-thirds of the way through the episode begins at the church with Shakil's brother Kush talking to the vicar, who has delayed the start of the funeral to wait for Carmel. Due to her deep grief, Carmel finds herself unable to attend the funeral, but Kush decides he cannot keep the attendees waiting any longer, so he tells the vicar to carry on with the ceremony. A fade-to-black then takes us to an unnamed woman seated in the community center, who speaks directly to the camera about the death of her son: "The moment you decide to carry a knife, you are taking a whole family into that grave with you. So Godwin was just one person. But then my whole family's life died with Godwin on that night." Then there's a straight cut to another unnamed woman, who tells the camera, "My pain is too much, and I do not wish another mother to go through my pain again." After another brief fade-out, we return to the fictional realm, as the vicar delivers an address about the pain of burying a child and having no soothing words to offer. Carmel then abruptly enters from the back of the church and takes a seat, and the vicar goes on to say that the mourners owe it to Shakil to surround his body with love and to retain their memories of the story of his life and death, as it is only through carrying forth his story that it will have sense and meaning. The vicar's words clearly resonate in both the fictional and real worlds. The family members in the interludes are offering exactly what she describes, while one is led to read Carmel's silent grief through the words offered by those mothers.

Therefore, the intercutting of testimonials with the fictional content brings to the fore key themes of coping with trauma, grief, and emotional paralysis in the wake of knife-crime loss, amplifying ideas expressed by the real participants through the fiction and vice versa. Langford contends: "We are able to dramatise it because people are invested in the characters and can see before and after, but I think it's just a way of telling you to turn your head in another direction to see that it's happening over there and over there and that this is real. . . . At this point, we are almost as a soap turning around and saying, 'here you go' and passing it forward. We are telling you our dramatising but this is the real thing."[15] This fits with the creators' stated goal of forcing the viewer to think about the larger consequences of knife crime and the collective societal responsibility that stems from its proliferation. Ideally, the soap opera format increases viewers' investment in the characters and provides the emotional pull necessary to prompt viewers to care about the plot developments, and the testimonials then transport them into the contemporary moment of reality. However, despite these good intentions, some viewers complained that the shifts between the fictional and the nonfictional were awkward or distracting and thus, despite any potential thematic resonances, the direct-address moments were too jarring to have the intended effect. Here we come to another question explored throughout this collection: does very special necessarily mean effective or even good?

Judging the Special

The fragmented episode fittingly made for divided feedback, as publicly available viewer and critical reaction to the testimonial interludes was mixed. The bulk of negative appraisals centered on the challenge of combining soap opera and documentary, as well as the presumed necessity to separate emotion and excess from truth and restraint in the case of such a serious topic. Those who applauded the show's unique storytelling approach especially praised the episode's moderation. The *Telegraph* reviewer Michael Hogan wrote, "The drama was stripped back and restrained, rightfully allowing reality to take the focus."[16] *Digital Spy*'s Sophie Dainty similarly lauded the episode for its choice to diverge from presumed soap opera tendencies: "Avoiding the usual drama that often surrounds soap funerals, the episode saw the fictional side of things completely stripped back—rightfully allowing the real-life accounts to be the most powerful focus."[17] Note that both critics use the phrase "stripped back," as if inherent soap opera tendencies had to be deliberately suppressed to achieve the desired result. Indeed, while these reviews offer praise, it's qualified by implying that the episode was not too soapy, as if those norms would be insufficiently somber for such an important topic. The negative reviews picked up on this same notion but found the attempt to juxtapose the separate formats ultimately too problematic. The *Radio Times* reviewer David Brown argued: "What this evening's *EastEnders* showed was that drama and documentary should remain two distinct mediums. Documentary's remit is to capture life as it is, drama's role is to take those specific experiences and present them in a creative way that we, as viewers, recognise but may have struggled to articulate had it not been for the skill of the writer."[18]

According to live tweets that unspooled as the episode aired, as well as posts in digital forums and review comments sections after the episode, the audience was similarly split, with many viewers respecting what the episode was trying to do by interweaving the testimonials but disagreeing on the effectiveness of the structural choice. Representative reactions can be found in the episode forum section on the *Digital Spy* website, which is one of the most popular TV-focused websites based in the United Kingdom. The forums allow users to start threads and post comments within broad categories, and the Soaps section features a separate thread for each *EastEnders* episode. These threads average about two hundred comments per day from well over half as many individual users, most of whom are devoted viewers who post regularly, but the thread on the July 6 episode contains nearly five hundred comments—another sign of its specialness, as well as its effectiveness at sparking conversations and debates. One of the most revisited issues in the thread is an argument over the conception of realism in soap opera mobilized for entertainment and character emotion versus realism in documentary mobilized for information and education.[19] "It's a soap, not a documentary," wrote one viewer, who also insisted, "[Soap opera] is NOT the place for real-life people with real life stories. . . . Who wants real life in a soap?"[20] Another complained, "I watch *EastEnders* because I am invested in the fictional characters. If I wanted to hear a real life knife crime storyline, I would pick up a newspaper or watch a documentary. . . . Soaps have never had to rely on using real life people to get their points across, so why start now?"[21] Others countered that the intermingling of real and scripted made the real-world relevance hit home in an entertainment medium. One forum user would have thrilled Reith by responding to those complaining that a soap opera is meant just for entertainment: "You do know that the programme is there to be used to inform and educate and not just entertain don't you?"[22] Similarly, another viewer responded to those who complained that this should have been a documentary rather than a soap opera episode: "Many people wouldn't seek out such a documentary because they want to watch soaps. This is soap giving up its own platform to tell real stories to an audience who wouldn't be arsed to hear them otherwise."[23]

Of course, the BBC has produced numerous documentaries about the knife-crime crisis, including one titled *EastEnders: The Real Stories*, which profiles the six families featured in the funeral episode testimonials.[24] This and related short films and text-based features are available on the BBC iPlayer online platform in the BBC Three portal, which targets audiences ages 16–34. It would be impossible to determine whether those documentaries are more or less effective at raising awareness and prompting action among youth groups or the general public than a soap opera episode, let alone whether they reached a receptive audience in the first place. It is similarly impossible to declare if the funeral episode was good or not based on the divergent cultural tastes communicated in an online forum or newspaper columns. But it is apparent that a common pivot point in judgments of the episode's efficacy consisted of the assumed divides between documentary and soap opera, the real and the scripted, and truth and emotion. These divides take on even deeper resonance when we consider how the episode ends.

The Very Special Ending

While there were mixed reactions to the bifurcated structure of the bulk of the funeral episode, there was virtually unanimous and unqualified praise for its final five minutes—itself a special segment within the VSE. The scene begins with Shakil's family carrying his coffin out of the church and toward a burial plot. The cemetery path along which the fictional characters move is lined by real family members (including those who appeared in the testimonials) silently holding framed photos of their murdered loved ones and alternately looking at the *EastEnders* characters and directly at the camera. The bulk of the shots in this sequence are of the real family members, with occasional glimpses of Shakil's loved ones walking past them. The sound track begins with the lone thump of a heartbeat, which is then joined by a rendition of the Christian hymn "Abide with Me," sung by Emeli Sandé. As the scene cuts to Shakil's coffin being lowered into the ground, the voice of the vicar delivering a blessing is overtaken by audio clips drawn from the family members' earlier testimonials. As we hear the anguished voices of devastated parents, the shots alternate between the grieving faces of Shakil's loved ones as they walk away and the real family members still standing and holding their photos. A long shot of Shakil's immediate family standing at his grave and a close-up of the grieving Carmel is followed by the final shot of the scene, a bird's-eye view of Shakil's burial plot surrounded by both fictional and real mourners, with the camera slowly tilting up to reveal the London skyline in the distance.

The image fades to black, and the credits roll with the names of the victims' family members who participated in the episode instead of the usual crew member names. The sound track in this final stage offers more testimonial clips underscored by news reports and police dispatches related to knife crimes, which are intended to express, in the words of the original script, "a sense of the sheer scale of this modern epidemic."[25]

FIG. 14.1 Shakil's family and friends mourn his death along with the many other victims of knife crimes across England and Wales.

Every critic and viewer response I could find praised the ending as powerfully effective, including those who said they disliked what had come before it. It also seemed apparent from how live Twitter feedback played out across the half-hour airing that some who commended the episode afterward for its powerful emotional impact did so primarily due to the final five minutes. The richest description came from Dainty, who wrote of the final scene: "This was a tear-jerking, traumatic reminder that knife crime is happening everywhere, in different ways, to different people—and that this is far, far more than a soap story. The show's decision to divert from its usual house style was a brave one, as is any attempt at combining art and reality."[26] The specification that a diversion from the usual house style to create more than a soap story encapsulates the core of the very special nature of this episode in both content and form. Even the sound track alone, with its combined voices of news reports and family grief, illustrates this reach for greater impact than the norm.

Also important is Dainty's observation about the attempt to combine art and reality. For an episode trying to incorporate reality into fiction, the most successful part of it, at least based on broad viewer reaction, is the least realistic part in terms of fidelity to the tangible world. It is also undoubtedly the most emotional part ("tear-jerking," as Dainty says) in an episode that critics praised for stripping back the soap opera's inclination toward emotional excess. But apparently, it is the haunting alchemy of both the fictional and real in this ending, both the emotions performed by actors and the poised grief of real people, as well as the viewer's accrued knowledge of both the real stories and the fictional story lines, that conjures up such powerful affect. Perhaps therein lies the power of a VSE of a soap opera like *EastEnders*—not necessarily in overtures toward unusual restraint or direct realism, but in finding unique formal means to express the deepest emotional core of a substantially important issue.

Conclusion

The most obvious signifier that this episode is a VSE is an absent one. Nearly every episode of *EastEnders* ends with the abrupt insertion of drumbeats, which leads into the series' theme song that plays over the end credits. Colloquially referred to as the duff duffs or doof doofs by viewers, these drumbeats are meant to emphasize the suspense or surprise of a cliff hanger moment at an episode's close. But there are rare times when the duff duffs don't intrude, and the episode instead ends in silence or alternative credits music. Out of the more than six thousand episodes aired at the time of this writing, only just over a hundred have not featured the duff duffs.[27] Usually, the absence is intended to mark the somberness of a moment, perhaps because of a character's death or a traumatic plot development. Rather than a few seconds of an emotional rush, the viewer instead receives an invitation to engage in quiet contemplation. *Metro*'s soap editor, Duncan Lindsay, used that invitation to contemplate what a very special soap opera episode can do: "We'll have our heightened drama, our scheming, our twists and everything back on Monday. But let's take this episode—and that poignant and devastating ending—to think about knife crime and what can so easily happen to any of us. . . . So what if it breaks the fourth wall of a soap for a few incidences of half an hour? We use soaps to switch off from the real world. But the real world is still here and we are all living in it. Soaps have a platform to raise these discussions. All soaps do it and so they should. *EastEnders* has a heartbreaking triumph here."[28] This viewpoint unquestionably recognizes the July 6, 2018, episode as very special, regardless of any dissent about its quality or appropriateness and particularly because of how substantially it breaks with formal norms.

However, in terms of the hope that one episode could help resolve an ongoing social crisis, we must also recognize limitations of the soap opera format. First, even if a soap opera tackles social issues, it rarely deals with them beyond an interpersonal level or offers tangible institutional solutions. The format is not set up to accommodate comprehensive explorations of the problems of poverty, austerity, inequality, mental health, policing, or other systemic problems at the heart of the knife-crime crisis. Not even the most well-meaning soap opera could reasonably narrativize, for instance, long-term economic investment in youth services. Additionally, daily soap opera episodes are by nature ephemeral and usually have little value or even visibility beyond their initial airing. One could also argue that a young person inclined to carry a knife is not the likeliest viewer of *EastEnders*. That said, a VSE is at least likely to be archived on sites like YouTube and thereby garner additional viewings, and *EastEnders*' initial stabbing-incident episode and the funeral episode have reportedly been screened in English secondary schools to prompt classroom discussion.[29]

Furthermore, presumably even just the single airing of the episode and the substantial press coverage it engendered did bring more attention to the issue and to the charitable services trying to help reduce knife crime and youth violence, thereby offering indirect benefits. One such service has a tie-in with *EastEnders*: the Ben Kinsella Trust was cofounded by Brooke Kinsella, a former *EastEnders* star whose brother was stabbed to death in 2008, as a vehicle for educating youth about the dangers of knife crime. Brooke Kinsella acted as a consultant for the knife-crime story line, Ben's father appeared in the funeral episode, and the publicity about both undoubtedly helped boost the visibility of the organization.[30] Unfortunately, Brooke Kinsella also implicitly affirmed the lack of impact of the *EastEnders* knife-crime story line with a March 2019 editorial in the *Telegraph* about how the knife crisis still hadn't been curbed and was spiraling even more out of control.[31] There was a record number of fatal stabbings in England and Wales in 2018, and the first quarter of 2019 brought no reduction in that pace.[32]

Notably, *EastEnders* itself foreshadowed this in the months following the funeral episode and, in the process, illustrated that soap opera and social problems alike are marked by the evasiveness of definitive resolution. After burying her son, Shakil's mother, Carmel, channels her grief into a single-minded mission to stop knife crime in her region, even just to get area youths to hand in a few knives, but basically she fails completely, as is most dramatically illustrated in an episode that aired on October 22, 2018.[33] As part of her crusade, Carmel gives cautionary talks to young offenders at the community center, the same one where real parents were seated in the funeral episode. During October 22 episode, Carmel encourages one thoughtful-looking teen to speak up, but a few other boys mock him for doing so, and he storms out angrily. Carmel pursues the teen and implores him to come back inside so they can talk about the pressures he's facing. But he declares, "it just is what it is," which is why he has to carry a knife to protect himself. She insists that this will get him killed. He responds before walking away, "People die on the streets every single day. They gonna keep getting killed. Don't waste your time, you ain't gonna change anything, it's just life now." The episode ends with no attempt to counter the teenager's bleak outlook, and Carmel gives up. Only two weeks later, she leaves the country (and the show) in despair to go live with another son in Dubai. This is a stunning and profoundly discouraging acknowledgment of the difficulty in curbing the knife-crime epidemic either on a personal level or via artistic intervention.

Whether or not Shakil's funeral episode produced any discernible intervention in the real-life crisis it addressed, it does stand as an emotionally powerful segment of soap opera storytelling. Of course, it is easier to identify the consistent aesthetic traits of the VSE than to determine its real-world impact—which is impossible to quantify. The actor who played Shakil, Shaheen Jafargholi, echoed a sentiment shared by many in an interview with the British newspaper *Metro* when he said of the episode, "It's hopefully going to help so many people and bring light to the situation." He also noted, "If even one person can stop carrying a knife, we've made a difference."[34] Until one person steps forward to admit that the episode made them stop carrying a knife, we cannot verify that any such difference was made. But the public attention fostered by the episode via the countless previews, interviews, and reviews that came out surrounding its airing certainly did bring light to a contemporary crisis. In the end, perhaps this is the most realistic outcome of a soap opera's VSE, a format that otherwise passes like a footnote in each day.

Notes

1 Alice Scarsi, "London Bloodbath: Victim of Latest London Stabbing Is Drill Rapper Incognito," *Daily Express*, August 2, 2018, https://www.express.co.uk/news/uk/997841/london-stabbing-crime-camberwell-incognito-rapper-crimewave.

2 Peter McKenna, email to author, June 4, 2019.

3 Sophie Dainty, "EastEnders Star Bonnie Langford Backs the Show's Special Knife Crime Episode," *Digital Spy*, July 4, 2018, https://www.digitalspy.com/soaps/eastenders/a860901/eastenders-bonnie-langford-shakil-funeral-episode-real-life-elements.

4 Quoted in Lesley Henderson, *Social Issues in Television Fiction* (Edinburgh: Edinburgh University Press, 2007), 39.

5 See "EastEnders: Information and Support," BBC, accessed January 29, 2021, https://www.bbc.co.uk/programmes/articles/DHjNLq6BdH5wV1p5bJ2ch9/information-and-support.

6 Sonia M. Livingstone, "Why People Watch Soap Opera: An Analysis of the Explanations of British Viewers," *European Journal of Communication* 3, no. 1 (March 1988): 56.

7 Henderson, *Social Issues in Television Fiction*, 32.

8 Dorothy Hobson, *Soap Opera,* (Cambridge, UK: Polity Press, 2003), 142.

9 See, for example, "EastEnders' Davood Ghadami Hopes Knife Story Will 'Make People Think Twice,'" BBC News, July 5, 2018, https://www.bbc.com/news/entertainment-arts-44722805.

10 Peter McKenna, Twitter direct message to author, June 4, 2019, 2:53 A.M.

11 Ibid.

12 Quoted in "Walford Web Asks . . . John Greening!," Walford Web, July 9, 2018, https://walfordweb.com/walford-web-asks-john-greening-t353478.html. Incidentally, Greening has directed far more episodes of *EastEnders* than any other director.

13 McKenna, Twitter direct message to author.

14 *EastEnders,* episode 5737, directed by John Greening, written by Peter McKenna, aired July 6, 2018, on BBC One.

15 Quoted in Dainty, "EastEnders Star Bonnie Langford Backs the Show's Special Knife Crime Episode."

16 Michael Hogan, "EastEnders Knife-Crime Special, Review: A Triumphant Tribute to Lives Lost Senselessly and a Plea for Sanity to Be Restored," *Daily Telegraph*, July 6, 2018, https://www.telegraph.co.uk/tv/2018/07/06/eastenders-knife-crime-special-review-triumphant-tribute-lives.

17 Sophie Dainty, "Why Shakil Kazemi's Groundbreaking Funeral Episode Was a Triumph for EastEnders," *Digital Spy*, July 6, 2018, https://www.digitalspy.com/soaps/eastenders/a861090/eastenders-funeral-knife-crime-episode-review.

18 David Brown, "Was EastEnders Right to Include Real Knife-Crime Stories at Shakil's Funeral? Our Verdict Revealed," *Radio Times*, July 6, 2018, https://www.radiotimes.com/news/tv/2018-07-06/was-eastenders-right-to-include-real-knife-crime-stories-at-shakils-funeral-our-verdict-revealed.

19 "*EastEnders* 06.07.18—Shakil's Special Send-Off @ 9:30PM," Digital Spy Forums, July 6, 2018, https://forums.digitalspy.com/discussion/2288512/eastenders-06-07-18-shakils-special-send-off-9-30pm.

20 SegaGamer, Digital Spy Forums, July 6, 2018, https://forums.digitalspy.com/discussion/comment/90576065#Comment_90576065. SegaGamer, Digital Spy Forums, July 6, 2018, https://forums.digitalspy.com/discussion/comment/90574006/#Comment_90574006.

21 londongirlGre, Digital Spy Forums, July 7, 2018, https://forums.digitalspy.com/discussion/comment/90575052#Comment_90575052.

22 Skp20040, Digital Spy Forums, July 8, 2018, https://forums.digitalspy.com/discussion/comment/90584533/#Comment_90584533.

23 BumbleSquat, Digital Spy Forums, July 6, 2018, https://forums.digitalspy.com/discussion/comment/90574150/#Comment_90574150.

24 See "EastEnders: The Real Stories," BBC, accessed January 29, 2021, https://www.bbc.co.uk/programmes/p06cr8j0.

25 Peter McKenna, "EastEnders 5737," undated shooting script, McKenna's personal collection, 46.

26 Dainty, "Why Shakil Kazemi's Groundbreaking Funeral Episode Was a Triumph for EastEnders."

27 "*EastEnders* theme tune," *Wikipedia*, accessed on July 10, 2019, https://en.wikipedia.org/wiki/EastEnders_theme_tune.

28 Duncan Lindsay, "Why *EastEnders* got their special knife crime episode so right by including devastating real life stories," *Metro*, July 6, 2018, https://metro.co.uk/2018/07/06/eastenders-got-special-knife-crime-episode-right-including-devastating-real-life-stories-7689713.

29 John Greening, Twitter post, May 19, 2019, 10:24 A.M., https://twitter.com/johnwg58/status/1130117036611461122.

30 Gurvinder Gill, "Brooke Kinsella: Why I Helped EastEnders on Knife Crime Story," BBC News, May 24, 2018, https://www.bbc.com/news/newsbeat-44154838.

31 Brooke Kinsella, "Why, Ten Years after My Brother's Death, the Knife Crisis Still Hasn't Been Dealt With," *Telegraph*, March 4, 2019, https://www.telegraph.co.uk/news/2019/03/04/ten-years-brothers-death-britains-streets-still-dangerous.

32 "Knife Crime: Fatal Stabbings at the Highest Level since Records Began in 1946," BBC News, February 7, 2019, https://www.bbc.com/news/uk-47156957; Alasdair Soussi, "UK 2019 Knife Crime Death Toll Passes 100," *Al Jazeera*, May 20, 2019, https://www.aljazeera.com/news/2019/05/uk-2019-knife-crime-death-toll-passes-100-190520161103796.html.

33 *EastEnders*, episode 5797, directed by David Moor, written by Kim Revill., aired October 22, 2018, on BBC One.

34 Quoted in Duncan Lindsay, "EastEnders Spoilers: Shaheen Jafargholi Reveals All on Shakil Kazemi's Death in Knife Crime Horror," *Metro*, May 15, 2018, https://metro.co.uk/2018/05/15/eastenders-spoilers-shaheen-jafargholi-reveals-all-on-shakil-kazemis-death-in-knife-crime-horror-7530638.

15

UnREAL, Sexual Assault, and the Very Special Season

JORIE LAGERWEY AND
TAYLOR NYGAARD

On January 28, 2019, *The Bachelor* (ABC, 2002–present) contestant Caelynn Miller-Keyes, discussed her sexual assault at length with bachelor Colton Underwood and by extension the series' approximately eight million viewers. NPR called it a "very special episode" of the reality TV dating competition show, and it was just plain gripping melodramatic television.[1] Clearly responding to #MeToo, the movement aiming to provide solidarity for survivors of sexual violence, and the increasing visibility of reemergent feminisms, *The Bachelor* was six months behind its fictional soap opera doppelgänger, *UnREAL* (Lifetime, 2015–2017; Hulu, 2018). In an effort to stand out in the massively overcrowded landscape of Peak TV, *UnREAL* has taken the ratings-grabbing social relevance strategy of the VSE and adapted it for prestige TV's contemporary bingeing and streaming environment, transforming it into a very special season.

As the introduction to this volume illustrates, the VSE was a mainstay of American broadcast television in the era before the massive proliferation of channels made possible by digital distribution. Often airing during ratings sweeps weeks, these episodes stand out for addressing an urgent contemporary social issue and consciously disrupting the normal tone and narrative patterns of a series in order to grab attention during those crucial weeks that set advertising rates for the coming TV season. Peak TV, the early twenty-first century era of streaming, binge watching, and overwhelming amounts of content from an apparently unending list of traditional channels as well as new digital distribution platforms, might have escaped the advertising-driven calendar that had dictated U.S. TV release schedules since the midtwentieth century, but it faces the same grueling demand for subscribers or viewers to sell to advertisers. In the bingeing and streaming culture of contemporary television,[2] programs are often consumed in season-long chunks rather than as individual episodes. In this climate, a single VSE could easily fade from memory. To gain traction with the fee-paying consumers of streaming services and to stand out in the glutted market of Peak TV, some programs turn to the very special season model, in which a whole (often short) season engages with what *UnREAL*'s fictional producer Rachel (Shiri Appleby) calls "this really important issue." For example, *Dietland* (AMC, 2018–present), *Handmaid's Tale* (Hulu, 2017–present), *Queen Sugar* (OWN, 2016–present), *Big Little Lies* (HBO, 2017), and *UnREAL* all follow this pattern, contributing to a contemporary televisual genrefication of "feminism" by addressing a diverse range of sociocultural phenomena and being united in their critiques of "women's oppression."[3] Thus as viewing culture has shifted to favor patterns of bingeing, and streamers and platforms pressure cable channels to have a steady stream of new socially engaged content rather than the formerly clearly defined seasons, the VSE strategy has in some cases morphed into the very special season strategy.

UnREAL's season-long arcs are each defined by a social problem and the self-conscious drive of its main characters (who are television producers) to create progressive social change through these social issue story lines. Throughout its run, *UnREAL* used its show-within-a-show structure to confront issues like coping with mental illness, coming out as gay in rural communities, TV's dominant whiteness, and gender inequality at work. In this chapter, we focus on the show's final season, in which the diegetic producers have assembled a cast of returning all-star contestants, supposedly so that they can find love, but really to resurface and publicize a socially relevant and still unresolved conflict from a previous season between a rapist and his survivor. *UnREAL*'s season-long arc, then, becomes a bleak, satirical, behind-the-scenes look at what goes on in creating a VSE about sexual assault for a reality television show. Breaking from the show's typical weekly release schedule of the previous three seasons, Lifetime studio executives chose to release all eight episodes of the final season at once on streaming platform Hulu to encourage binge watching and a condensed, all-consuming viewership experience. This amplifies *UnREAL*'s use of a very special season structure in its depiction of the process of creating a very special episode for broadcast television, and thus offers a neat case study for a comparison of using social relevance to stand out in broadcast versus postnetwork, Peak TV programs.

Peak TV and Lifetime's Move to Prestige

Peak TV, a term coined in 2015 by John Landgraf, FX network's CEO,[4] describes both the massive overcrowding and the celebrated narrative complexity and aesthetic innovation that characterize the televisual landscape of the 2010s.[5] In the environment of channel and streaming platform proliferation, audiences shrink, and any individual program has to work harder to attract attention from marketers, gatekeepers (critics and award-granting organizations), and viewers. In some ways, the need to stand out in the newly crowded marketplace created by technological innovation echoes earlier eras of channel proliferation caused by deregulation and satellite and cable television technologies. The Lifetime network, whose original tagline was "television for women," was born in that environment and marketed itself to a specialized audience of middle-class white women and the advertisers hoping to reach them.[6] To survive in the streaming era and compete for the most desirable (that is, affluent and loyal) audiences, Lifetime now creates programming with social relevance, high production values, seriality, and character and narrative complexity: the marks of so-called quality TV that have become the dominant modes of televisual distinction.[7] In particular, Lifetime has opted to invest in a small number of prestige programs (following AMC's *Mad Men* [2007–2015] strategy),[8] hoping to create a viable lasting rebranded identity that distances the network from its schlocky, gimmicky, and overly emotional (read: feminine) reputation—a reputation solidified by the camp appeal of its dominant programming lineup featuring reality dramas like *Dance Moms* (Lifetime, 2011–present) and *Married at First Sight* (FYI, 2014–2016, Lifetime, 2017–present); women-in-peril films like *Mother, May I Sleep with Danger?* (1996; 2016) and *Surviving R. Kelly* (2019); and its biopics with low production values and starring struggling or first-time actresses, like *Liz and Dick* (2012) and *Harry & Meghan: Becoming Royal* (2018).[9] The bleak, self-reflexive satire *UnREAL* is Lifetime's best effort at this rebranding strategy, playing on the of-the-moment feminist credentials of the show's cocreator, Marti Noxon (best known for her writing on feminist television darling *Buffy the Vampire Slayer* [The WB, 1997–2001; UPN, 2001–2003]), to create an aura of auteurism. In addition to the prestige provided by Noxon's name, *UnREAL* benefited from the real-life experiences of her cocreator, Sarah Gertrude Shapiro, who had worked as a producer for four seasons on *The Bachelor* in a role she strongly disliked.[10] Together, the two created a series that uses the very special season narrative structure to achieve social relevance, complexity, and ripped-from-the-headlines contemporaneity. Like a traditional VSE, it selects an issue of immediate social relevance, but it also reflects the heavily serialized structure of twenty-first-century prestige TV by creating a very special season. And like a VSE, its emotional stakes are heightened. Its aesthetic choices might be excessive, but its season-long story line about creating a VSE offers a note of self-reflexivity and self-awareness that once again reflects Peak TV's drive for "narrative complexity."[11]

Where the VSE has historically been, by definition, an episode out of the ordinary run of a (typically episodic) television show, the very special season uses what Todd Gitlin called CBS's "social relevance" strategy of the 1970s.[12] Following this strategy, despite being the highest rated network at the time, CBS canceled its entire slate of popular rural comedies and replaced them with programming like *The Mary Tyler Moore Show* (CBS, 1970–1977), *All in the Family* (CBS, 1971–1979), and *Maude* (CBS, 1972–1978) that addressed the nation's social and political conflicts, particularly those related to gender and generational conflict, head-on. The new programming strategy reflected a shift away from programming that appealed to the entire country and toward the more urban, socially liberal viewers who would eventually become understood as "quality audiences."[13] In an era of emerging feminisms[14] and increased visibility of certain "popular" feminist issues,[15] American television culture has seen a fracturing of the previous three decades' hegemonic postfeminist sensibility.[16] The same period has witnessed increased visibility of both racialized state violence and protests against it. In an effort to attract a culturally discerning, socially conscious audience and the critical publicity needed to stand out in a saturated market of prestige programming, *UnREAL* devoted its four very special seasons to, respectively, a feminist interrogation of reality television dating shows; police violence against unarmed Black men; the ineffectiveness of neoliberal corporate feminism; and finally, a sexual assault revenge story line intended to speak to the #MeToo movement.

Over the course of its run, the series represented these issues with greater or (more often) lesser success and insight. The series' first season was met with lavish critical praise[17] and won a 2015 Peabody award for "build[ing] an unorthodox platform for delivering biting social commentary . . . critiqu[ing] the placement of women in today's media environment . . . [and] delivering incisive views on key social issues—gender stereotypes and sexism, class inequality, addiction, mental illness, the vagaries of power, the underside of kinship and the blinking glow of celebrity."[18] In other words, it was rewarded precisely for achieving the goals of a VSE: to highlight an important contemporary social issue. It simply did that using serial structure rather than a stand-alone episode. Together, this social commentary and the series' various narrative concerns fit well with Lifetime's history of co-opting liberal feminist discourses[19] to attract their desired quality audience of affluent, educated women. Yet in its unique mixture of satire, dramedy, and soap opera, *UnREAL* marks both a somewhat contradictory extension of and a departure from Lifetime's legacy as the network for VSEs and other melodramatic, saccharine, and gimmicky content that has led to the dismissive and pejorative assumptions about the VSE and its lack of artistic or ideological contributions described in the introduction to this collection. Similar to Jillian Báez's description of Lifetime's earlier effort at prestige melodrama, *Devious Maids* (2013–2016),[20] *UnREAL* adheres to Lifetime's long-standing generic convention of female-centered dramas and, more specifically, taps into formulas used by popular prime-time soap operas and reality series to attract younger female audiences. It draws on the conventions of soap operas in its focus on interpersonal conflicts, romance, and melodramatic tropes like unplanned pregnancies, suicide, drug use, eating disorders, and love triangles, negotiating them in a satirical mode that lightens the show's more serious issues with elements of knowing humor. In the midst of the unfolding sexual assault that we analyze below, for example, a very pregnant woman is hired for an extortionate fee (she receives college funds for all her children, and a raise and promotion for her husband, who is a camera operator on the show-within-a-show) to go into labor on camera. Later, two male contestants who just happen to be a pediatrician and a doula, coach her through her screaming birth while producers watch and cackle: "Oh my god, did she just shit herself? You shit yourself??" This interlude—clearly played for laughs given its blatant scatological humor, with the camp value amplified by a bizarre barn set, the impossible handsomeness of the competing birth coaches, the woman's own cavalier attitude, and the jokes from onlookers—is intercut with a sinister, violent scene of sexual assault. The juxtaposition is seemingly intended to remind viewers that they're watching a silly soap opera rather than a serious social issue drama. The intercutting asks viewers to draw parallels to the obvious contrivance and producer manipulations needed to create both of the ratings-grabbing "very special" televisual moments on the series, thereby highlighting and critiquing Rachel's role in instigating the assault. Yet in intercutting these scenes the sequence also links, and therefore can't help implying a kind of equation between, the mild embarrassment of defecating while giving birth in front two attractive, compassionate men and the traumatic reality of being sexually assaulted and having one's post-traumatic stress disorder intentionally triggered in front of millions of viewers.

In their comprehensive cataloguing of date rape as a televised social problem, Francesca Polletta and Christine Tomlinson note the trend in the 1990s away from "the earnestness and didacticism of the 'special episode'" and toward integrating rape as a secondary plot in more serialized drama.[21] They argue that this narrative trend works to normalize rape even while treating it as a serious issue: "one effect may have been to make the rape less significant. Made into one among many plotlines . . . rape became even less 'the' plot of the story."[22] This intercut *UnREAL* sequence, like much of the show's tone, creates an uneasy marriage between continuous plot threads, where parody or excessively soapy melodrama detracts from the seriousness and indeed criminality of staging a sexual assault. Furthermore, the show's central arc is about main character Rachel's mental state and character deterioration. The assault she stages is a function of that narrative drive rather than receiving its own story line. It's important to note that some of these tensions stem from the fact that *UnREAL* was very purposefully created to critique the televisual strategies of distinction (like the very special season) needed to stand out in Peak TV. Nonetheless, it uses those strategies in its own attempts to stand out in a glutted TV environment. Thus, both

FIG. 15.1 Left: an extravagantly staged birth. Right: monitors show a sexual assault in progress.

Everlasting, the show-within-a-show, and *UnREAL* ultimately reify the status quo of representational exploitation and cultural power. This is particularly the case when it comes to the televisual history of sexual assault—which, as Polletta and Tomlinson point out, has trended in precisely this direction: toward being a plot point in the service of other continuing stories or character development rather than the focus of the story.

In the same vein, Báez notes that the development of *Devious Maids* was fueled by competition from other cable networks that cater to female audiences such as WE, OXYGEN, and OWN, and reflected Lifetime's branding strategy to develop edgier programming that foregrounded sex and scandal in an attempt to capture lucrative younger audiences.[23] Yet Báez contends that *Devious Maids*'s dependence on postfeminist and postracial sensibilities—including its overt sexualization and centering of individualized ambition with its lead Latina characters and its resistance to naming or engaging with racial inequality—sharply limit its transgressive possibilities,[24] in the same way that incorporating sexual assault as one of several intercut story lines limits *UnREAL*'s political potential. *Devious Maids* and *UnREAL* both reflect Lifetime's early twenty-first-century programming strategies and reproduce what Kristen Warner calls the contemporary era's reliance on "plastic representation."[25] Warner defines "plastic" in relation to race, where the mere (frequently hollow or obviously contrived) visibility of racially diverse casts erases the need or even desire for more meaningful or culturally specific representations, while nonetheless attracting superficial praise and audience interest. "Plastic" can easily extend to other socially relevant issues like the fodder for *UnREAL*'s very special seasons and Lifetime's other key prestige programs. The network's development of *UnREAL* pushes its edgier programming strategy beyond *Devious Maids*'s postracial and postfeminist plastic representations by directly incorporating progressive gender and racial politics. This was necessary because, as Amanda Lotz notes, the typical strategies of distinction common to the postnetwork era needed to be "revolutionized" to compete with the changing viewing habits and content offerings ushered in by streaming platforms' massive investments in original television series.[26] Nonetheless, *UnREAL*'s use of the very special season and social relevance strategies that incorporate explicit political themes should not be uncritically celebrated. Its representational patterns, reflecting Polletta and Tomlinson's survey, trend toward the plastic and the secondary plot, using the very special season as an effective *televisual* strategy that is nonetheless a toothless *political* strategy for shifting understandings of, in this case, rape and sexual assault.

UnREAL's explicit incorporation of feminist politics—its apparent effort to push past plastic—is visualized from the pilot episode's opening shots with Rachel's "This Is What a Feminist Looks Like" T-shirt, and vocalized through her consistent challenges to the perpetuation by the showrunner, Quinn, of tired feminine stereotypes and hegemonic ideologies about the lack of women's worth outside of heterosexual marriage, as well as women's overemotionalism, cat fighting, use of feminine beauty as power, and so on. The show was initially praised for, among other things, this overt critical exposure of television's role in perpetuating these damaging myths of the advertiser-friendly postfeminist sensibility (the idea that women had achieved equality, and therefore feminist cultural and political interventions were no longer needed)[27] to garner ratings and advertising revenue. Yet as a television product itself, *UnREAL* borrows from other established quality TV conventions and modes of distinction—including its high production values, celebration of auteurism, and ripped-from-the-headlines social relevance—to attract audiences in other ways. The series' satirical tone relies especially on the self-reflexivity and intertextuality that Dana Polan argues have been key to attracting a certain type of "quality" intellectual viewer interested in "television about something."[28] Polan describes prestige cable shows like *The Sopranos* (HBO, 1999–2007) that throw out references to the culture at large (especially allusions to high culture such as art, literature, or philosophy) to flatter the viewers who catch the reference, especially urban professionals who increasingly define themselves in cultural terms and flaunt their cultural capital. In an era of Peak TV, when more original television content is being produced than ever before, watching television is still the number one leisure activity in America.[29] Countless blogs and fan sites are devoted to television recaps and cater to active fandoms; in that context, the self-reflexive and intertextual references Polan refers to are increasingly based on television programming.[30] Writing in 2007, Polan suggests that so-called insider shows about the behind-the-scenes workings of the culture industries had yet to gain popularity. Yet the proliferation of reality TV in the twenty-first century has produced spectators with increasingly sophisticated reading practices, including those critical of how their experiences are depicted on screen.[31] *UnREAL* exploits some of the known spectatorial pleasures in trying to gauge authenticity and contrivance in reality television programming, painting a bleak, parodic portrait of producing reality TV that appeals to those savvy, TV-literate audiences whose members seek socially relevant programming. Working at maintaining the balance between meaningful social relevance and more plastic representations of social issues, the show catches and keeps viewers with heavily serialized, binge-friendly, and issue-focused very special seasons.

As a behind-the-scenes satire of reality TV production, *UnREAL* offers a unique look at the cultural and industrial conceptions of VSEs, rendering visible and critiquing (but also reinforcing) the genre's seemingly inherent tensions as both a cynical marketing ploy and an attempt to make serious important television that serves the public interest. These tensions are embodied in the series' central relationship between Rachel, the hopeful optimist with big ideas about the potential to use television for progressive social change, and Quinn, who is bluntly cynical and unequivocally driven to improve the show's ratings and financial success. The contrast is repeatedly vocalized through the characters' lines from the pilot, which are often replayed during the "previously on" segments before each episode: Quinn gleefully shouts from the control room, "I want nudity, I want tears, I want 911 calls!," and the enraged Rachel responds, "you're pumping toxic sludge into the minds of young women!" As this exchange illustrates, Rachel often becomes the audience's mouthpiece for socially conscious critique, and Quinn is represented as the unapologetic id of guilty pleasure TV, promoting spectator delights whatever the cost. Yet Quinn also frequently mocks as much as celebrates broadcast television's penchant for excessive style, or what John Caldwell has called crisis televisuality.[32] In the episode following the on-air birth described above, for example, Quinn strides through the *Everlasting* set rolling her eyes and shaking her head at an antique baby stroller, surrounded by thousands of pink flowers and prominently on display, and jokes dismissively, "where did we get this, from the set of *Downton Abbey*?" And she continuously mocks the host's corny themed costumes and hokey pontifications about true love, romance, and living happily ever after, which are always underscored with the overly romantic *Everlasting* theme music. The excessively bright and cheerful on-set lighting also continually contrasts with the dark, low-key, harsh lighting of the control room, where Quinn wears chic but severe, tight, and perfectly tailored black suits—thus framing her parodic enthusiasm in a critical as opposed to a loving homage.

This visual contrast further separates the melodramatic reality TV show *Everlasting* from the quality, socially relevant series *UnREAL*. But more often than not, Quinn (perhaps like the intended audience?) relishes the contrivance of excessive and outlandish melodrama, gimmicks, and blatant or obvious appeals to sexuality and emotionality, paying her producers extravagant bonuses to manufacture ratings-grabbing moments for the show, regardless of the physical or psychological harm they might cause contestants. For example, in the final season, Rachel has enthusiastically returned to her role as producer after finally (and inexplicably) rejecting the reclusive cabin in the woods that she earned at the end of season three, and that would supposedly have saved her from the cycle of feminist guilt and emotional breakdowns she has been experiencing since the pilot episode. Quinn zealously praises Rachel's idea of having the women contestants walk across a bridge and having the male contestants judge them on their looks and whether they should be "humped or dumped [into the water]." "This is the most sexist, most misogynistic shit we have ever done," she says, "and I love it. It's so dark and demented." When Rachel explains somewhat surprisingly that she has no lingering feminist guilt and that she is "all in" for the exploitative schlock of the season, the camera lingers on Quinn. The now seemingly contrived or forced exuberance has drained from her face, replaced by a doubting, trepidatious look. Quinn's skepticism speaks to the series' overarching narrative shift in the fourth and final season of the show (which we explore in depth in the rest of this chapter). In this final season, the central dynamic between Quinn and Rachel has altered, and the writers seem to give Rachel the now almost hegemonic "quality TV" antihero character arc established with Walter White on

Breaking Bad (AMC, 2008–2013): pushing a once empathetic character to revoltingly despicable lengths to see if or when audiences would stop rooting for him.[33] As a result of *UnREAL*'s generic mixing, and particularly this soap-operatic villainization of Rachel, the show's very special season, socially relevant critiques, and particularly the targets of its satirical lens become muddled and, we argue, ultimately fail, suggesting that, like the once-and-done nature of the VSE, the very special season is ultimately no more memorable or effective at social issue television than its predecessor.

UnREAL's Feminist Failure

UnREAL's final season, with #MeToo-related story lines on both the show and the show-within-a-show, participates in the hypervisible contemporary discourses of consent, assault, and harassment. Despite this of-the-moment social relevance, the very special season is ultimately a feminist failure. The burden of representation, aiming to be both popular melodrama fitting with Lifetime's historical brand and cutting-edge complex quality TV narrative, ultimately created characters who were just despicable rather than satirical or self-critical antiheroes. And because it was those characters who voiced the supposed feminist critiques of rape culture and patriarchy, in our view, they ultimately worked to maintain rather than disrupt the status quo of representational cultural power. To be clear, as a televisual strategy, the very special season structure had worked for the series' first two seasons, as evidenced by positive reviews, strong ratings, Emmy nominations, and a Peabody award. But in our feminist and antiracist view, it then failed as a political and cultural strategy. We've written previously about the failure of its second season narrative—which featured *Everlasting's* first Black suitor, something *The Bachelor* had yet to show—and particularly its narrative of police brutality against Black men, which ended up centering the emotional suffering of the show's white women protagonists at the expense of physical violence against Black bodies.[34] The fourth season continued this centralization of white emotionality at the expense of violence against Black bodies and ultimately botched its representations of rape, particularly its critique of television's complicity in perpetuating rape culture. The season centralized the actions of deranged, erratic individuals instead of pointing to larger institutional culprits, while trading in stereotypical rape culture narratives and myths about rape that feminists have been trying to dispel since the 1960s. Ultimately *UnREAL*'s attempts at relevance and its intended contributions to expanding the dialogue about sexual assault conflicted with and were usurped by the series' empty dramatic shock tactics—which are necessary for a very special season to stand out in Peak TV.

By the fourth and final season, *UnREAL* had established that Rachel is a survivor of sexual assault, having been raped at the age of twelve in her home by one of her psychiatrist mother's clients, who was visiting her mother's home office.

UnREAL's third season traced Rachel's unsuccessful attempts to confront her rapist and her parents' complicity in her rape: in avoiding responsibility, the parents end up blaming Rachel's undiagnosed and untreated mental illness for her assault and her subsequent supposed misremembering of a Lolita-style initiation of her own statutory rape. This parental betrayal and Rachel's failure to get closure or catharsis becomes the personal narrative motivation for her to bring back the *Everlasting* contestants "Roger the rapist" (Tom Brittney) and his survivor, Maya (Natasha Wilson), whom he date-raped in a season one subplot of *UnREAL* after *Everlasting* producers plied her with enormous amounts of alcohol (making her too drunk to consent to sex). Although the act was caught on camera, the diegetic producers convinced Maya not to make formal accusations either on camera or in the media, and not to press official charges against Roger, for fear it would bring bad publicity to the show and negatively affect its ratings. This fictional sexual assault represented on *UnREAL* spoke intertextually to the alleged sexual misconduct scandal involving alcohol and a potential lack of consent that occurred on *The Bachelor*'s 2017 summer show, *Bachelor in Paradise* (ABC, 2014–present).[35] Yet rather than questioning and rejecting dominant myths about rape or portraying the rape realistically by focusing on the effects of the experience for the victim, *UnREAL*'s narrative complexity sacrificed the depth implied by a very special season.

Bachelor in Paradise later organized a sober, full-cast discussion (moderated by the host, Chris Harrison) about the sexual assault allegations, consent, and the pressures to drink and hook up on the show, creating a more conventional VSE of *Paradise*. In contrast, as a parodic fictional soap opera trying to stand out in an era of Peak TV, *UnREAL* pushed for a more exaggerated melodramatic and serialized confrontation—one that simultaneously critiqued and exploited strategies of televisual distinction. Rachel states that "she wants Roger and Maya locked in a room by episode four [of *Everlasting*]." That is, she wants to script and stage a dramatic VSE about rape retribution. Quinn exuberantly describes this as a "girl-power rape revenge witch trial," a phrase that humorously captures the VSE's inherent tension between being a cynical marketing ploy and serving the public interest (in this case, favoring the former). When Maya fails to follow the confrontational "script" that Rachel has set up by the prescribed deadline in episode four (that is, she refuses to directly accuse Roger of rape on camera or provide any melodramatic televisual fodder, with Quinn frustratedly asking, "Why is this criminal sounding reasonable? I have rape revenge blue balls"), it's clear that Rachel is being positioned by the *UnREAL* narrative less as a rational television producer who addresses the issue with the care and sensitivity it deserves, and more as a woman scorned, with a personal investment in what happens and a vendetta she wants to carry out on Roger through Maya. In the dark control room, Rachel is depicted fuming and staring unblinkingly in amazement at the glowing monitor that displays Maya's physical withdrawal and emotional retreat from Roger and the rest of the female contestants, who are demanding an explanation of what happened between them. The harsh blue directional lighting from the monitors distorts Rachel's facial features and makes her appear monstrous as she rages at everyone and no one in particular: "I busted my ass for this moment and I'm not going to let some weak, damaged-ass pussy take it away from me. This is my moment!" While Quinn takes the moment as a loss and works to reframe the VSE as "Baby *Everlasting*," staging the aforementioned live on-air birth, Rachel doubles down on trying to stage a rape revenge VSE and decides to manufacture an on-screen sexual assault for Maya to witness. She encourages "America's sweetheart"—the only Black contestant, Noelle (Meagan Holder)—to "loosen up" and drink to excess while cozying up to Roger, whom she's also encouraged to flirt with Noelle, knowingly and purposefully creating the circumstances for Roger to rape Noelle.

Rachel's actions are an exaggerated extension of the satirical manipulation represented throughout the show's run and could be read as a critique of the way Hollywood treats women, both physically and symbolically, in today's media environment. Yet throughout season four Rachel is treated less like a surrogate for or symbol of the media industry and its perpetuation of rape culture and more like a deranged individual experiencing a psychotic breakdown. Thus, the series reifies what Lisa Cuklanz calls some of the traditional misconceptions or assumptions about rape instead of offering the type of counterformulations encouraged by feminist scholars and antirape activists.[36] Susan Berridge writes about sexual assault on teen programming as typically being presented as an episodic interruption to a series' narrative.[37] Assault happens, is confronted, and is resolved (with no lingering character consequences) in the space of a single episode. In other words, sexual assault, in her view, is often the subject of a VSE. On this season of *UnREAL*, the only on-camera assault takes place in episode five, midway through the season, illustrating its use as a peak inciting incident for the narrative and character resolutions that will wrap up *UnREAL*'s final season in the remaining four episodes. In other words, its position within the season's plotting already positions it as subsidiary to Rachel, the protagonist's, character arc, an arc that traces her most recent mental breakdown, signaled by her blonde highlights, false eyelashes, and seeming disavowal of her feminist principles as she seeks to use *Everlasting*'s contestants to garner a marriage proposal for herself (and, by extension, a sense of self-worth). So despite Rachel's self-professed feminism and directly stated goal of changing the world via the representations of race and gender she orchestrates on *Everlasting*, sexual assault is clearly instrumentalized via *UnREAL* in the service of a "crazy soap opera lady" character arc reminiscent of Lifetime's earlier movie-of-the-week melodrama branding. It also aligns "crazy" Rachel with the quality television convention of pushing a once empathetic character to despicable and seemingly unforgiveable limits in an effort to distance that person from the heroism and aspiration of conventional television protagonists or the sympathetic victims common in *Lifetime*'s movies of the week.

This instrumentalization of sexual assault is also conveyed aesthetically. While one woman goes into labor and is giving birth live on camera on one set, Rachel and Tommy (her lover and coproducer) watch the sexual assault that Rachel has stage-managed unfold on the control room monitors. Having kicked the rest of the staff out of the room, Rachel and Tommy look over the screens (with a woman in labor screaming from one of them in the background) before the camera cuts to the single monitor showing an angled shot from an overhead surveillance camera of stumbling, drunk Noelle being ushered down the corridor by Roger. The camera cuts to Rachel's face scanning the monitors, and when it cuts back to the panel of monitors, miraculously four now show different overhead views of Noelle and Roger, while the pregnant woman still screams on the sound track. After a cross-cut to another story line, we see Rachel watching the monitors, and then the camera cuts to the interior of the bedroom where Roger is easing Noelle onto the bed and pulling off her underwear. These shots within the space where the assault is taking place are rare within the scene, with the sequence favoring instead the surveillance camera footage that presumably will make it into the finished reality television episode. The erratic accidental-seeming framing, multiple cameras, and overhead mounted-camera angles all indicate surveillance, the incidental recording of a private event or crime scene. They doubly mediate Noelle's experience, distancing her from any agency or narrative centrality, and attribute them instead to Rachel, who is always shown in medium shots or close up and in a straight angle and center frame as she watches the scene unfold with the almost rabid gleam of a maniacal puppet master in her eye. Eventually Maya bursts into the room and stops the assault by stabbing Roger in the shoulder and nearly slicing off his penis. Rachel is ecstatic about the ratings bonanza VSE television she's just captured, and it falls primarily to two male producers to voice concern and ultimately rush into the bedroom to stem Roger's bleeding and check whether Noelle is conscious. Berridge notes that it is most often male characters who rush in to stop assaults and men who voice the feminist articulation of active consent, forestalling again the feminism of representing rape and sexual assault as a women's issue.[38] Aligning with the analysis of both Berridge and Polletta and Tomlinson, *UnREAL* follows representational patterns more than it challenges them, despite its relatively novel very special season structure that centralizes the social issue.

Given that Rachel is both a rape survivor and a television producer, her actions read as inexplicable, unfathomable, and psychotic—even monstrous. She revictimizes Maya and is criminally complicit in Noelle's near rape, and therefore she completely undermines any altruistic intention she may have had to create a VSE about sexual assault to inform viewers and contribute to accurate and sensitive discourse about the social issue. This monstrosity is exacerbated throughout the rest of the season when, in an effort to conceal her and the network's criminal complicity in the rape, she doesn't even air this VSE footage. Ultimately the footage is reedited to make Maya appear like a jilted ex who violently attacks Roger not in defense of Noelle, but in a jealous rage. Rachel convinces Noelle to support the reedited story by threatening her with the many misconceptions and assumptions about rape victims against which Noelle would have to defend herself if she were to formally accuse Roger: women who report rape often lie, rape takes place only between people who don't know each other, women who dress or behave in particular ways are "responsible for their own attacks," all rapists are "abnormal, depraved, or marginal men," and women who are raped are placed on trial and forced to prove their moral purity through discussions of their previous sexual activities.[39] The central story line of Rachel's monstrous vilification—and, by extension, *UnREAL*'s very special season—offers no counterformulations to these dominant misconceptions about rape or sexual assault that are perpetuated by a postfeminist media culture. Instead, it reifies the cultural power of these myths by centralizing them in the season's melodramatic conflict. Even though in a surprise twist on the show-within-a-show, Quinn sets the record straight about the rape and Maya's violent defense of Noelle, the series nonetheless ends with Quinn also unjustly placing the blame of criminal complicity and manipulation on Tommy, letting Rachel, the network, and the television industry off the hook for their role in perpetuating and exploiting rape culture.

Conclusion

In Sarah Projanksy's thorough analysis of media depictions of rape, she illustrates how representations of sexual assault are ubiquitous and versatile and often communicate ideas about gender, race, class, nationality, sexuality, and feminism.[40] The sexual assault narrative of *UnREAL*'s very special season clearly communicates hegemonic ideas about gender and race, as well as about contemporary television. In particular, we argue that *UnREAL*'s very special season reveals the tensions and ultimate limitations in how quality television represents feminism and particularly sexual assault in the early twenty-first century. Even though *UnREAL* was created to self-reflexively comment on and critique the televisual strategies of distinction needed to stand out in Peak TV, it uses those same strategies in its own attempts to stand out. By focusing on Rachel's despicable actions and her point of view, the series borrows directly from the conventions of quality TV, but it also "augment[s] women's vulnerability and social isolation as individuals . . . perpetuates a textual neglect of women's experiences of rape," and adheres to conventional postfeminist rape narratives that demonstrate no racial specificity—that is, where women are racially undifferentiated, yet almost always white.[41] The series thus avoids a critique of present-day racialized gender relations in relation to rape, which is central to the #MeToo movement and the social issue it purports to be addressing. Like the common popular culture depictions of rape that Projansky traces, *UnREAL* presents Black women as highly visible in rape narratives but rarely heard. Even though Noelle is the central rape survivor in season four, the narrative of *UnREAL*'s very special season is not specifically about her and seems to marginalize her intersectional perspective, soliciting spectators' empathy with the despicable but ultimately forgiven central white protagonist. While *UnREAL* contributes to the visibility of discourses about consent, rape, and the plight of survivors and could be read as offering a critique of television's treatment of women, the show seems more interested in instrumentalizing sexual assault narratives to produce superficial claims of social relevance and sensationalized melodramatic distinction that will attract both its traditional viewers and discerning quality audiences. It ultimately gives up the political potential of its very special season structure in favor of repeating the VSE's flaws—in which an urgent social issue is put in service of plot, character, and viewership rather than careful, nuanced, complex representations of its central problem.

Notes

1 Ari Shapiro, "How 'The Bachelor' Confronted the Issue of Sexual Assault," *All Things Considered*, NPR, January 29, 2019, https://www.npr.org/2019/01/29/689760967/how-the-bachelor-confronted-the-issue-of-sexual-assault. See also Will Thorne, "TV Ratings: 'The Bachelor' Finale Up from Last Year, Wins Tuesday," *Variety*, March 13, 2019, https://variety.com/2019/tv/news/tv-ratings-the-bachelor-finale-wins-tuesday-1203162381/

2 See Mareike Jenner, "Is This TVIV? On Netflix, TVIII and Binge-Watching," *New Media & Society* 18, no. 2 (February 1, 2016): 257–273; Robyn R. Warhol, "Binge Watching: How Netflix Original Programs Are Changing Serial Form," *Literatur in Wissenschaft und Unterricht* 47, nos. 1–2 (2014): 145–158.

3 Jana Cattien, "When 'Feminism' Becomes a Genre: *Alias Grace* and 'Feminist' Television," *Feminist Theory* 20, no. 3 (2019): 324.

4 Meg James, "2015: Year of 'Peak TV' Hits Record with 409 Original Series," *Los Angeles Times*, December 16, 2015.

5 Amanda Lotz, *Portals: A Treatise on Internet-Distributed Television* (Ann Arbor, MI: Maize Books, 2017), and *We Now Disrupt This Broadcast: How Cable Transformed Television and the Internet Revolutionized It All* (Cambridge, MA: MIT Press, 2018); Taylor Nygaard and Jorie Lagerwey, *Horrible White People: Gender, Genre, and Television's Precarious Whiteness* (New York: New York University Press, 2020).

6 Julie D'Acci, introduction to "Lifetime: A Cable Network 'for Women,'" special issue, *Camera Obscura* 11–12, no. 3-1 (1994): 7–12; Heather Hundley, "The Evolution of Gendercasting: The Lifetime Television Network—'Television for Women,'" *Journal of Popular Film and Television* 29, no. 4 (Winter 2002): 174–181.

7 Lotz, *We Now Disrupt This Broadcast*; Jason Mittell, *Complex TV: The Poetics of Contemporary Television* (New York: New York University Press, 2015); Taylor Nygaard and Jorie Lagerwey, "Broadcasting Quality: Re-Centering Feminist Discourse with *The Good Wife*," *Television and New Media* 18, no. 2 (2017): 105–113.

8 Described in depth in Lotz, *We Now Disrupt This Broadcast*.

9 For a thorough discussion of this rebranding, see Kathleen Battles, "This Is *UnREAL*: Discourses of Quality, Antiheroes, and the Erasure of the Femininized Popular Culture in 'Television for Women,'" *Feminist Media Studies*, Online First,

(2019): 1–15, https://www.tandfonline.com/doi/full/10.1080/14680777.2019.1668450

10 Kate Stanhope, "*UnREAL* Co-Creator Sarah Gertrude Shapiro: How I Made It in Hollywood," *Hollywood Reporter*, June 1, 2015, https://www.hollywoodreporter.com/live-feed/unreal-creator-sarah-gertrude-shapiro-798923.

11 Mittell, *Complex TV*.

12 Todd Gitlin, "The Turn Toward 'Relevance'" in *Inside Prime Time* (Berkeley: University of California Press, 2000), 203–220.

13 Jane Feuer, "MTM Enterprises: An Overview" in Jane Feuer, Paul Kerr, and Tise Vahimagi, eds., *MTM: Quality Television* (London: British Film Institute, 1985), 3–4.

14 Jessalynn Keller and Maureen Ryan, *Emergent Feminisms: Complicating a Postfeminist Media Culture* (New York: Routledge, 2018).

15 Sarah Banet-Weiser, *Empowered: Popular Feminism and Popular Misogyny* (Durham, NC: Duke University Press, 2018).

16 Rosalind Gill, "Postfeminist Media Culture: Elements of a Sensibility," *European Journal of Cultural Studies* 10, no. 2 (2007): 147–166, and "Post-Fostfeminism? New Feminist Visibilities in Postfeminist Times," *Feminist Media Studies* 16, no. 4 (2016): 610–630.

17 Emily Nussbaum, "Doll Parts: *UnReal* Deconstructs *The Bachelor*," *Atlantic*, June 25, 2015, https://www.newyorker.com/magazine/2015/07/06/doll-parts; Willa Paskin, "Reality Check," *Slate*, June 29, 2015, https://slate.com/culture/2015/06/lifetimes-unreal-reviewed-this-riff-on-the-bachelor-is-the-first-antihero-show-that-is-created-by-women-stars-women-and-at-times-brutally-satirizes-women.html; Emily Todd VanDerWerff, "3 New Summer Shows You Should Be Watching," *Vox*, June 24, 2015, https://www.vox.com/2015/6/24/8839461/summer-tv-shows-new.

18 "UnReal (Lifetime)," Peabody, 2015, http://www.peabodyawards.com/award-profile/unreal.

19 Eileen R. Meehan and Jackie Byars, "Telefeminism: How Lifetime Got Its Groove, 1984–1997," *Television and New Media* 1, no. 1 (2000): 33–51.

20 Jillian Báez, "Television for *All* Women? Watching Lifetime's *Devious Maids*," in *Cupcakes, Pinterest, and Ladyporn: Feminized Popular Culture in the Twenty-First Century*, ed. Elana Levine (Chicago: University of Illinois Press, 2015), 55.

21 Francesca Polletta and Christine Tomlinson, "Date Rape after the Afterschool Special: Narrative Trends in the Televised Depiction of Social Problems," *Sociological Forum* 29, no. 3 (2014): 541.

22 Ibid., 543.

23 Báez, "Television for *All* Women?," 55.

24 Ibid., 61.

25 Kristen Warner, "In the Time of Plastic Representation," *Film Quarterly* 71, no. 2 (Winter 2017): 32–37.

26 Lotz, *We Now Disrupt This Broadcast*.

27 Gill, "Postfeminist Media Culture."

28 Dana Polan, "Cable Watching: HBO, *The Sopranos*, and Discourses of Distinction," in *Cable Visions: Television beyond Broadcasting*, ed. Sarah Banet-Wriser, Cynthia Chris, and Anthony Freitas (New York: New York University Press, 2007), 266.

29 Joe Pinsker, "How Do American Families Have 8 Hours of TV Every Day?," *Atlantic* December 6, 2018, https://www.theatlantic.com/family/archive/2018/12/tv-popular-americans-free-time/577468/.

30 Nygaard and Lagerwey, *Horrible White People*.

31 Robin M. Boylorn, "As Seen on TV: An Autoethnographic Reflection on Race and Reality Television," *Critical Studies in Media Communication* 25, no. 4 (2008): 413–433.

32 John Caldwell, *Televisuality: Style, Crisis, and Authority in American Television* (New Brunswick, NJ: Rutgers University Press, 1985).

33 For a description of this trope in general, see Mittell, *Complex TV*. For *UnReal*'s intentional incorporation of the trope, see Battles, "This Is *UnREAL*."

34 Jorie Lagerwey and Taylor Nygaard, "Liberal Women, Mental Illness, and Precarious Whiteness in Trump's America," *Flow*, November 27, 2017, https://www.flowjournal.org/2017/11/whiteness-in-trumps-america/.

35 Shapiro, "How 'The Bachelor' Confronted the Issue of Sexual Assault."

36 Lisa Cuklanz, *Rape in Prime Time: Television, Masculinity and Sexual Violence* (Philadelphia: University of Pennsylvania Press, 2000).

37 Susan Berridge, "Personal Problems and Women's Issues," *Feminist Media Studies* 11, no. 4 (2011): 467–481.

38 Ibid.

39 Cuklanz, *Rape in Prime Time*, 10.

40 Sarah Projansky, *Watching Rape: Film and Television in Postfeminist Culture* (New York: New York University Press, 2001).

41 Ibid., 19.

Notes on Contributors

APRYL ALEXANDER is an associate professor in the Graduate School of Professional Psychology at the University of Denver. Her research and clinical work centers on violence and victimization, human sexuality, and trauma-informed and culturally informed practice. As a public impact scholar, she enjoys bringing psychology to the public through popular culture. She is a frequent presenter at Denver Pop Culture Con and has contributed to *The Joker Psychology: Evil Clowns and the Women Who Love Them* and *Black Panther Psychology: Hidden Kingdoms*.

CHRISTINE BECKER is an associate professor in the Department of Film, Television, and Theatre at the University of Notre Dame who specializes in film and television history and critical analysis. Her book *It's the Pictures That Got Small: Hollywood Film Stars on 1950s Television* won the 2011 IAMHIST Michael Nelson Prize for a Work in Media and History. She is working on a research project that explores issues of cultural taste in contemporary American and British television. She also cohosts and coproduces the *Aca-Media* podcast for the *Journal of Cinema and Media Studies*.

RON BECKER is a professor in the Department of Media, Journalism and Film at Miami University of Ohio. He is the author of *Gay TV and Straight America*. His work has appeared in *The Television Studies Reader*; *Queer TV: Theories, Histories, Politics*; *The Great American Makeover: Television, History, Nation*; *How to Watch Television*; *The Craft of Media Criticism*; and *Television and New Media*.

JONATHAN COHN is the director of the Digital Humanities Program and an assistant professor of digital cultures in the English and film studies department at the University of Alberta. He is the author of *The Burden of Choice: Recommendations,*

Subversion, and Algorithmic Culture (Rutgers University Press). His work has appeared in various collections and journals, such as *Television and New Media*, *Camera Obscura*, and *JCMS*.

DAVID SCOTT DIFFRIENT is a professor of film and media studies in the Department of Communication Studies at Colorado State University. His articles have been published in *Cinema Journal*, *Historical Journal of Film, Radio, and Television*, *Journal of Fandom Studies*, *Journal of Film and Video*, *Journal of Popular Television*, *Journal of Popular Film and Television*, *New Review of Film and Television Studies*, *Quarterly Review of Film and Video*, *Post Script*, and *Velvet Light Trap*, as well as in several edited collections about film and television topics. He is the editor of *Screwball Television: Critical Perspectives on Gilmore Girls* and the author of three books: *M*A*S*H*, *Omnibus Films: Theorizing Transauthorial Cinema*, and *Movie Migrations: Transnational Genre Flows and South Korean Cinema*.

ERIN GIANNINI has a PhD from the University of East Anglia and is an independent scholar of television studies. Her recent work has focused on portrayals of and industrial contexts related to corporate culture on television, including a monograph on corporatism in the works of Joss Whedon. She has also published and presented work on religion, socioeconomics, and technology in series such as *Supernatural*, *Dollhouse*, *iZombie*, and *Mystery Science Theater 3000*.

LINDSAY GIGGEY is a lecturer in the communications department at California State University, Dominguez Hills. She holds a doctorate in cinema and media studies from the University of California, Los Angeles, where her dissertation examined the relationship between contemporary reality television and celebrity as sites for network and individual branding. Her work has appeared in *The Lifetime Network: Essays on "Television for Women" in the 21st Century*.

JORIE LAGERWEY is an associate professor of television studies at University College Dublin. Together, she and Taylor Nygaard research and write on gender, feminism, and critical race theory in prestige television. Most notably, they are the authors of *Horrible White People: Gender, Genre, and TV's Precarious Whiteness*. Their collaborative work has also appeared in *Television and New Media* and *Flow*. Separately, Lagerwey is the author of *Postfeminist Celebrity and Motherhood: Brand Mom* as well as further work on celebrity and genre in programs including *The Real Housewives*, *The Great British Bake Off*, and *Outlander*.

BRETT MILLS is a professor of media and culture at the University of East Anglia. He is the author of *The Sitcom*, *Television Sitcom*, and *Animals on Television: The Cultural Making of the Non-Human*. He is also coauthor of *Reading Media Theory: Thinkers, Approaches, Contexts* (with David M. Barlow) and *Creativity in the British Television Comedy Industry* (with Erica Horton). His funded research projects include "Make Me Laugh: Creativity in the British Television Comedy Industry" and "Multispecies Storytelling: More-Than-Human Narratives about Landscape" (with Claire Parkinson). He reviews stand-up comedy for *Fest* magazine and television for BBC Radio Norfolk.

TAYLOR NYGAARD is a faculty associate in film and media studies at Arizona State University and a freelance documentary story producer. Together, she and Jorie Lagerwey research and write on gender, feminism, and critical race theory in prestige television. Most notably, they are authors of *Horrible White People: Gender, Genre, and TV's Precarious Whiteness* (2020). Their collaborative work has also appeared in *Television and New Media* and *Flow*. Separately, Nygaard has published work on gender, media industries, digital technologies, and youth culture in *Feminist Media Studies* and several anthologies.

JENNIFER PORST is an assistant professor in the Department of Media Arts at the University of North Texas. Her work on the media industries has been published in journals and anthologies including *Film History*, *Television and New Media*, and *Hollywood and the Law*. Her book, *Broadcasting Hollywood: The Struggle Over Feature Films on Early TV* is forthcoming from Rutgers University Press.

PHILIP SCEPANSKI is an assistant professor of film and television at Marist College. His research interests include television history, cultural theory, comedy and humor, trauma, and temporality. He is the author of *Tragedy Plus Time: National Trauma and Television Comedy* and is working on a second book project that examines temporality in film and television comedy. His work has appeared in *Television and New Media*, *The Comedy Studies Reader*, and *How to Watch Television*, among other venues.

BARBARA SELZNICK is an associate professor in the School of Theatre, Film and Television at the University of Arizona. She is the author of *Sure Seaters: The Emergence of Art House Cinema* and *Global Television: Co-Producing Culture*. Her work has also appeared in edited books as well as journals such as *Science Fiction Film and Television*, *Quarterly Review of Film and Television*, *Spectator*, and *Global Media Journal*.

ERIN COPPLE SMITH is an assistant professor in media studies at Austin College. Her work on media industries has been published in various anthologies, including *From Networks to Netflix: A Guide to Changing Channels*, *Beyond Prime Time: TV Formats in the Post-Network Era*, and *Popular Communication*.

MIMI WHITE is a professor of screen cultures at Northwestern University. She is the author of numerous essays as well as *Tele-Advising: Therapeutic Discourse in American Television*, coauthor of *Media Knowledge: Popular Culture, Pedagogy,* *and Critical Citizenship*, and coeditor of *Questions of Method in Cultural Studies*.

REBA WISSNER is an assistant professor of musicology at Columbus State University. She received her MFA and PhD in musicology from Brandeis University and her BA in music and Italian from Hunter College of the City University of New York. She is the author of articles on music history pedagogy, seventeenth-century Venetian opera, Italian immigrant theater in New York City, and television music of the 1950s and 1960s, and she has presented her research at conferences throughout the United States and Europe. She is also the author of three books, *A Dimension of Sound: Music in The Twilight Zone, We Will Control All That You Hear: The Outer Limits and the Aural Imagination*, and *Music and the Atomic Bomb on American Television, 1950–1969*.

Index